This book is a treasure of God's glory, grace, and hope for the pastor's wife. Mary Somerville has written with biblical and practical clarity all-the-while weaving in personal glimpses of her own life and what the Lord has taught her. This book is most certainly a tribute to the "praise and glory of His grace." I loved reading this exceptional book and believe it will be beloved by pastors' wives for many years to come.

Martha Peace, Biblical Counselor
Author of *The Excellent Wife*

Mary Somerville has written the best work on the role of a pastor's wife. She deals with every issue that a pastor's wife encounters and gives numerous helps that are valuable. I wished I had read it before entering that role myself. Having been a pastor's wife for 46 years, I know the burdens and struggles they bear. I now have the joy of mentoring many of them and Mary's book is a must when doing so. May this excellent work be used to encourage many pastors' wives and leadership wives throughout the world.

Susan J. Heck, Author and Speaker
With the Master Ministries

It is always a joy to recommend sound advice and biblical teaching written by someone who lives it. In this helpful volume you will find both! As a former teacher of both seminary and pastors' wives, I wholeheartedly recommend this book. It will help you to glorify our Lord, and to improve and better understand your ministry marriage.

Elizabeth George, Author and Speaker

Mary was a precious voice to me as a young pastor's wife trying to find my way in ministry. As a seasoned ministry wife Mary walks you through some of the major issues and questions many wives deal with in the ministry, like what is my role? Are there special qualifications for a shepherd's wife? How do I handle difficulties and criticism? How do I balance my home, husband, children, and church life? I commend this book to you as a treasured resource as you seek to honour Christ in being One with a Shepherd.

Erin Coates, Pastor's Wife and Women's Ministry Director
Gracelife Church of Edmonton

What a blessing to be one with a shepherd! I know that now, but when I married Wayne I only knew that it was a blessing to be married to him. I would have known the blessings of being a shepherd's wife earlier in our ministry if a book like this had been available to instruct, encourage, teach, and challenge me. I certainly recommend it for all pastors' wives. It will help you know the blessing of being a shepherd's wife and also help you to be a blessing!

Carol Mack, Wife of author Wayne Mack

Mary Somerville has written a book which has helped me personally and will help many other women married to pastors. She shares personal experiences which help her readers to glorify God and bless others. She is "able to teach what is good and so train...women." I heartily recommend her book.

Caroline Newheiser, Biblical Counselor
Reformed Theological Seminary, Charlotte NC

MARY SOMERVILLE

ONE

WITH A

SHEPHERD

The Tears and Triumphs
of a Ministry Marriage

WITH STUDY QUESTIONS BY MARY BEEKE

One With a Shepherd: The Tears and Triumphs of a Ministry Marriage
Mary Somerville

316Publishing.com

Published in partnership with

kressbiblical.com

Printed in Korea by codra.com
28 27 26 25 24 / 1 2 3 4 5
ISBN: 978-1-63664-418-9

To the Chief Shepherd,
whose I am and whom I serve.

To my dear husband Bob,
whose love and companionship has
been my dearest earthly treasure.

To our flocks,
who have been patient with us
as we've learned shepherding.

Table of Contents

INTRODUCTION

"Will you give up your independence on Independence Day and become my wife?" was Bob's proposal of marriage. When I said yes, I said yes to being in ministry. I knew what I was getting into because he was studying to be a pastor. I entered my new role as a pastor's wife believing that God had prepared me and given me the desire to help a man called to ministry. It was the fulfillment of a lifetime desire and prayer.

Perhaps you never dreamed of being a pastor's wife and you were caught by surprise when your husband changed careers and entered the ministry.

I'm assuming that if you are reading this book, however you arrived, here you are—a wife of a man in ministry! Whether or not you see yourself as especially gifted or prepared for your role, God put you together with your husband intentionally and purposefully so you could partner with him, as your husband's helper "suitable for him" (Genesis 2:18). God gave you to your husband just as certainly as He gave Eve to Adam. You were given to him so as to uniquely help him perform the ministry to which God has called him.

After conversations with many ministry wives, I know that sometimes it is hard to see our supporting role as significant. So much of what we do is done behind the scenes, so no one sees or hears about our service. And a big part of our service is supporting our husbands, which again, often goes unnoticed by others. But the Bible holds up our role as extremely vital to the kingdom of God and my hope is to encourage you and affirm your valuable contribution to the Lord's work.

God has chosen to place the care of His precious flock into the hands of pastors and elders who are His under-shepherds (1 Peter 5:1-4). Those men who are married cannot fully carry out their mission without the support of their wives. But with the partnership of their wives, they can fulfill their role to protect and nourish the flock so that "when the Chief Shepherd appears, you will receive the unfading crown of glory" (1 Peter 5:4). That means you have a part in the rewards your husband will receive for his service.

What an honor and privilege to be in union for life with a man devoted to serving Christ for the highest of all possible purposes— building His church! For me, that blessing has spanned over three decades and I wouldn't change my life for any other. There have been days, however...

The truth is, you may need some encouragement—a booster shot. You may be weary from being on the front lines. You may just be starting out like my daughter, who is a young missionary wife, and need someone who has been down the road to point out the obstacles and shed some light on the journey ahead. As one missionary wife from the past wrote a friend,

> I love to converse, write, and reflect. It is a duty incumbent on the children of God, to reprove, encourage, and animate each other on their journey to the upper world. Every Christian has difficulties to overcome, temptations to encounter, and a warfare to accomplish, which the world are strangers to. If pilgrims in the same country can in the least console each other, and sweeten the thorny journey, by familiar intercourse, they ought not to neglect it.[1]

My primary source of encouragement will be God's all sufficient Word for its timeless encouragement, direction, and counsel, which is still relevant in the twenty-first century. Scripture must be our compass in a world of changing social and cultural climates and ethical and technological challenges. I will share experiences and lessons that I have learned along the way in my life as a pastor's wife. And I will also

---

1 Harriet Newell, *Memoirs of Her Life* (Baltimore, Maryland: Abel Brown, 1830), 88.

share insights and inspiration from the lives of wives out of church history, who have made a lasting contribution.

One such wife is Maria Taylor. Every quality looked for in a missionary wife Hudson found in Maria. She loved Christ so much that she said that despite her great love for Taylor, she would not be willing to marry him if he loved her more than Jesus, or if he were to leave the Lord's work for the world's honor.

She was a help to him in numerous ways. She spoke fluent Chinese and ran a little school, which provided the trifling income for Hudson to establish their first church. They received no fixed income as missionaries. They pioneered the great work in China, which set the course for all faith missions. Hudson and Maria were a team. "Undoubtedly, the overriding factor in their marriage was an equal uninhibited loyalty to their vocation. Without Maria, Taylor never could have embarked on his life's work."[2]

You too, dear sister, have a significant part to play in your husband's life and ministry. You too can see God do great things through your faithfulness and loving support. Because I've been in your shoes I know it isn't easy. It is a demanding role. But we are all in this together. We have a kind of sisterhood because of what we share. Our challenges are very much the same, no matter what the type, location, or size of our ministry.

We have many hard things to bear along with our joys and rewards. In this fulfilling yet demanding role, we need each other to share both burdens and successes. It is a vision worth our lives. We can live to our utmost potential for the kingdom of God through the power of the Holy Spirit.

The title of this book, "One with a Shepherd" sums up what I believe is the key to a fulfilled life as a ministry wife. It expresses your relationship to your husband and to Christ. Unity with each is the key. As Christians, we are one with the Good Shepherd who purchased His flock by His death on the cross. Apart from Him we can do nothing. If we abide in Him we can do all things. Likewise, the more unity that exists in our marriages to under-shepherds of Christ's flock, the more effective we will be in our particular calling.

---

2 John Pollock, *Hudson Taylor and Maria* (Fearn, Rossshire, Great Britain: Christian Focus Publications, 1996), 99.

What strength there is in unity with each other and with our God! "A cord of three strands is not quickly torn apart" (Ecclesiastes 4:12b). The more unity that exists in our marriages, the more joy we will find, the more effective our husbands will be, and the stronger Christ's church will be. I hope this book is an aid to that end. I do not have all the answers. I am on this journey with you, seeking to be faithful, looking to God and His Word for guidance—all for God's glory, gloriously one with a shepherd!

—Mary Somerville

UNDERSTANDING OUR ROLE

A Noble Role

Many daughters have done excellently, but you have gone above them all.
(Proverbs 31:29)

She is a precious treasure, one of sterling worth and possessed with an untiring zeal for the good of this poor people.[3]
—Hudson Taylor about his wife, Maria

"Well done, good and faithful slave … enter into the joy of your master."
(Matthew 25:21)

As wives of pastors or men in church ministry, these are the accolades that we would all love to hear. But sometimes we are so busy trying to meet the expectations of everyone besides the Good Shepherd that we are overwhelmed with an insurmountable task.

---

3 Pollock, *Hudson Taylor and Maria*, 78.

A Confusing and Impossible Role?

> Wanted: women to work full-time for no pay at their husband's office. Long hours. Frequent relocation required. Must be polite and understanding at all times. Thousands of women, driven by love and devotion to God and their families, work at this job—that of a minister's wife. But the strain of loneliness, financial struggles, and heavy church demands, can sap the joy from their marriages.[4]

So states an Associated Press release entitled "Ministers' Wives Face Challenge."

Does this describe you? Do you feel the constant strain of ministry and overwhelmed by the pressures and demands of your role? According to the article quoted above you're not alone. Thousands of other ministry wives feel that way, too.

Are you confused about where you fit in? Or how you are to meet all the needs that exist within your husband's sphere of ministry? With each job come requirements and expectations. There are usually clear performance guidelines for the senior pastor and youth pastor, as well as for those over music, Christian education, missions, worship, and family ministry. The same goes for missionaries, para-church ministers, church executives, and others who work outside the local church setting. But very rarely is there a job description for their wives. That's not to say there are no expectations, though.

"The pastor's wife (youth pastor's wife, missionary's wife) must _____." How do you fill in the blank? Maybe the former pastor's wife did it all. As a result of the precedent she established, the church might have high expectations of what their next pastor's wife should—and should not—do.

All this is compounded by the fact that as a pastor's family, you live in a fishbowl. You are expected to be an example in everything you do. You are scrutinized and criticized. Then there are the expectations that you put on yourself.

Maybe you've found yourself saying to others, "I know the parents of our youth expect me to be more involved, but I just can't with two

---

4 "Ministers' Wives Face Challenge", Associated Press, June 8, 2001.

preschoolers. It makes me feel bad most of the time that I can't help my husband more with the youth work. I often feel left out of his life because I can't participate more." I've been there, too, and I remember how it feels to experience that.

Another wife shared, "I feel torn. I don't know how to balance my involvement in church, care for the needs of my husband, homeschool my three children, and spend time with my mom, who is alone since Dad passed away. I know the church expects more of me but I just don't have it to give." Sound familiar? I have felt this way myself, especially when we cared for my invalid father in our home. There is pressure from every side.

How can the wife of a man in ministry know when she has carried out her task and done a good job? How does she deal with everyone's expectations including the expectations she puts on herself? It has been my observation that wives of men in ministry are usually high achievers. Their husbands are out to change the world and the wives are right there with them. We want to do and be our best for the glory of Christ.

If you want to be free from the burden of false guilt, you should first determine if you have yielded to non-biblical expectations. Make it your aim to discover and fulfill your God-given calling, knowing that He will not give you more than you can bear. Realize too that we do not answer to everyone else; we answer to God alone for our actions. Paul said that what people thought of him was unimportant and that even his own opinion of himself was inconsequential. He realized that God was the only one to please (1 Corinthians 4:1-5, 1 Corinthians 3:13, 2 Corinthians 5:10). "So then each one of us will give an account of himself to God" (Romans 14:12). This means turning a deaf ear to the complaints and criticisms that are ungrounded. And when we decide upon a course of action before God, we need to know that everyone will not agree with our plans. Sisters, we need not be "man-pleasers" but God-fearers. "Whatever you do, do your work heartily, as for the Lord rather than for men" (Colossians 3:23).

Now, sometimes people will have valid criticisms that will point us back to God's expectations for us. In these cases, we should not be intimidated by confrontation, but thankful for the help. Let's admit it, we aren't perfect! We need not try to make everyone think that we are. We can step out and be the women that God has created us to be without fear or intimidation of what others think. We live in the mercy and grace of God. As we fail, we admit it and obtain forgiveness from God and those whom we may have offended. There's radical freedom in the grace of God! "It was for freedom that Christ set us free" (Galatians 5:1a). So let's clarify our role as ministry wives and then step out with confidence and be the women that God has created us to be.

Clarity in Your Role

Some churches may be surprised to hear this, but the Bible does not teach that a pastor's wife must play the piano, run the women's ministry, and host all social functions. Actually, Scripture does not give a job description for the wife of a man in ministry. So how do we know what God expects of us? What is our role? Paul does give some character qualifications that are necessary for a deaconess or wives of deacons. "Women must likewise be dignified, not malicious gossips, but temperate, faithful in all things" (1 Timothy 3:11).[5]

As wives of men in ministry, you and I must be sure that we have this kind of exemplary character. But what are the "all things" that we are supposed to be faithful in? Scripture makes it plain that our calling is exactly the same as that of every other woman in the church—to be a godly woman, wife, mother, and faithful member of the body of Christ.

Let's take a close look at one key Bible passage that defines the roles of all women in the church. As we carefully examine these practical instructions, we will be able to see our own role more clearly.

> Older women likewise are to be reverent in their behavior, not malicious gossips nor enslaved to much wine, teaching what is good, so that they may instruct the young women in sensibility: to love their husbands, to love their children, to be sensible, pure, workers at home, kind, being subject to their own husbands, so that the word of God will not be slandered.
> (Titus 2:3-5)

---

5 Some interpret "Women" in 1 Timothy 3:11 as either deacons' wives or female deacons.

Character Qualities for Your Role

Notice that above all God is concerned about the character of the exemplary women in the church. If your children are grown, then the teaching for older women applies to you directly. But no matter what your age is, as a wife of a man in ministry, you are looked to as an example. So we all must pursue the character qualities of the older woman.

The very first character quality that we must focus on is reverence. The term reverent is taken from the word revere, which means to regard with affectionate awe or veneration. God wants us to exemplify behavior that exhibits affectionate awe for God. One way for us to keep that focus is to dwell on the attributes of God and His Son. It is easy to let the demands of life and the culture around us draw us away from our greatest privilege as women—knowing and revering God. Obedience will flow naturally from that loving respect. We need to constantly keep our eyes on the awesome God we serve.

One older woman whom I sought to follow was my dear mother-in-law who was 97 years old, and still demonstrating her reverence for God by seeking to grow in her understanding of His Word and obedience to it. I asked her to write her prayer requests in my prayer journal about a year ago. This is what she wrote:

> Pray for my disposition—that I'll be loving, and kind and thoughtful and wise in my use of words. Pray that I will be thankful for my health and place to live and such dear children. That I'll be a good example to them and show my appreciation for all everyone does for me. That God will help me to be patient and willing to give up and give in and content when I should be content and wise if I need to disagree—to be kind and loving when I disagree. Pray that I'll never forget who is in control.

God has answered that prayer. It was apparent that this woman had walked with God and revered Him for many, many years, and I want to be like her!

Next, we must be sure that we have control over our speech and our appetites. Being a malicious gossip, or enslaved to wine can tear down our lives and ministries. It is easy to mask gossip as "needs for prayer" and to pass on confidential information about what others have done or said that hurt us.

This sin can do damage to the name of Christ and hurt our husbands' ministry. What damage an uncontrolled tongue can cause! God can manifest the fruit of the Spirit—namely self-control—in our lives as we yield this area to Him. As He gives us a controlled tongue and controlled passions, that makes us stand out from the world and makes us ready for ministry.

The Role of Older Women

Continuing in Titus 2:3 we see that Paul addresses older women as the main ones leading in church ministry. If you are free from your child-rearing responsibilities, then you fit into this category of older women like me. This is not the time for retirement, it is the time for "teaching what is good." Put on your work boots and get ready to use all of the wisdom you have accumulated through years devoted to your character and your home. Free up the younger women to focus on their main ministry in the home. Get active in women's ministries, whether one-on-one or in large groups. We cannot excuse ourselves from service thinking that the younger women won't want to hear our outdated opinions. The younger women need encouragement from those who have walked the road. They need to be discipled by those who are more mature in their faith. As a ministry wife this job will probably fall to you naturally. So go for it and recruit as many other older godly women in the church as you can to join you. Now listen in as I address the younger women because this is what you older women need to be teaching them.

The Role of Younger Women

Paul teaches us that the ministry of younger women is to focus on their home. So even as a wife of a man in ministry, your main role is to love your husband and children, to guard your purity, to be a worker—a kind worker—at home, and to be subject to your own husband so that the Word of God may not be dishonored. Any other ministry that you pursue in the church must not interfere with these priorities.

To be "workers at home" simply means being homemakers. This

is how we fulfill our callings to love our husbands and children. Our priority task as wives and mothers is to make home a prepared place for them. The greatest ministry that you can have to your church is the provision of a home for their pastor where he can receive the rest and rejuvenation he needs to be able to serve effectively as their spiritual shepherd.

I love the people in our church dearly, but I think they need to understand that my relationship with Bob takes precedence over all of my other relationships. My first ministry is directed toward him, before the church and all its demands. My family is the Lord's work.

I think that you and I as wives and mothers are the essence of home. Our presence in it to care for the family is what constitutes home. A member of our fellowship who lost his wife said it most poignantly: "Our house is no longer a home so I'm going to sell it."

We also make our homes a place of love and training of our children and a place of order. We serve a God of order, not confusion. To have a home characterized by order, we must be disciplined ourselves to have a place for everything and to train our children to put things in their place when they are through with them, to clean their rooms, and to live harmoniously with one another.

The question comes up about working outside the home. Many wives of men in ministry are college-educated women and may have worked in a career before marriage. Should they give that up to work at home? That's an issue that must be grappled with before the Lord, taking into account our needs versus our desires. The couple must determine how she will fulfill her God-given roles.

Bob and I agreed that my place was in the home and not in the workplace. I have found that the role of wife and mother, plus pastor's wife, is very demanding and rewarding. It has been my career. My counsel to women seeking direction is that they should make their home their career unless their husband is not able to earn enough to meet the necessities of life and they need to help out temporarily. But it may also be possible to supplement the income without seeking an outside career. If you look at the Proverbs 31 woman, you will see that there are many ways that the industrious and creative wife can help provide for her family and even earn money from the home.

A missionary wife from the past that I deeply admire is Mary Moffat who, with her husband, was a pioneer missionary to South Africa where our children serve. Her son-in-law, David Livingstone, is more famous. Mary had 10 children and managed the mission station, much of the time single-handedly. She learned Bechuana, traveled with her husband into very hostile territory when he went to preach and supported her husband through times of frustration and gloom when he was left alone to fight against overwhelming odds. She gave him the strength to carry on. He called her his "beloved partner."

So many of Mary's tasks involved menial labor to run the household. At one point early on in their ministry she became frustrated and depressed saying, "Is this the sort of work I've left home and friends to spend my life doing, in this uncongenial heathen land?" Her biographer said,

> Inside her, out of the strength of her faith and the depth of a commitment which she had almost forgotten, a voice said, 'If I may be a hewer of wood and a drawer of water in the temple of my God, am I not still blessed and privileged?' It was a turning point. Nothing was changed as far as the physical efforts were concerned, but her sense of priorities was restored.[6]

She used her practical, administrative, and teaching gifts to the full as she served beside her husband, which turned out to be a very fulfilling role for her.

What an incredible example Mary is to me! She faithfully served and went through horrendous hardships alongside her husband for 50 years—and only one furlough! They buried five of their 10 children in Africa. She would have been outraged at the suggestion that Robert Moffat should have pioneered alone. I can hardly identify with such sacrificial service; but it motivates me to a deeper level of commitment.

As we follow Christ and serve alongside our husbands we set the example for the women in our flock. Whether or not we like it, we are their models. Whatever you and I do, the women in the church are

---

6 Mora Dickson, *Beloved Partner: Mary Moffet of Kuruman* (P.O. Box 34, Kuruman, South Africa: Kuruman Moffat Trust, 1989), 49.

likely to do it, too. So we want to be careful about the choices we make. For example, when we came to plant a church and had no money for a down payment on a house, we let the church know that I was going to teach for a couple of years. Our children were three and six years old. Immediately, a young mother in the church used my situation as a reason to insist to her husband that she should go out and get a job. Later, Bob and I changed our minds about me teaching and I stayed home after all. The woman who was using my example to justify her working outside the home then said that she had lost her bargaining power with her husband.

It sometimes seems more productive to get a job and bring in supplemental income. But Proverbs 31:27 speaks of the importance of the wife's role as a household manager. "She watches over the ways of her household". The Hebrew word for "watches" is the one used of a watchman who guards a city from enemy assault. Just as you would not want a watchman to come on duty tired and strained from another job, you do not want the watchman of your home expending all her effort and energy on other pursuits and giving her leftover attention to her family. However, each couple must decide before the Lord what is the best way for that wife to fulfill her responsibilities as a homemaker and be a sterling example for the flock. As we seek first God's kingdom and His righteousness, He promises to supply all of our needs. It doesn't mean that we are exempt from suffering.

Your Role in the Body of Christ

As we have seen, our first calling is to our Lord and Savior, then to our husbands and children. Are we merely to let our husbands do all the serving in the church? Just what is our role? We also have a calling to use our spiritual gifts as members of the body of Christ. We all have gifts. Some sample lists are in Romans 12:3-8; 1 Peter 4:10-11, and 1 Corinthians 12. Some are communication gifts and some are serving gifts. If anyone is not using his or her gifts, the church is crippled. So don't try to be an ear if you are an eye. If you are an eye, be the best eye you can be, don't try to taste and hear too. You are free to serve with all your heart and soul to God's glory as any other member of the church would, in the power of the Spirit.

The Joy of Fulfilling Your Biblical Role

Don't you see my dear sister, that there is actually wonderful freedom that comes from understanding your biblical role? When you "limit" yourself to pleasing God, you are freed from the pressures of fulfilling unattainable expectations. You are freed from the pressure to try to juggle two or three careers. You have discovered that the role of a wife of a man in ministry is no different than any other exemplary woman in the church. You are freed to focus in on your own character, your husband, your home and then your specific areas of spiritual giftedness. Keep in mind that you are not on a pedestal because of your position as the wife of a man in ministry. You and I are but sinners saved by His matchless grace, not having to prove anything in ourselves.

Yet even the responsibilities we have in fulfilling just these few essentials could appear terribly daunting. That is because it is impossible to do this in our own strength. Fortunately, we have God's promise that He will enable us. Aren't you thankful that you have God's grace, not only to survive, but also to thrive in your role? He called you to it, and He will enable you for it. This is the promise: "And God is able to make every grace abound to you, so that in everything at every time having every sufficiency, you may have an abundance for every good deed" (2 Corinthians 9:8).

By faith, you can daily appropriate God's amazing grace to fulfill your biblical role as a ministry wife. Then as you focus in on the essentials, you will find the joy of a job well done. You will be able to sift through the varying expectations and evaluations of the crowd and hear the voices that you long to hear: your husband saying, "Many daughters have done excellently, but you have gone above them all"; and most precious of all, your Lord commending, "Well done, good and faithful slave" (Proverbs 31:29, Matthew 25:23).

DEALING WITH THE PHYSICAL DEMANDS OF MINISTRY

Pastoral ministry is living life with a flock and being available. No matter what size flock you serve, you feel like you have always left things undone that would be good to do. At times you may become physically drained—"maxed out." You have always been one to serve with your husband wholeheartedly, bearing the concerns that your husband bears. That includes counseling and comforting those in need, visiting the sick and new people, being with people in the midst of their problems, and reaching out to neighbors. Perhaps you take on all the tasks that no one else wants or can do—nursery duty, the bulletin, clean-up, informing people of upcoming events, women's ministry, Vacation Bible School and so on. As a result, you find yourself under the constant weight of ministry.

You want to have the simple, focused life that we discussed in the first chapter but you don't know how to keep your life from being swallowed up by the demands of ministry. In this chapter I want to give you twelve practical tips for dealing with the physical demands of ministry. If you follow these tips that we have discovered over the years, you will find your ministry life to become much more balanced, enjoyable, and rewarding.

TWELVE WAYS TO LESSEN THE PHYSICAL DEMANDS OF MINISTRY

Focusing on Your Role in the Body of Christ

We will find our greatest joy when we use our God-given gifts effectively in the church.

> whoever speaks, as one speaking the oracles of God; whoever serves, as one serving by the strength which God supplies; so that in all things God may be glorified through Jesus Christ, to whom belongs the glory and might forever and ever. Amen. (1 Peter 4:11)

What positions are open to us as women seeking to use our gifts in the church? God has directed us through the apostle Paul that we are first to be learners within the church with an attitude of submission toward the church leaders (1 Timothy 2:9-15). As with all believers, it is our responsibility to submit and support those whom God has put in leadership within the church.

God has also directed us: "I do not allow a woman to teach or exercise authority over a man" (1 Timothy 2:12), which would be over the pastor and elders whose role is to shepherd the flock. We are free to serve in every area not excluded to us by Scripture.

So many vital areas of service are open before us. As we have seen, the mature women are specifically commanded to teach the younger women in the faith. We can have a special role in counseling and teaching women and children. We can be involved in the music ministry of the church, secretarial work, direct women's ministries, help with visitation, and so on.

Just look at the early church. We are given examples of women who had key roles and worked mightily for God. Phoebe was a servant in the church whom Paul praised and by whom he sent his letter to the church at Rome (Romans 16:1-2). Priscilla participated in evangelism with her husband Aquila. They were close friends of Paul and may have risked their lives for him (Romans 16:3-4; Acts 18:2). Lydia was a successful businesswoman in Philippi and one of the founding members of the church there. When she came to know Christ as her Savior, she opened her home for the team of missionaries and for the church (Acts 16:14, 40).

If you aren't sure what your gifts are, study the passages on spiritual giftedness (Romans 12:3-8; 1 Corinthians 12:1-14:40; 1 Peter 4:10-11). Then enlist your husband's help in identifying your particular giftedness. Others within your circle of friends can also give input. What are your interests? What needs stand out to you the most? What are one or two areas of service you do that are bearing the most fruit? These are probably the things that you enjoy doing the most and that's a strong sign of the areas in which God has gifted you. I know that as you pray and ask the Lord to reveal to you what your gifts are, He will. Then use those gifts!

Whatever your spiritual giftedness, work on developing it to the greatest extent. Many wives attend leadership and counseling conferences and take courses to further equip themselves for ministry. My seminary training was a huge blessing as Bob and I entered the ministry together and I used it in my support role as a pastor's wife. Many godly women, through their counsel and others through the books they've written, have also mentored me.

Focus in on your area of giftedness. Do not expend your energies elsewhere. As difficult as it is for us to do, we must trust the Lord with the things that are not our responsibility. If it is not your gift to speak, trust the Lord to bring those who can teach and lead groups. I have seen that happen even in small churches. I have never directed the women's ministry programs in our churches, but I've encouraged other women to use their giftedness to direct the programs. This freed me to focus on my strengths—visitation with my husband Bob and using my giftedness for administration and counseling. Just in these later years I've been writing and speaking more often.

For 14 years now, my husband has encouraged me to use my gifts to develop and administer a program for matching single teen mothers with mentors for the purpose of evangelism and discipleship through Young Life. The mentors are not only from our church, but also from other churches within the community, which provides me with a wealth of friends. It is a joy for me to use my gifts two days a week for the body of Christ as a whole. I greatly esteem my husband for his selflessness in supporting me in this ministry.

If we just serve in our area of giftedness, does this mean we should automatically turn down other opportunities that do not involve the use of our gifts? Not always. We are instructed, "So then, while we have opportunity, let us do good to all people, and especially to those who are of the household of the faith" (Galatians 6:10).

In our first church in New Jersey, I served in the nursery a great deal. Our children were babies and it was the natural place to be exercising the gift of helps. While it's not my strongest gift, it was needed. Thankfully, we had the sermon piped in, so I didn't miss too many of Bob's messages.

When we came to California to start a church of eight families, the church office was in our home for ten years. That meant that there were many opportunities for me to do several things for the church that were not in line with my gifts and education. I was needed to answer the phone so my husband could study, and the children were small and I homeschooled them for several years.

Was it a challenge to balance home, and school, and office, and ministry? Certainly! There were plenty of those "I'm exhausted!" moments. Were there times that I felt overwhelmed? Many! We were often compelled to claim the promise of His strength in Isaiah 40:31, waiting on Him moment-by-moment and His strength was always there for us. I give testimony to the fact that God gave us His supernatural strength and enabling power during those hectic years.

Have you found that when you are called upon to give beyond your own resources and to wait upon the Lord, He enables you to do it? It's a "soaring on eagles' wings" experience. God carries us along and we look back and ask how did we do it all? It was God!

Recruiting and Training Others

Despite the fact that God will enable you to do things beyond your abilities or endurance, if they are in areas that do not fit with your giftedness, you should see service in that area as a transitional role. Constantly look for someone who is better suited to that task. Then you can bring that person alongside and equip her to use her gifts in that area. When she is ready, she can take over, thus freeing you up and allowing the whole body to work better.

Prioritizing and Organizing

Jesus gives us the principle of putting first things first—prioritizing. He said to seek first His kingdom and His righteousness and all the other things would be added to us (Matthew 6:33). What comes first? Our relationship with Christ comes first. If we have no time for Him, then we are too busy. One pastor's wife lamented that she doesn't have enough time for the kind of prayer life that she would like to have. She said, "I pray as I go and go and go!" I can relate.

Let me encourage you to take a very careful look at all the commitments you've made in your life. Do you need to say no to some things? Yes, you do! You must say yes only to the things that are a part of your God-given calling, and say no to the extras. That may be difficult to do at first. But it's much better for us to do our priorities well than to try to do everything poorly.

There is the possibility of "burn-out"—physical exhaustion—which can bring on other emotional responses that we don't want to experience. Instead of being trapped by the tyranny of the urgent, we need to create a plan for making the best use of our time.

Moreover, as homemakers, we need to be organized (cf. 1 Corinthians 14:40). You can make a graph showing the hours of the week and map out a schedule. On my schedule, the first thing I do is fill in the important things that I must accomplish each day. Since we do not punch a time clock, our time can easily get away and we may find that we haven't accomplished the most important things on our to-do list. Because God comes first, we can let Him write over our schedules at any time, and we need to let Him do that without hesitation.

There are good books written on organizational skills so that we can accomplish more with less stress. I'm sure that you, like me, want to study to be the best you can be for your husband and ultimately for God's glory. See my *Recommended Resources* in *Appendix E.*

Keeping Family a Priority

When you participate in your husband's calling, you want to do it in a way that doesn't dominate your family life. You do not need to live, breathe, eat, and sleep his ministry. Paul told Timothy that an elder must manage his own household well; if he doesn't, how will he manage the church of God (1 Timothy 3:4-5)? The household and church are two distinct responsibilities, and your husband is to manage both of them effectively. Under his authority you are to manage the home.

You as a wife can try to ensure that your family does not end up focusing on the needs of your congregation all the time. The children can know some of the needs and they can be prayed for together and ministered to as a family; however, these do not need to dominate your family life. We must maintain our priorities: both ministry and family are important, and then lastly, recreation and other interests. We don't want our children to feel like they're less important to us than ministry. It takes conscious effort to continue to assure them that they are a priority and blessing.

Caring for the needs of sick or elderly parents will often take priority. We had my dad in our home the last year of his life when he needed constant care. Needless to say, that dominated most of my time, but the family and church understood that and encouraged us in it.

Not Adding to Your Husband's Load

Could this be played out in your home? "Honey, did you notice that the nursery needs painting? I've noticed that the church down the street has catchy sayings on their sign in front. Shouldn't we do that? When are you going to get someone to clean up the leaves on the side of the office?" And on and on we go! If you are like me, you will bring up needs that you think your husband should be made aware of—people who need visiting or calling, things in the church that need fixing, and events that should be on the church calendar.

Our husbands do not need extra pressure from us. It is their responsibility to manage the church of God, not ours. Scripture tells us, "But each one must examine his own work, and then he will have reason for boasting in regard to himself alone, and not in regard to another. For each one will bear his own load" (Galatians 6:4-5). Yet, too often, we as wives can take on burdens that we were never meant to carry and then pass those on to our husbands.

How then can we lighten our husband's load, not add to it? On Sunday, you may want to take care not to bring up any topics that might stir relational conflict. To help out my husband, on Monday mornings I often make a list of needs that I became aware of during church on Sunday. During the week, I'll add to the list (and I like to send get-well cards, notes of encouragement, sympathy cards, and baby cards.) This helps to take some of the responsibility for ministry without burdening my husband about it.

If we still see a need to bring up a suggestion, we must be careful to find the appropriate time. It is especially important not to bring the ministry to bed. We need to let our husbands go to bed in peace without a reminder of things left undone. This is a real temptation because many times it is the only time we have our husband's ear. But at this time of day, when nothing productive can be done, suggestions are seen more as nagging.

It's good to set limits. Enough is enough. We can only do so much. Therefore, we need to trust people in the church to take care of certain needs or get to them another time. A well-taught flock will regularly meet people's needs before the pastor even hears about it.

Accepting Help from Others

While we receive more joy from giving to others than from receiving, we must allow others to minister to us as a family. Then they can experience that joy, too. Paul writes about the churches of Macedonia,

> For I testify that according to their ability, and beyond their ability, they gave of their own accord, begging us with much urging for the grace of sharing in the ministry to the saints, and this, not as we had expected, but they first gave themselves to the Lord and to us by the will of God.
> (2 Corinthians 8:3-5)

Paul allowed the Christians to minister to his needs. He went on to tell them that they would be enriched by their liberality in giving (2 Corinthians 9:11). If we don't allow our flock to minister to our needs, we are robbing them of a blessing.

It would be good to examine ourselves in this area. Do we sometimes stifle people's desire to minister to us by not letting anyone know about our needs?

One way to receive help and encouragement is to ask an older pastor's wife to mentor us either in person or over the phone. What an incredible blessing this can be to both parties!

Resting One Day in Seven

Bob and I were very interested in hearing what our seminary president had to say in his seminar entitled: "How to Overcome Stress in the Ministry." His main point was that the best way to manage stress is to observe one day of rest every week—that is, obey the fourth Commandment. What a basic solution to a big problem!

Resting one day in seven is not only a nice idea; it is God's idea—a creation ordinance.

> Six days you shall labor and do all your work, but the seventh day is a sabbath of Yahweh your God; in it you shall not do any work, you or your son or your daughter, your male or your female slave or your cattle or your sojourner who is within your gates. For in six days Yahweh made the heavens and the earth, the sea and all that is in them, and rested on the seventh day; therefore Yahweh blessed the sabbath day and made it holy.
> (Exodus 20:9-11)

God always knows what's best. I can't overstate this truth. We must rest. It is for the good of our own body and soul and increased productivity that we must follow the pattern that God established. It is especially important because of the constant weight of ministry responsibilities upon our shoulders. Understanding our bodily limitations is part of taking care of our body, which is the temple and sanctuary of the Holy Spirit (cf. 1 Corinthians 6:19-20). There is no doubt that we need to make a priority of getting the proper amount of rest.

Since Sunday is not a day of rest for us in ministry, as it should be for the others in our churches, it is wise to have another day off.

The reason for taking the last day off is that all the preparation for Sunday is done and the pastors can relax more completely than if they took Mondays off. Many pastors choose to take Mondays off because they need the rest after the busy day preaching and teaching. We have found that it's important to do something fun and relaxing together on our day off, such as taking a drive to the mountains, reading in our lawn chairs, going for a walk, or playing tennis. A change of pace is important for our emotional and spiritual well-being—especially because we're involved with people all the time. Outdoor activities seem particularly refreshing as our husbands are in an office most of the time.

One goal I have is to get the household chores done so Bob doesn't have to help me with them on his day off. There are times when we do them together if it has been an extra busy week for me. We then treat Saturday like everyone else does. We use it to get things done at home, do maintenance work, or go shopping. It is part of the six days that we are to labor and do all our work. When our work for Saturday is done, we may have some time left for recreation.

What should a wife do when her husband won't take a day off? One pastor is known to have said, "The devil doesn't take a day off, so why should I?" To that the answer was given, "I didn't know the devil was our example." That's true. God is our example in resting from all of His labors on the seventh day.

Unfortunately, some men in ministry do not take time for their families. Their life is their ministry, and the family fits in the cracks—and sometimes falls through the cracks. One wife expressed, "To have any time with my husband, I would need to have a problem. Then I could make an appointment and get an hour of his time." This is so very sad because the first ministry a minister has is his family.

If your husband won't rest, you should appeal to him in the spirit of meekness and pray that God will make him sensitive to your concerns. You could say, "I would like to have the chance to ask you about something. Is this a good time?" If it is, then proceed by saying something like this: "How do you think you and I could plan on taking one day in seven as a day of rest? Is there a way that I could help that happen? Because you carry such a heavy load in all that you do, I think it is especially important for you to get rest. I know that I need it too."

This should initiate a good discussion about this concern of yours. If your husband is still not convinced of the importance of rest, you have two choices. You can "cover" it and ask God for the strength to continue on in support of your husband (1 Peter 4:8), or you can confront it lovingly. But no matter what you do, it's very important not to let anger or bitterness creep into your heart. God can give you His patience, perseverance, and gentleness (cf. 1 Peter 3:4) as you trust Him to work in your husband's heart. You may also choose to humbly ask for the help of a trusted church leader. If you ask a church leader to go with you to talk to your husband about this issue, be careful not to do this in a way that disrespects him by going behind his back or undermining him (cf. Ephesians 5:33). Most likely your husband will listen before the problem goes any further. Godly church leaders are concerned that the needs of the pastor's family are cared for and would gladly encourage the pastor to take a day of rest.

Caring for Your Body

Let's face it—ministry is taxing physically. We get tired and worn out. Paul compared our bodies to a treasure in a clay jar. A clay jar is fragile and easily broken or chipped. We get tired and ill and are subject to sicknesses and diseases that limit our ability to minister.

Sometimes, because we are so busy we don't get the proper food, rest, or exercise for God's optimum use. Bob and I have found that we feel better and have more energy when we work out several times a week. Exercise improves our energy, endurance, and physical well-being.

If we are overweight, we need to examine the cause because being overweight puts greater strain on our bodies. If we have an eating problem, we need to bring it under the control of the Holy Spirit. Being in ministry often means being offered meals, which include rich desserts. In our first church, the Ladies Aid thought it was their job to fatten up their young pastor. We must think of polite ways to turn down foods that would be detrimental to our health. Paul said, "I discipline my body and make it my slave, so that, after I have preached to others, I myself will not be disqualified" (1 Corinthians 9:27).

We're called to be good stewards of our bodies and that means asking God for self-control and disciplining ourselves for the purpose of godliness (1 Timothy 4:7). While our appearance is not the most important factor in life, we do want to care for ourselves in a way that reflects positively on God and thus brings glory to Him.

The great reformer John Calvin is said to have gone to his grave relatively early, at age 55 because of his sedentary life, that conspired along with his tremendous workload, to make him the victim of disease.[7]

As one pastor has said we must strive for *sustainable sacrifice*. We want to pace ourselves for the marathon of life. Lord willing, by properly caring for our bodies, we can enjoy a long and healthy ministry for God's glory.

Taking Vacations

Some may view vacations as a luxury, but they are a must for ministry families. Most churches recognize the need for a complete rest from the pressures of ministry and allow the pastor a month or more off. We get five weeks of vacation and use part of that time to go to conferences where Bob and I often serve as speakers. However, when we do that, the purpose of the vacation is not fulfilled because we didn't take a complete break from our responsibilities in ministry.

Is it extravagant to travel or vacation? I don't think so. God "richly supplies us with all things to enjoy" (1 Timothy 6:17b). The world is ours as believers and is for our discovery and enjoyment. Vacations may be comparable to Old Testament feasts, which God commanded His people to celebrate throughout the course of their year. There was the Feast of the New Moon, The Feast of Pentecost, The Feast of Purim, The Feast of Tabernacles, The Feast of the Passover, The Feast of Trumpets, The Anniversary Feasts, The Sabbatical Year Feast, and The Feast of Jubilee. He was so generous in giving them times to stop work and celebrate as families and as a people of God.

Also, vacations need not be expensive. When our budget was tight we went camping or traveled to visit friends or relatives. Camping is not only affordable, it provides beautiful places to explore and enjoy such as the ocean or lake. As often as we could, we would pack up the rolling suitcases and head out of town on an adventure. From the

---

7 *The New Schaff-Herzog Encyclopedia of Religious Knowledge* (Grand Rapids, Michigan: Baker Book House, 1955).

time our kids were little, Bob and I have taken them off to far-flung places to experience the flavors of different parts of the country. Relatives and friends welcomed us with open arms. Of course, we didn't go to their homes just out of monetary reasons. We put a priority on spending time with our families and have tried to see them regularly, even though we are on opposite sides of the continent.

Another form of vacation is to attend Christian camps and conferences. You may need to do some research, but some places will allow pastors and their families to use their facilities as a retreat for free. My parents invested in a cabin at a Christian conference center in the mountains where we spent most of my summers growing up. It was a wise investment for every member of the family. In following my parents' example, Bob and I have experienced some of our greatest family vacations at Christian camps where we have been refreshed spiritually as well as physically.

Some might argue that you have nothing to show for all you spend on vacations except pictures in an album. I would say that you have built into the lives of your children the unity, love, and enjoyment of the family that is so important in today's world—along with the albums of pictures.

Our children are both married now but they still vacation with us as couples—a highlight of our year. Sometimes we are required to travel to the other side of the world to vacation with our missionary kids, but it is worth it. The importance of taking breaks from ministry to get refreshed and rejuvenated cannot be over-emphasized.

Taking Mini-Breaks

It's great to take a small break with your husband to just get alone with the Lord for a day or part of a day. We go to a park or the mountains and take our Bibles and meet with God. In the rush and hurry of our busy lives this is a time to be still and listen to God, enjoy His presence, and get focused on why we are doing what we do. As we go to Him, away from the clamor of our lives, and listen for His voice, we receive rest and refreshment for our souls.

Jesus set the example with this practice. He often would slip away from His busy ministry to commune with His Father. On one occasion,

"He said to them, 'Come away by yourselves to a desolate place and rest a while.' (For there were many people coming and going, and they did not even have time to eat.) And they went away in the boat to a desolate place by themselves" (Mark 6:31-32).

Another purpose of a mini-break would be to spend time alone as a couple to set goals and evaluate. Some friends of ours take a day every six months to see how they are doing on keeping the goals that they set as a couple.

Bearing One Another's Burdens as a Staff

If you work with other staff members in your church or with other missionaries, it is so important to regularly meet together as wives to fellowship and share each other's burdens. Our husbands have staff meetings and see each other often so they feel like a team, but we as wives can feel isolated and alone with our burdens and responsibilities. This is especially true if your children are small and you are housebound much of the time.

The oneness we have through ministry doesn't just happen; it takes conscious effort to have a close camaraderie because we are each busy in our own particular area of ministry. Weeks and months can go by without connecting with other wives of pastors in your church. It is important for someone on the staff to initiate this vital fellowship.

The wives of our pastoral staff come to our house for breakfast at 6:30 A.M. once a month. We meet early in the morning so that our husbands are able to be home with the children. It is a sweet time of fellowship as we share and hear what is going on in each other's lives. We also pray for one another with sympathetic prayer out of our mutual position as ministry wives.

Since our husbands hold each other accountable in their weekly staff meetings for certain things, we have chosen to also hold each other accountable by asking some questions to spur each other on in our walk with God. See *Appendix A* for a list of questions.

Recognizing the Different Seasons of Life

We can take comfort in knowing that there are seasons in life for different focuses. Your role in the body of Christ will change over the years. Bob and I are in the "empty nest" season which enables me to do much more church-related work. I remember when Daniel went off to school after eight years of having at least one child in the home all day long; I felt a new freedom. I could be more involved in Bob's life and ministry. Even with children in school I couldn't do as much as I can now. When the children both went off to college there was another big adjustment to redirect the focus of my life from our children to other pursuits. But God's grace is there for us and I can honestly say that this season is equally rewarding.

Below is an excerpt from my journal of a typical week in this current season of life:

Sun. After church hosted the membership class at our home. Served 9 people—lasagna, French bread, salad, and homemade apple pie. Worked in Awana.

Mon. Went shopping with a friend who is new in town and who visited church in order to get her acquainted with our community. Had a couple from church over for dinner.

Tue. Teen-mom-related work. Attended our home Bible study (Impact Group) in the evening with Bob.

Wed. Led small group at Ladies' Bible Study. Attended the luncheon, which followed the study. Visited a lady in the hospital who is battling cancer.

Thu. Hosted pastors' wives for breakfast. Did teen-mom work.

Fri. Had the day off with Bob.

Sat. Had a Mentor Mom training day. Bob had an elders' retreat.

At one stage of our ministry, when our children were babies, my husband asked me to give over all my ministries in the church and merely care for the children and responsibilities in the home, which involved hospitality. Now that the children are grown, I can be especially active in the work of the church. If your children are young, let me encourage you that this season of life—devotion to their care—is just as valuable in God's eyes as working alongside your husband in church-specific activities.

One young missionary wife who is a mother of seven children (nine and younger) finds comfort in calling these her "underground years." If she devotes herself to nothing but raising godly children, think of what a platform she will have in years to come. Women will want to know how she did it and how they can learn from her.

Whatever season of life you are in, savor it and enjoy it to the full, because it won't last.

I encourage you to use these tips to guide you to lessen the physical demands of ministry. Instead of being defeated, may you—by God's grace—have His strength for your journey. Let's review. I encouraged you to:

◊ Focus on Your Role in the Body
◊ Recruit and Train Others
◊ Prioritize and Organize
◊ Keep Family a Priority
◊ Do Not Add to Your Husband's Load
◊ Accept Help from Others
◊ Rest One Day in Seven
◊ Care for Your Body
◊ Take Vacations
◊ Take Mini-breaks
◊ Bear One Another's Burdens as a Staff
◊ Recognize the Different Seasons of Life

I hope you will look at each of these areas and see what practical steps you need to take to evaluate your life as a ministry wife and couple. Plan now to sit down with your calendar or planner and evaluate with your husband what changes you'll make—and then commit to making those changes to enhance your life as a ministry couple.

HANDLING THE SPIRITUAL AND EMOTIONAL BURDENS OF MINISTRY

In the first two chapters we discussed the role of a wife of a man in ministry. We've breathed a great sigh of relief, realizing that we do not have to bear the weight of everyone's expectations. But now what about the burdens that we carry as we serve alongside our shepherding husbands?

As the wife of a man in ministry you share the weight of all the trials and tests that the flock is experiencing—everyone's physical and spiritual burdens. This is because the shepherd of the flock is always apprised of the condition of the sheep so he can pray for them. Your husband can't begin to minister to all the needs. He has hopefully trained his flock in the work of ministry—to visit and pray with those who are experiencing difficulties, and to seek to meet physical needs (Ephesians 4:11-12). However, just knowing those needs for the purpose of prayer is a huge burden.

Your role involves feeling with those whose marriages are breaking up, those whose children are going astray, those who are battling life-threatening diseases, or those who have lost a loved one. It includes weeping along with your husband over unfulfilled desires for growth in individuals and sorrow over those who are wandering. It means standing with your husband by the grave of someone in your flock that you had to part with. I have come to realize that being a pastor's wife is not for the faint-hearted!

Just as Laura Bush became the "Comforter in Chief" for our country after the 2001 terrorist attacks, we are there with our husbands to comfort those who are experiencing trials of any kind. In the first interview with the press after the 911 attacks, President Bush said, of Laura, "She couldn't have been more calm, resolved, almost placid, which was a very reassuring thing."[8] The whole country was looking to the president and his wife in the face of national danger and disaster.

Our churches look to their pastors and wives in the same way. We represent unwavering faith, courage, and resolve in the face of tragedies and heartbreaking circumstances. Yet, these expressions of grace under pressure don't come easily.

One pastor's wife said that her top challenge is to be happy in God amid the pain. She explains,

> My greatest challenge is loving and delighting in the sovereign God who often chooses not to cause fruit from my labors of love even, and especially, right within my own family. This is not so much the sacrifice of pouring out my time and tears on people, but the startling bewilderment of watching people grow worse despite years of prayer, fasting, support, and encouragement. I've seen men who I've battled for in prayer and fasting leave their wives for someone else. I've seen children I've poured myself into nurturing decide there is no God and walk away from the faith. I've seen children whose protection I've prayed for endure the atrocity of sexual abuse. These things are my worst struggles.

Our husbands carry an awesome responsibility as under-shepherds of Jesus who is the Chief Shepherd, and we, as their companions also bear a heavy load—spiritually and emotionally.

Loving and Delighting in the Sovereign God

Just how can we handle these weights? We cannot! God is the only one who can bear the grief of the world because He is the One who has

---

8 Tamara Lipper and Debra Rosenberg, "This is our Life Now", *Newsweek*, (3 December 2001), 24-25.

determined it for good. He sees the end from the beginning. Although God is never the author of evil, He uses it for His ends, for His glory. Even the wrath of men shall praise Him (Psalm 76:10). What was the worst crime that was ever committed? The murder of the innocent Son of God. This great evil became the source of the greatest good for humanity.

Peter proclaimed this truth:

> Men of Israel, listen to these words: Jesus the Nazarene, a man attested to you by God with miracles and wonders and signs which God did through Him in your midst, just as you yourselves know—this Man, delivered over by the predetermined plan and foreknowledge of God, you nailed to a cross by the hands of lawless men and put Him to death. But God raised Him up again, putting an end to the agony of death, since it was impossible for Him to be held in its power.
> (Acts 2:22-24)

We will not be able to understand all the reasons for all the sin and hurt and pain in our world, but we know that God is God and that is all we need to know. We are not exempt from our own struggles of faith just because we are wives of men in ministry. Even Asaph, a godly writer of many of the Psalms, almost lost his faith seeing the prosperity of the wicked and the apparent lack of reward for those who live for God. He admits that if he gives public expression to his doubts, he would be causing younger believers to stumble (Psalm 73:15). So instead he runs into the presence of God. There he sees the end of the story. He says, "My flesh and my heart fail, but God is the rock of my heart and my portion forever... I have set Lord Yahweh as my refuge, that I may recount all Your works" (Psalm 73:26, 28b).

What about Job? He had no idea of the great glory that would come from his loss of family, wealth, reputation, and health. Job bore His suffering righteously. But when he wanted to question God's purposes, he was humbled into silence as God reminded him who laid the foundations of the earth and stretched out the heavens and enclosed the sea with doors, who commands the morning and causes the dawn to know its place. God asked him, "Can you send forth lightnings that they may go and say to you, 'Here we are'?" (Job 38:35). At the end of

God's overwhelming revelation of Himself, Job answers, "I know that You can do all things, and that no purpose of Yours can be thwarted … I have heard of You by the hearing of the ear; but now my eye sees You; therefore I reject myself, and I repent in dust and ashes" (Job 42:1-2, 5-6).

Our hurting pastor's wife quoted above knew the answer. When our hearts are aching with disappointment, we must love and delight in the Sovereign God, trusting that He always does what is wise and good. But how do we do that?

Knowing Christ Personally

We must know God in order to trust Him like Job did. The only way to know God is through His Son Jesus Christ. If we truly get a glimpse of Jesus, we will be compelled to prize Him and delight in Him above all else.

God's Word tells us, "Test yourselves to see if you are in the faith; examine yourselves!" (2 Corinthians 13:5). Yes, even as wives of men in the ministry we must test ourselves.

A dear friend of mine came to faith in Jesus Christ as her Savior after she was married to a seminary graduate. She was a sweet woman whom this man had fallen in love with, but she had never come to acknowledge the painful truth of her inadequacy to meet God's standard of perfection and to trust in Christ's death on the cross for her. She had all her life trusted in her own goodness not realizing her own wretchedness before God and need for His grace for salvation. What a joy it was for both of them when she was born again into the family of God through faith alone (John 3:1-21).

It's not a matter of being good enough or even religious—a sort of bootstrap religion where we do it ourselves. It is all by the grace of God. Like Job, we must repent of our sin and trust in the saving grace of God. It is our inner poverty of spirit, realizing it isn't our ability to make God love us because all our righteousness is like filthy garments in His sight (Isaiah 64:6). We must come into a personal experience of the awesome love of God and confess Him as Lord and Savior. Salvation is the gift of God (Ephesians 2:8-9).

How do you test yourself to see if you are in the faith? Ask yourself the question, "Have I responded to His overture of love by personally trusting in the cross where Jesus, who is God in human flesh, paid the full penalty for my sin? Have I confessed Christ as my Lord and Savior—the only One who could forgive my sin and give me right standing with God?"

When you are united with Christ through the new birth, moment-by-moment fellowship with Him is the most satisfying thing in your life and you have a passion for bringing God glory in everything you do.

King David had that soul-satisfying relationship with his God. He had come to know the Shepherd of his soul personally and intimately as a young shepherd boy. Can you say with David in his heartfelt psalm, "Yahweh is my shepherd, I shall not want" (Psalm 23:1)?

Because the Shepherd became the sacrifice and paid the penalty for our sin, you and I have all we need. We shall not want for any good thing—forgiveness, restoration, guidance, protection amid danger, comfort, blessing, joy, goodness, mercy, and heaven besides. He is our wisdom, righteousness, sanctification, and redemption (1 Corinthians 1:30). He is all we need for salvation and to live the life of faith that pleases God and satisfies our own soul.

In the wonderful treatise about the supremacy of Christ in all things Paul writes, "And He [Jesus] is before all things, and in Him all things hold together. And He is the head of the body, the church; Who is the beginning, the firstborn from the dead, so that He Himself will come to have first place in everything" (Colossians 1:17-18).

Dear friend, do you seek to make Jesus Christ the preeminent One in your life? We can't do it on our own. But as we abide in Him, He becomes our all in all.

Abiding in Christ

Just before Jesus went to the cross, His parting words were directed to the disciples who were facing the devastation of His coming death. He gave them the beautiful picture of Himself as the vine and His disciples the branches (John 15:1-17). There could be no closer relationship than that. The branch gets its life and nourishment from the vine—all it needs to grow and be fruitful. Jesus told His disciples they were to abide in Him as the branch abides in the vine. It pictures the dependency and constant communion between Christ and us and that it is He that is producing the fruit in our lives through that living connection.

Fruit bearing is important. Jesus says, "Every branch in Me that does not bear fruit, He [the Father] takes away" (John 15:2). If we have that intimate connection to Jesus, we will see visible fruit—the fruit of the Spirit growing in our own experience and other people coming to Jesus and their lives being built up and changed as we work with them. But if our lives are barren of fruit we will be taken away—judged. The heavenly Gardener gets rid of dead wood so the living branches can be shown to be truly His. He prunes or trims every branch so that it bears more fruit. No fruit-bearing branch is exempt. This can be a painful process, but it is a loving purpose for which He prunes us—so that each branch will be even more fruitful. We are impelled from this teaching of Jesus to examine our lives for fruit-bearing.

Are we seeing fruit? Keep in mind that fruit will often be produced when there are trials. Those trials we may be experiencing in our ministry are producing fruit for His glory for which He will reward us. Isn't it amazing that He is the One who produces the fruit and then rewards us for it! He wants us to do even greater things than Jesus did when He was on earth and this brings glory to Himself (John 14:12-14; 15:7, 16; 16:23-24, 26).

How wonderful to realize that we do not have to produce fruit out of our own reserves! He is living His life in and through us. Apart from Him we can do nothing—not some things, but nothing! But through Him we can do all things (Philippians 4:13). He is our source of life, joy, and comfort. As one with Christ, we as His disciples can fulfill His commission to go and make disciples of every nation and teach them all that He has commanded.

Abiding in the vine is the same as being filled with the Spirit as we are admonished in Ephesians 5:18. If I am living in obedience to His Word by living a life of purity, confessing all known sin, and depending upon His power to produce the fruit in my life, I am being filled with the Spirit.

Jesus Christ is in us in the person of the Holy Spirit but do we bring Him into everything we do? Do thoughts of Him dominate our life?

Are our waking thoughts of Him as well as our last thoughts before we go to sleep? Why do we constantly and consistently let our minds dwell on lesser things if there is nothing else to compare with knowing Him and dwelling on His beauty?

As we set Him always before us, we will be able to do all that we do as an act of worship. We will be bursting forth with a heart full of praise as we constantly think about His great grace and love. It is living in the conscious presence of the Lord Jesus that gives us joy in our journey.

In order to sustain the constant weight of ministry and to grow in the fruit of the Spirit we must have this vital connection to Jesus Christ. There is no other way to sustain this kind of life.

Living by the Word of God

How do we nurture that oneness with Jesus Christ? What does it look like in daily practice to be prizing Christ above all else and abiding in Him?

Jesus said, "If you abide in Me, and My words abide in you, ask whatever you wish, and it will be done for you" (John 15:7). His words are important for us to listen to and obey.

So that we can better grasp the importance of this we need to look at the account where Jesus took three of His beloved disciples up to a mountain to pray. While Jesus was praying, His glory became unveiled and His clothing became white and gleaming. Moses and Elijah came to speak with Him about His impending death. After falling asleep during the prayer time, the disciples awoke to see Jesus' glory and the two men with Him. When the men were leaving, Peter said to Jesus, "Master, it is good for us to be here; let us make three booths" (Luke 9:33). He wanted to do something great. What happened? "While he was saying this, a cloud formed and began to overshadow them; and they were afraid as they entered the cloud. Then a voice came out of the cloud, saying, "This is My Son, My Chosen One; listen to Him!" (Luke 9:34-35).

It was more important to listen to Jesus than to build something. It is the most important thing in our lives—more important than what we accomplish for Him. Out of that intimacy with Him may come things for Him, but it is more important to hear God's voice and obey

Him than to do great things for Him. I need to constantly keep that in mind because I tend to be like Peter—"let's do something." Because of our busy lives it is imperative that we spend time with our Lord in reading and meditating on His Word so we don't grow cold and weary in well-doing.

It may take some real planning to find time alone to spend with the Lord—time away from the pressures of life and ministry. We all need some time to be still so we can hear His voice through His Word.

Journaling is the primary way I have sought to hear His voice and sustain my walk with Christ. Over 45 years ago I began keeping a quiet time journal and I can't begin to tell you what a blessing it has been in my life. Please realize that I haven't done it perfectly, but it has been my goal.

To begin my time in the Word, I pray the prayer offered by the author of Psalm 119—the longest chapter in the Bible exalting God's Word: "Open my eyes, that I may behold wonderful things from Your law" (Psalm 119:18). Since God is the ultimate Author, He can open our eyes to the meaning and application of His precious Word to our lives.

I read consecutively and record a "wonderful thing" each day in my journal. I also seek to respond to what I have read by writing a prayer praising God and asking Him to work in accordance with what I have read—to change me more into the likeness of Christ. For instance, my response to the passage about the Transfiguration of Jesus might be, "Lord, You're awesome! Jesus, You are greater than Moses and Elijah. In you the Law and the prophets are fulfilled. You are the Word made flesh. Oh, to get a glimpse of Your glory! I pray that you will help me to constantly listen to You and to obey Your voice today."

My husband also journals and we begin our day often by sharing our "wonderful things" with each other. It is our spiritual food. It keeps us alive and growing spiritually. It keeps our relationship with Christ fresh. There is no substitute for God's Word.

I hope you too, have a plan for getting into God's true and unfailing Word each day. It is the surest way to truly build your relationship with Christ.

Living by Communion with God in Prayer

We also nurture our oneness with Christ through prayer. As we pray God imprints His own image of Christ's character on our lives—His love, His wisdom, and His compassion toward those for whom we pray. We surrender to His will as we pray, "Lord, Your will be done." We don't pray for our own gain but for God's glory.

Sometimes, however, when we want to go to God in prayer we feel inadequate or we've just blown it—failed Him in a significant way. We feel like God wouldn't want to hear from us and He certainly wouldn't want to answer my prayers.

We need to keep in mind that our rightness before God is not based on our ability to live up to what we know is right. We come to God because of Jesus' sacrifice on the cross to a "throne of grace." It is all of grace that He saved us, and all of grace that He hears our prayers. We can come boldly before His throne because Jesus has made the way (Hebrews 4:16)! As we enter God's presence, we can call God "Abba" or Daddy, because we have the spirit of adoption—that awareness that we have been adopted into His family. We are His children (Romans 8:15).

In Jesus' model prayer, He included confession. "And forgive us our debts, as we also have forgiven our debtors" (Matthew 6:12). When we come into the presence of our holy Father we are to come seeking forgiveness and cleansing, and that is what He gives us (1 John 1:9). Then we enter just as pure as Jesus, without fear or hesitation.

Not only do we come to Him with confession, but with thanksgiving and praise. The psalmist wrote, "Enter His gates with thanksgiving and His courts with praise. Give thanks to Him, bless His name" (Psalm 100:4). And "He who offers a sacrifice of thanksgiving glorifies Me" (Psalm 50:23).

We glorify God through our thanks and praise of Him. Let's pour out our grateful hearts for who He is. As we read His Word we see His character portrayed in so many ways—His sovereignty, His love and forgiveness, His omnipotence and omnipresence. We see His beauty and perfection, His holiness and justice. We see His mercy and grace. This results in a heart of praise and thanksgiving for all He is and has done for us.

Jesus said, "Ask whatever you wish, and it will be done for you" (John 15:7b). I want to take Jesus up on His desire for us to ask of Him and to be challenged to pray for God-sized prayers—things that only He can do. God gave Sarah a child when she was 90 and her husband 100. That's God-sized. God put His Son in Mary's womb. That's God-sized. Is there anything too hard for God? If the answer is no, then let's go to Him in prayer, expecting great and mighty things!

It has been my practice to keep a prayer journal. This is where I record my requests and the dates when they are prayed for and answered. If you don't have a structure for prayer, why not try this faith-building exercise? It encourages not only your own faith but also those for whom you are praying.

Here is one answer to prayer for which I praise the Lord. Matt and Margie were very dear to us; Bob performed their wedding. Margie had a difficult pregnancy with suspected birth defects, but they were strong in resisting the doctors' insistence that they abort their son. Their son's problems were corrected with some minor surgeries and we rejoiced with them over all God had seen them through. As things got comfortable again, they drifted away from the Lord, stopped coming to church, and even got involved in a cult. This led to the breakdown of their marriage and eventual separation. They were on my prayer list for six years when one day I received a call from Margie. She wanted to get together. What a cause for rejoicing when she came back to Christ! That same day Matt called Bob and he also recommitted his life to Christ! They were reunited and joyously returned to the fellowship.

This is a dramatic story, but there are many other testimonies to God's faithfulness, that could be multiplied in journal after journal. Just as it was a delight for the apostle Paul to intercede for the believers whom he had led to faith in Christ, it is a joy for us (Philippians 1:3). They were his children and grandchildren in the faith. He knew God would work in their lives as he prayed for them. It's not a burden but a privilege to bring these precious ones before the throne of grace. As God answers prayers for them it brings Him glory.

In my journal I also keep a "Bonus Prayer List" based on the promise, "Delight yourself in Yahweh; and He will give you the desires of your heart" (Psalm 37:4). I ask God to grant these requests only if it would delight His heart to delight mine. At the bottom of the page I put this prayer, "Lord if this wouldn't be good for me or bring glory to You, please withhold it." I do not want Him to grant something that might be dangerous for me to receive. It has been a joy to see God answer many of these special requests.

Here is an example of one of these bonus prayers. I requested of the Lord to be able to go overseas with my husband to minister. This was a sincere request because we have always been deeply interested in foreign missions. However, it was quite a leap of faith because Bob was not in demand as an international speaker.

One day as Bob was flipping through my journal he glanced at my Bonus Prayer List. "What? Is somebody going to ask me to speak overseas?" he laughed. It was just a few weeks later that a man came to our church representing the Biblical Counseling Association in Germany to ask my husband to speak for three weeks all around his country. "And by the way, we want your wife to come too," he added.

As it turned out, the seminary where my husband earned his doctor of ministry degree in biblical counseling recommended him. While we were in Germany speaking on biblical counseling we were also able to meet with missionaries for our mutual encouragement. Bob called that venture "Operation Isaac" because he laughed.

Since that time, knowing the desires of our heart in this area, God has given us the privilege of ministering to missionaries in all parts of the world. He delights to delight us as we delight ourselves in Him.

Bob and I also take "prayer walks" several times a week. We pray together for our personal, family, and church needs. If the weather is bad, we walk on the treadmill and use our church directory to lift up the needs of our church family. What a release it is to know that God has the power to work in each situation. He answers prayer. There is no way we could begin to meet the needs, but God can!

Cultivating the habit of daily praise and intercession is the best way for the wife of a man in ministry to cope with all the burdens. We cast all our cares upon the Lord, who alone is able to carry them in the ultimate sense (1 Peter 5:7). Prayer becomes like breathing. Each need that we become aware of should be cast over on the Lord. We are to pray about everything. When we are told a need, we pray about it then and there—if it is over the phone, on the street, or in a restaurant. It can be done silently or audibly. We shouldn't carry a burden a minute longer than we need to but rather cast it upon the Lord. He will show us our part in caring for the need, but He is the ultimate burden-bearer.

I challenge you to increase your "knee exercises." Start with five minutes, 20 minutes, a half hour, an hour a day, and see what God will do!

Sharing in Christ's Sufferings

We've discussed how we must strive to draw near to Christ through the daily spiritual disciplines of Bible reading and prayer. Now I want to share with you how Christ actually draws us nearer to Himself through the trials and opportunities that He brings into our lives. Are we willing, like Paul, to thank God for opportunities to die to ourselves? We can be willing if we see the prize.

> More than that, I count all things to be loss because of the surpassing value of knowing Christ Jesus my Lord … that I may know Him and the power of His resurrection and the fellowship of His sufferings, being conformed to His death, in order that I may attain to the resurrection from the dead.
> (Philippians 3:8, 10-11)

Paul wrote about the hardships that he endured in ministry. "Apart from such external things [and these were many], there is the daily pressure on me of concern for all the churches" (2 Corinthians 11:28, bracketed portion mine). Paul invited young Timothy to "suffer hardship with me" in the work of the ministry (2 Timothy 2:3). If we didn't carry some of the weight of ministry, it would be doubtful if we should be in ministry. This seems contradictory to what we have just said about casting all our cares upon Christ.

We experience the cares and pressures of ministry, but then cast them on Christ through prayer. The concern for the church is at the heart of a pastor and his wife. This is part of knowing Christ in the fellowship of His sufferings.

Weights can be a good thing. I use weights to increase my strength when I work out. It's not particularly fun. I have noticed that when I slack off and don't consistently use the weights I become flabby and out of shape. We don't want to be flabby saints. We want to use the weights to develop our spiritual muscles of trusting Christ more and drawing closer to Him.

We can claim the Father's promise to work together for good all the things that are happening in our church family, knowing that He is both loving and sovereign (Romans 8:28). We can thank Him in advance for each distressing situation, for each thing that causes us pain, each pressure and disappointment, each interruption that may come into our day, and week. This is in spite of how we feel. It is by faith. We can choose not to resist our trials as intruders, but to welcome them as friends, to consider them to be a joy, to thank God for them (James 1:2-4). God knows what He is doing. He is conforming you and me more into the likeness of Christ. This is part of His will, which is "good and pleasing and perfect" (Romans 12:2).

Just think of it, God is at work to beautify your character through each struggle; to expose your weakness, sin, selfishness, and pride, and to perfect you into what He wants you to be in Christ! That is God's ultimate aim for us (Romans 8:29).

Yes, we are under the constant weight of ministry and it involves sacrifice, but the great part about sharing in His sufferings is that then we can share in His glory. "For I consider that the sufferings of this present time are not worthy to be compared with the glory that is to be revealed to us" (Romans 8:18).

Knowing Christ in His Resurrection Power

Women, we could have no greater hope because of our oneness with Christ in His death and resurrection! Paul grasped the truth of oneness with Christ when he wrote these words, "I have been crucified with Christ, and it is no longer I who live, but Christ lives in me. And the life which I now live in the flesh I live by faith in the Son of God, who loved me and gave Himself up for me" (Galatians 2:20).

We died and rose again with Christ. Because of His victory over sin and death we have hope for the wandering child and the abused child. We have hope for the drunkard and the adulterer. If God can raise the dead, then He can change those lives in answer to our prayers.

We are not on a "mission impossible." We have the power of the risen Christ. We can do more than we imagine in our lives and ministries through the power of Christ.

Having Hope

We can get up in the morning with hope and we don't need to fear what may happen next in our congregation, family, or world. What is the worst that can happen to us as believers? Our last and worst enemy is death. We will have power over the worst enemies that we have to face.

My dear mother chose Romans 8:28 for her "life verse" when she came to Christ at age 16. She trusted in the goodness and sovereignty of Christ throughout the rest of her life. She would say, "Let's trust God. He is working it together for good." When she was in her 50s that faith was put to the test when she was diagnosed with terminal cancer. As was her practice, she turned to God's promise without wavering. She showed me how to live trusting the Shepherd and she showed me how to die—full of faith and hope that she would dwell in His house forever. Her homegoing exalted the Savior.

Three months after her death my father wrote our home church the following letter that I keep in the album of his life story.

Dear Pastor Dick and Family and Beloved Friends,

Enclosed is a little Thanksgiving gift to the church in appreciation for the blessing that you and your people have been to my family and me through the years—through times of joy and through times of bereavement.

I thank God at this Thanksgiving season for sins forgiven, for a great Priest touched with a feeling for my infirmities, for the privilege of being a small tool in His mighty hand, for His guidance, for His ear that hears my prayers, for His arm on which to lean, for His precious Word in which He speaks to us explicitly and for the blessed, blessed hope of His soon coming!

I thank Him, more than all else, for utter safety. In the past I have known what it was to be afraid, but now I know that I am entirely and perfectly secure. I feel that I have come into a safe place, a safe harbor. Nothing, absolutely nothing, not my own deeds nor those of others, not the works of devils, or circumstances, or so-called fate, nothing can separate me from the love of Christ. Sorrow and bereavement can come, death can even put my body and that of my beloved in the grave, but whatever comes, it passes first through His tender hands, and so I can love it because it comes from Him!

Nothing can keep me out of heaven. I am as safe now as though I were already there. Just a few years to live, a few tasks yet to be done and then to be forever with Him and our beloved gone on before, our daily portion glory beyond infinite glory! Thankful? My cheeks are often wet with happy tears. Why He gives all this to a poor creature like me I do not know, but I know that I shall need all eternity in which to thank Him for it!

As you fellowship in Him on your Harvest Festival to thank Him for His bounty, may your expectation and every desire be found in Him and the Blessed Hope.

Affectionately yours till He comes,
—Robert L. Gates

What a legacy of faith! My dad finished his "few years to live" at the ripe age of 90 and is now with Jesus also. Nothing can separate our loved ones or us from the love of Christ—"...neither death, nor life, nor angels, nor rulers, nor things present, nor things to come, nor powers, nor height, nor depth, nor any other created thing" (Romans 8:38b-39a).

That is the kind of peace and assurance we have to model and share with those in our churches. Do you find yourself forgetting the riches that are in Christ and like me going down the path of self-pity, self-justification, self, self, self? Do you battle with discouragement? Do you often feel like quitting? (My husband says he does about once a week.) Does your mind center on all the problems instead of the goal—God's glory?

Dear sister, the answer is Christ. He is before all things and in Him all things hold together. He is the Chief Shepherd who will care for His flock. He is the vine and you are the branch. Be one with Him through His Word. Be one with Him through prayer. Be one with Him in His sufferings. And be one with Him in the power of His resurrection. If you are one with Him, there is no defeat.

I love Paul's prayer for the Ephesian believers because it tells us how God works, not to just get us by, but abundantly:

> that He would give you, according to the riches of His glory, to be strengthened with power through His Spirit in the inner man, so that Christ may dwell in your hearts through faith; and that you, being firmly rooted and grounded in love, may be able to comprehend with all the saints what is the breadth and length and height and depth, and to know the love of Christ which surpasses knowledge, that you may be filled up to all the fullness of God. Now to Him who is able to do far more abundantly beyond all that we ask or understand, according to the power that works within us, to Him be the glory in the church and in Christ Jesus to all generations forever and ever. Amen. (Ephesians 3:16-21).

He will sustain you in your role! It is only for this short life and then you'll spend eternity with Him. Peter looked forward to Christ's second coming with these words, "And when the Chief Shepherd appears…" (1 Peter 5:4), and that is how he spurs the shepherds on in shepherding the flock entrusted to them. Jesus is coming back! Our husbands will turn over their flock to the Chief Shepherd.

4

NOT FALLING PREY TO THE SUCCESS SYNDROME

"Pastor Wright built that church up from nothing to two thousand in six years!" "You should see their multimillion dollar church! They prayed the prayer of Jabez and look what happened!"[9] "I know the Barnburners and they finished their translation of the New Testament in five years" (while it's taking you 25). "You don't have a preschool in your church? Don't you know the tremendous outreach that is into the community?" These are some of the comments that may trigger discouragement to you as a wife of a man in ministry. You see other churches or other ministries flourishing while you are plodding along. You start to wonder what you are doing wrong, what you can change. You become consumed with a desire to see more results from your labors. Before you know it you have fallen prey to the "success syndrome."

The success syndrome is a downward spiral of sinful desires and actions that stems from a worldly definition of success and ends in depression or burn out. It is conquered through replacing the passions for achievement, fame, prosperity, and success with passions to please Christ, to exalt His name, to contentedly sacrifice self, and to bear true fruit through faithful service.

---

9 The "Prayer of Jabez" was a trend based on a book of the same title. This prayer had many elements that are similar to the heretical prosperity gospel.

SYMPTOMS OF THE SUCCESS SYNDROME

◊ Going through the motions spiritually
◊ Discontentment with your husband's ministry
◊ Desire to change churches or ministries or to get out of the ministry
◊ Putting pressure on yourself or your husband to have more vision, add more programs, expand your territory
◊ Discouragement
◊ Depression
◊ Lack of zeal for your ministry
◊ Feelings of failure
◊ Envy and jealousy
◊ Pride
◊ Burnout

If these symptoms are left unchecked, your ministry and even your life will be destroyed. We must discover the source of the devastating success syndrome.

How do such good desires, desires to see your ministries succeed and your life count for something, turn into such a harmful downward spiral? The process occurs slowly and subtly as we allow the world to creep in and start turning our hearts to seek after its deceptive version of success.

When we look at the way people in our consumer society shop for churches, it would appear that they approach the church in the same way that they shop for goods. The bigger the store, the more it has to offer—so shop there. Churches respond by employing good marketing techniques, bigger budgets, and larger fancier buildings. Preaching must be kept short and non-confrontational so as not to turn anyone off. Success is name recognition—having a pastor with a radio ministry and who writes books and speaks internationally. It is having a state-of-the-art worship facility. It is having every kind of program imaginable to meet the needs of people.

The American Heritage Dictionary (third edition) defines success as the achievement of something attempted; the gaining of fame or prosperity.

If you find yourself striving for your church to achieve the approval of the majority of twenty-first century Christians and seekers, you may be caving in to worldly definitions of success. Do numbers, growth, applause, fame, prosperity, or goal attainments define success in God's eyes?

What about you personally? What spells success for you—being the perfect hostess, succeeding as a "real" person in a "real" career, having a beautiful home? Are you letting the world's definition of success creep in? You may be if you find yourself demanding quick quantifiable achievements, some sort of fame or prosperity. If you really look at your underlying motives, could there be some lust for self-promotion and advancement?

If this is the case, when you do not get the results that you want, you become depressed, judgmental and more determined than ever to get some approval. Then you know that the success syndrome has you in its grasp (James 4).

WHAT IS THE CURE FOR THE SUCCESS SYNDROME?

Is there a drug that we can take to calm our ambitions and depressions? Are there some rose-colored glasses that we can put on to make us see our current situation as ideal? Maybe we just need to speak more positive words over our ministries and have more faith that God will accomplish those goals for which we long.

No, the success syndrome must be attacked at its source. It is driven by a lust for worldly success, achievement, fame, and prosperity. It can only be conquered through transformed passions. The success syndrome is not a disease but a cycle of sin that can be broken through repentance. Health comes through humility as we replace the passion for self-exaltation with a renewed passion for God-exaltation.

Put off a Passion for Personal Achievement and Approval • *Put on* a Passion to Please Christ

The success syndrome says that you must achieve your own goals; you must achieve the approval of men. God says we must choose to seek to please Him. Rather than seeking to be a man-pleaser, I need to be like Paul, who did not seek the favor of men but God. He said, "For am I now seeking the favor of men, or of God? Or am I striving to please men? If I were still trying to please men, I would not be a slave of Christ" (Galatians 1:10).

It's natural for us to want the plaudits of people, but we only need the applause of heaven. Who is the one to judge success? Paul's concern was only what the Lord thought. "For I am conscious of nothing against myself, yet I am not by this acquitted. But the one who examines me is the Lord" (1 Corinthians 4:4). This gives us an even higher standard by which to measure ourselves.

Paul's ambition was to be pleasing to God knowing that, "...we must all appear before the judgment seat of Christ, so that each one may be recompensed for his deeds in the body, according to what he has done, whether good or bad" (2 Corinthians 5:10). We only need to please the Lord.

We all like to be loved and appreciated by everyone all of the time. I have battled the desire to have all the women of our church count me as their best friend. I love each of them and desire to be close to them. However, that is just not possible. Does it prevent me from reaching out to each one? No. Knowing that I am completely loved and secure— safe in my relationship with Christ should help me deal with slights, rebuffs, criticism, and misunderstandings that come up.

Instead of looking for the praise of men, God directs His children to work heartily as for the Lord because His rewards are what matters. Some ministry couples work themselves into a state of burnout seeking to become a mega-church, thinking that is success. We must find that balance of working hard, resting and making time for our family. Jesus said that His yoke is easy and His burden is light (Matthew 11:30). We have to pace ourselves for the long race that is set before us. We as wives can help our husbands with this, helping them balance work and rest.

In order to defeat the success syndrome we must take our healthy dose of humility as we realize that God is the judge and His standard is perfection. There is nothing that we can do to merit His approval. But by God's grace we have been justified and can serve Him with a clear conscience (2 Corinthians 1:12).

He (Jesus) must increase and I must decrease. God gets more of the glory when He uses nobodies, not some-bodies. Paul wrote that God gave him a thorn in the flesh, to keep him from exalting himself. Through that he learned another lesson about the "backwards kingdom"—God's power is perfected in weakness (2 Corinthians 12:9). The more we recognize our own weakness, the more God's power shines through.

This is the success to rejoice in—His power at work in our lives. Do we love Christ so much that we are willing to serve Him when no one sees or appreciates us, or even when we gain enemies for the sake of the gospel? Then that's success in His eyes.

Put off a Passion for Fame • *Put on* a Passion for Christ's Name

The success syndrome says that you must seek fame—to be widely known and esteemed or acclaimed. You must be better than someone else in order to promote yourself. Scripture tells us that it is pointless to compare ourselves with others. "For we do not dare to classify or compare ourselves with some of those who commend themselves, but when they measure themselves by themselves and compare themselves with themselves, they are without understanding" (2 Corinthians 10:12).

As pointless as this is, we are prone to do it anyway. Do you see your ministry as less successful than that of those who have large ministries? It seems like the ones with the large ministries are esteemed more highly and therefore must be more successful. I've felt that way. My friend Pat Palau, who was a roommate in college, had a husband with a successful ministry. Luis had ministered to millions. He had written books and was on the radio all over Latin America and around the world. I remember thinking how insignificant our little church ministry was compared to the vast ministry Luis had preaching to millions and seeing thousands turn to Christ. I admitted that to my friend Pat years ago when we were together at a conference where her husband was the speaker. I remember her words. She said, "You shouldn't feel that way. Your husband has a different calling—that of a pastor-teacher to equip the saints for the work of ministry. Luis has another calling—that of an evangelist. Because you aren't touching thousands, doesn't mean you are less successful. Luis's ministry is only the first step. The believers have to be nurtured in churches. The work of pastors is vital. Your faithfulness in the local church is invaluable to the kingdom of God." Pat believes this so much she has written a book about the importance of the local church. Her words have encouraged me over the years.

It's important to keep in mind that a larger church or sphere of ministry means more responsibility. It means being held accountable for more people. Scripture says that those who exercise rule over the church will give account to God for those under their care (Hebrews 13:17). We need to constantly go back to the fact that Jesus is the Lord of His church. He leads people to different churches. He has led the ones to our church that He desires our pastors to shepherd.

The Lord has given our church slow but steady growth since its inception. We have four emphases—solid preaching of God's Word, small groups for discipleship and caring, world missions, and a strong caring emphasis to demonstrate the love of Christ. We now have five pastors to carry the load of the people whom God has brought to be a part of the ministry. We also have a biblical counseling ministry where lay counselors are trained, which ministers to the whole community. What about all those many years when Bob was the only pastor? Were we less successful then? No!

Perhaps you are feeling that your husband is less successful because he has a behind-the-scenes ministry and receives little recognition or thanks. It all seems to go to the senior pastor or worship pastor who is up-front every week.

When you start to compare yourself with others, stop and ask, "Am I seeking fame for my name or Christ's name?" The apostle Paul could rejoice even when people preached Christ out of selfish ambition seeking to cause him distress. He said, "What then? Only that in every way, whether in pretense or in truth, Christ is proclaimed, and in this I rejoice. Yes, and I will rejoice" (Philippians 1:18).

As much as we think our husband is the best expositor of the Word in the community or the best missionary or best worship pastor, we must walk humbly before our God. "God is opposed to the proud, but gives grace to the humble" (James 4:6b). As much as we think our church is faithful to God's direction, we have to keep in mind that other churches are doing the job equally well or better, and confess the pride of our hearts as sin. We should be praying regularly for other pastors and their wives and missionaries and their wives, for God's blessing upon their ministries. We are not in competition but workers together. Sometimes we feel resentful as our people change churches and those churches grow through people we have trained for ministry. There is a danger for bitterness to creep in.

I know this from experience. When we had the exodus to another church in our community, I was hurt and felt like a failure. I felt "humbled." Humbling ourselves is not the same. I wanted to change places of ministry, to escape this place of humiliation.

Fortunately, I learned from my husband that humility was one thing that God was trying to teach us. We fell on our faces before Him and sought to learn the lessons He had for us. I read *A Chance to Die*, the story of Amy Carmichael. Her life demonstrates God's "backwards kingdom. Through death comes life. He calls us to die to ourselves, and our ideas of success. Jesus said, "For whoever wishes to save his life will lose it, but whoever loses his life for My sake, he is the one who will save it" (Luke 9:24). Amy Carmichael rejoiced in the disappointments and trials, knowing that it was her chance to die to self. By dying to self, she was living more completely to Christ. This was Amy's prayer when one of her most trusted colleagues died:

> *From prayer that asks that I may be*
> *Sheltered from winds that beat on Thee,*
> *From fearing when I should aspire,*
> *From faltering when I should climb higher,*
> *From silken self, O Captain, free*
> *Thy soldier who would follow Thee.*
>
> *From subtle love of softening things,*
> *From easy choices, weakenings,*
> *(Not thus are spirits fortified,*
> *Not this way went the Crucified,)*
> *From all that dims Thy Calvary,*
> *O Lamb of God, deliver me.*

Give me the love that leads the way,
The faith that nothing can dismay
The hope no disappointments tire
The passion that will burn like fire,
Let me not sink to be a clod:
Make me Thy fuel, Flame of God.[10]

When you are tempted to seek fame for yourself—stop! Remember that your goal is to promote Christ and His name. Trust His sovereignty to give you the role that is best for you. Humble yourself and find a way to consider others more important than yourself (Philippians 2:3-4). Rejoice when Christ is preached. Be zealous for Christ's name!

Put off a Passion for Prosperity • *Put on* Passionate Satisfaction with Christ and Emptying of Self

The success syndrome says that we must seek prosperity. We can overcome this drive for worldly success by being content in Christ and in His place for us. Paul's ministry of traveling and establishing churches was curtailed by his imprisonment. Did that lead to discontent? It certainly could have! He had been evangelizing the then-known world. But he said,

> Not that I speak from want, for I learned to be content in whatever circumstances I am. I know how to get along with humble means, and I also know how to live in abundance; in any and all things I have learned the secret of being filled and going hungry, both of having abundance and suffering need. I can do all things through Him who strengthens me. (Philippians 4:11-13)

What an example of contentment! He was fully satisfied with all he had in Jesus and knew his situation would work out for the advancement of the gospel. Even in prison he was content—he had all he could wish for.

I have to confess, much to my shame, that I did not exemplify

---

10 Elisabeth Elliot, *A Chance to Die* (Tarrytown, New York: Fleming H. Revell Company, 1987), 221.

that kind of contentment during the 15 years that our church was in rented facilities—a Christian school. Our Sunday School shared the classrooms of the school. They put things away every weekend and we tried to leave them just as they were when we found them. That was difficult. We had a portable nursery in a huge cabinet on wheels. Our auditorium was a school multipurpose room that in no way resembled a church. It was on the extreme edge of town with no visibility whatsoever. We put up our sign and took it down each week.

At conferences, when we were in "real" churches, I often would go down this trail, "If only we had a church like this. If only it were downtown. If only we didn't have to do all this extra work of setting up each week. If only we could grow faster, we could get our own place sooner." The "if onlys" weren't glorifying to God in that they were not demonstrating contentment.

Contentment is such an important virtue. It demonstrates trust in God's sovereignty. I was envying the pastor and wife in the church with the building. That was sin. When I recognized the sin and confessed it, I could enjoy being in those churches. Now I have found that since we have a beautiful large church of our own on the main street of town, I can still find other pastors and wives to envy. It is a continual battle.

I must rest in the loving sovereignty of God realizing that He is building His church. He has set some pastors in large churches and most pastors and missionaries in small works. According to some surveys, 70% of all churches in the United States are 100 or less in attendance.[11]

We do not have to have the most popular or progressive church in town. We don't have to have every possible outreach a church could have. We don't have to have a church building to be a success. I can be content in Christ.

I do not have to consider myself a second-rate pastor's wife because my husband is not ministering to thousands or even hundreds. I am content in Christ.

---

11 Aaron Earls, "Small Churches Continue Growing—but in Number, not Size," *Lifeway Research*, https://research.lifeway.com/2021/10/20/small-churches-continue-growing-but-in-number-not-size/. Accessed September 5, 2024.

I do not need everyone in church to consider me his or her best friend. I am content in Christ.

Nor do I need a "real" job to get the recognition of others to be content.

My relationship with Jesus Christ satisfies. I find contentment in Him and am able to be the encouragement to my husband that God wants me to be. Jesus plus nothing equals success—all I need.

When we are fully satisfied with Christ we are willing to sacrifice everything so that others can have that same prosperity (2 Corinthians 5:18-6:10). Instead of striving for our own comfort we can actually seek self-sacrifice and self-denial for the sake of the gospel. Paul wrote to one church where he had ministered, "So I will most gladly spend and be fully spent for your souls. If I love you more, am I to be loved less?" (2 Corinthians 12:15). He had invested in the lives of the believers at Corinth to the fullest but they believed some ridiculous rumors about him. It was hard for him. However, his zeal for ministry was not abated. Paul considered it a privilege to suffer for Christ and His church (Philippians 3:7-14; Ephesians 3:8-13). "Now I rejoice in my sufferings for your sake, and I fill up what is lacking of Christ's afflictions in my flesh, on behalf of His body, which is the church … so that we may present every man complete in Christ" (Colossians 1:24, 28b).

When you are tempted to seek prosperity and comfort—stop! Remember that in Christ are hidden all the treasures of wisdom and knowledge. You can be content in Him.

Put off a Passion for Worldly Success • *Put on* a Passion for Fruitfulness through Faithfulness

The world defines success as achievement, fame, financial gain, wealth, and comfort. God defines prosperity differently. A prosperous life in God's eyes is a fruitful life, a faithful life, and a life that is given away. Just what does it look like? It looks like our seeking for the Word of God to spread rapidly and to be glorified (2 Thessalonians 3:1-2), for eternal souls to be saved (2 Timothy 2:10), for every man to be found complete in Christ (Colossians 1:28), for the crown of righteousness (2 Timothy 4:8). The rewards that we seek as Christians far outshine the temporary glitter of gold.

We have the reward of being a part of raising up faithful disciples of Christ. "For who is our hope or joy or crown of boasting? Is it not even you, before our Lord Jesus at His coming? For you are our glory and joy...for now we really live, if you stand firm in the Lord" (1 Thessalonians 2:19-20; 3:8).

Do you value faithfulness in your husband and the people within the church? I thank my husband over and over for being faithful to me. I don't express thanks to people within our church enough for their faithfulness. We have some saints still active in our church that were part of the original group 25 years ago. When I get discouraged over people leaving the church, I've made it my practice to think of the faithful ones and get encouraged.

In our first church there were people who had been faithful over 50 years to that one congregation. Louise Nilsen typed the bulletin and ran it off on an old mimeograph machine for over 30 years! One of the elders, Lewis Larsen, had served for as long.

My father modeled faithfulness. He directed the choir in a little Baptist church for 30 years. He taught history with excellence for 56 years. What a legacy to pass on to the next generation—faithfulness! If this brought great joy to the leaders in his church, think of how much more joy it brings to the heart of God. I believe that these humble servants will reap more rewards than many people who are seemingly more successful in the eyes of the world.

Jesus brought this point home when He gave the parable of the talents. Those who invest their gifts wisely and responsibly receive the commendation, "Well done, good and faithful slave. You were faithful with a few things, I will put you in charge of many things; enter into the joy of your master" (Matthew 25:21). The slaves were given different resources and expected to produce accordingly. Some gained a greater profit than others, but all who were faithful to use what they were given were praised.

God values faithfulness very highly. We must, by His power, remain faithful to Him, our husbands, families, and the church, no matter what. We must run this race to win the imperishable prize. We must discipline ourselves so that we are not disqualified in the end (1 Corinthians 9:23-27).

As we are each faithful to our own particular calling (as we discussed in Chapter 1), and as we abide in Him, we will see fruit. How is this different from the success syndrome? Instead of seeking achievement, fame, and prosperity, we seek God's approval, the fame of Christ's name, contentment, and self-sacrifice.

As we faithfully lay down our lives, we know that we will be rewarded with the imperishable rewards of being a part of building Christ's kingdom. The difference is in the motive and the means. At the beginning of Paul's ministry he said, "But I do not make my life of any account nor dear to myself, so that I may finish my course and the ministry which I received from the Lord Jesus, to testify solemnly of the gospel of the grace of God" (Acts 20:24). True success is achieved for God's glory not self-exaltation. True success is achieved through humility and faithfulness.

At the end of Paul's life he was able to say,

> For I am already being poured out as a drink offering, and the time of my departure has come. I have fought the good fight, I have finished the course, I have kept the faith. In the future there is laid up for me the crown of righteousness, which the Lord, the righteous Judge, will award to me on that day, and not only to me, but also to all who have loved His appearing.
> (2 Timothy 4:6-8)

This, my friend, is what it is all about! Let's line up our passions and practice with Paul's, and the success syndrome will have no power over us. We will be able to run the race to truly win the prize.

OVERCOMING THE HURTS THAT PEOPLE INFLICT

Someone has said, "Being in the pastorate would be great, if you didn't have to work with people." Wouldn't that be ideal? Our husbands could study the Word of God all week and get up on Sunday morning and preach or teach or lead worship. There would be no problems to deal with, no heartaches to bear, and no hurts or misunderstandings. However, that is not ministry. It is not life. We are called to work with people, who like ourselves, are sinners who offend one another. We can sink into depression at this fact or we can overcome.

Some of God's choicest servants almost went down—their despair was so bad that it resulted in desiring God to take their lives. If you want company in your misery, read about Job (Job 6:8-9), Moses (Numbers 11:11-15), Elijah (1 Kings 19:4), and Jeremiah (Jeremiah 20:14-18); they all viewed their situations as hopeless.

Moses may have thought that shepherding the sheep on the backside of the desert was better than shepherding a million or so rebellious humans. (Now that's a large flock!)

In fact, Moses was so sick of the peoples' complaints that he wanted to die. He said,

> So Moses said to Yahweh, "Why have You allowed this evil toward Your slave? And why have I not found favor in Your

sight, that You have laid the burden of all this people on me?
… I alone am not able to carry all this people because it is too
heavy for me. So if You are going to deal thus with me, please
kill me at once, if I have found favor in Your sight, and do not
let me see my wretchedness."
(Numbers 11:11, 14-15)

Likewise, Paul had a hard ministry seeking to reach God's chosen
people who had rejected their Messiah. Then he uses Elijah's situation
as an example to not give up in his own ministry (Romans 11:2-4). The
divine response to Elijah's discouragement was telling him that He had
seven thousand men who had not bowed the knee to Baal. God has
His remnant. Paul concluded, "for the gifts and the calling of God are
irrevocable" (Romans 11:29).

God would sovereignly accomplish His will in the Jews as well
as Gentiles. Then Paul bursts out with this doxology of praise, "Oh,
the depth of the riches and wisdom and knowledge of God! How
unsearchable are His judgments and unfathomable His ways!" (Romans
11:33) Paul would leave the results in the hands of the all-wise God,
which is what we must do.

In this chapter I am going to address three of the main ways that
people hurt us when we are trying to serve them. We suffer from people deserting us by changing churches. At other times they hurt us by
staying in the church and attacking us with criticism, complaints, and
gossip. Finally they may completely reject our ministry and us. We are
tempted to give up in despair, but God actually wants to use these hurts
that people inflict to strengthen us.

The Pain of Church Members Changing Churches

I don't know if you've ever identified your top struggle in ministry but I definitely know mine. I really feel like throwing in the
towel rather than taking it up when people in our church change
churches within our community. This is a continuing struggle for
me.

Just what makes this such a deeply distressing trial? I believe it
is because of the feeling of rejection by the people whom we love so
deeply. We have poured our lives into them, maybe even led them

to the Lord and discipled them. They are like family. We have gone through all kinds of circumstances with them over the years seeking to be there for them—comforting and encouraging them for all we were worth. They might have been great encouragers to us in the ministry. We thought they would always be by our sides. Then they decide to change churches. It is inevitable that we are affected by it if we have any emotional involvement at all with our people.

According to a recent survey, one out of seven adults switches churches every year. We all know how these moves can hurt the entire church in many ways. The church counts on their support to pay salaries. There is a need to fill ministry positions. The whole congregation feels the loss, almost like they have been divorced, because relationships that have been valued have been torn out of their lives. It is just plain discouraging.

Probably the hardest trial that we have experienced in ministry was when ten families left our young church of just a few years for a large church with a good youth program. These were some of our closest friends and we thought they would never leave us. When this happened it was like the wind had gone out of our sails. We were stopped short in the water wondering if the church that we had moved across the country to plant would survive.

I wanted to move away, thinking that I could escape the hurt. I felt that if our best friends weren't supporting us in ministry, who would? I went into the depths of discouragement. Although Bob was receiving criticism from the elders for the decline in the ministry, he was holding steady in the gale and looking for the lessons God was trying to teach us. I have never wept so much in our ministry. I cried out to the Lord. "Lord, why are these people going to the large church, when we need them so desperately in our church? Can't they make some sacrifices for the sake of this church that they have been such a vital part of up until now?" And on and on my cries to the Lord went.

Just how do we handle this situation and come out like Paul who wrote, "in every way afflicted, but not crushed; perplexed, but not despairing; persecuted, but not forsaken; struck down, but not destroyed" (2 Corinthians 4:8-9)?

Keep Your Focus on Jesus

During this trial I just described, the one passage of Scripture that I clung to was,

> fixing our eyes on Jesus, the author and perfecter of faith, who for the joy set before Him endured the cross, despising the shame, and has sat down at the right hand of the throne of God. For consider Him who has endured such hostility by sinners against Himself, so that you will not grow weary, fainting in heart. You have not yet resisted to the point of shedding blood in your striving against sin. (Hebrews 12:2-4)

In order to sustain myself spiritually, I meditated on these verses, which I had on cards throughout the house. I kept reminding myself, "Keep looking to Jesus, Mary; don't grow weary and lose heart. You haven't resisted to the point of shedding blood!" I prayed, "Lord, you will never leave me. You love me. I'm yours. You endured the cross with such pain and hostility of sinners to purchase me for Yourself. Give me Your peace. Help me to be satisfied in You."

John Piper writes,

> Christ does not exist in order to make much of us. We exist in order to enjoy making much of him... Christ is not glorious so that we get wealthy or healthy. Christ is glorious so that rich or poor, sick or sound, (successful church ministry or not), we might be satisfied in him.[12]

I saturated myself in God's Word. I began in Genesis and underlined in red all the references to Jesus Christ and His atoning work for us throughout the whole Old Testament. I read the Gospels seeking to draw closer to Jesus. With my increased knowledge of His love for me, my love for Him grew.

I read books about strong women who kept their focus on Jesus such as *A Chance to Die*, the story of Amy Carmichael, who saw the disappointments and trials in her life as an opportunity to die to self (John 12:24). The only lack of success would be not dying to self nor

---

12 John Piper, *Seeing and Savoring Jesus Christ*, (Wheaton, Illinois: Crossway, 2001), 27.

living to Christ. I saw that through Jesus' example and teaching I needed to die to myself and my idea of success. Elisabeth Elliot's life and writings were also an inspiration and I read many of her books.

Let God's Peace Rule in Your Heart

Instead of a downward spiral into self-pity, I went to Paul's directive to have God's peace in Philippians 4:4-9. What is his prescription for peace?

Rejoice in the Lord (v. 4). This is a command. Rejoice is in the present imperative and could be translated, "Rejoice in the Lord always; again I will say, rejoice" (Philippians 4:4)! This is repeated. Let's just think about all we have to rejoice in. We rejoice in the cross of Christ where God the Father poured out His wrath on His own Son so that we could become His children. We rejoice that we are His blood-bought children because of His great love for us. We rejoice in all the riches we have in Christ. We rejoice that He is sovereign, perfectly holy, just, loving, wise, and powerful and is working everything in our lives together for good.

When my life is not turning out the way I had hoped, I can rejoice because my joy and peace are totally unrelated to my circumstances, rather, they are related to my unchanging relationship to my sovereign Lord. If Paul could rejoice from a prison cell, then I can rejoice anywhere, at any time!

How do I rejoice? I talk to the Lord and tell Him how much I love and trust Him, if need be, through my tears. Consider the trial to be a joy, because it is a way to fellowship in His suffering. I know more of the rejection He went through. Sing a praise song, a hymn. Write Him a psalm. Turn on praise music. Remind myself of how much He cares for the precious people who hurt us. He loves them more than we could ever love them. He is directing their lives. It is His church. I must learn to release people to other parts of His vineyard with less sorrow. Any love that I poured out on the people who left, I did for Jesus. He saw it and was pleased.

Resolve to be gentle, patient, and have a forbearing spirit (Philippians 4:5). This means that I must be willing to submit to injustice or mistreatment without retaliating. When I feel like lashing out I must walk in the Spirit, exhibit the fruit of patience and wait on God to accomplish His will.

Remember the Lord is near. (Philippians 4:5) I have His presence living within me to comfort me on a moment-by-moment basis.

Refuse to be anxious about anything (Philippians 4:6a). This, too, is a command. I must put off anxiety about our church going under and my friends leaving us, because He is in control, loves me and is working for my good.

Rely on prayer (Philippians 4:6b-7). I must pray about the situation—lay my hurts and disappointments before the Lord who already knows all about it. He wants me to do it with thanksgiving—gratitude that He will take care of it. What a promise I have: "And the peace of God, which surpasses all comprehension, will guard your hearts and your minds in Christ Jesus" (Philippians 4:7).

Rest my mind on whatever is excellent or praiseworthy (Philippians 4:8). Here Paul summarized everything worthwhile for me to think about. I must keep my mind on the things of moral and spiritual excellence if I am to have peace. These thoughts will crowd out all the other thoughts that cause me to worry and doubt God's goodness.

Reach out and practice what is good (Philippians 4:9). The thinking that Paul just talked about has a purpose. It leads me to action. I hear what God wants me to do, think on it until I understand it, and then I must act on it—put it into practice. The result is what Jesus said would happen to the house built upon a rock: when the storms come, it will stand firm.

Draw Comfort from Your Husband

Satan would like to divide us by tempting us to blame our husbands for perceived failures on their part and cause these trials to pull us apart. It's important to draw closer together as a couple as you weather the storms.

My husband, in comforting me in my grief said, "Honey, I'll never leave you. You're stuck with me!" I seemed to have forgotten that and those words brought me comfort. The important thing was that we weather it together. God designed marriage for these very times. "Two are better than one because they have good wages for their labor. For if either of them falls, the one will lift up his companion (Ecclesiastes 4:9-10).

Give Unfulfilled Expectations to God

We have certain expectations of the flock. We expect them to be as passionate about serving Christ in our church as we are. Some are and some aren't. When they aren't, we feel let down, disappointed, discouraged, and ready to give up. Our feelings tell us, "If they don't care, why should I? I can't continue to carry the burden of this alone! I'm tired of being the one to always encourage others to serve. Why can't they encourage me some of the time?" See this for what it is, a "pity party" and the beginning of a downward spiral.

Contrast that with giving these expectations to God. When we do that He will give us His grace to continue alone if need be. Paul wants us to get it straight. He writes, "Who are you to judge the servant of another? To his own master he stands or falls; and he will stand, for the Lord is able to make him stand" (Romans 14:4). If I could only remember this!

Keep the Big Picture in Mind

Dear friend, you and I need to remind ourselves that our church is just one row in the vineyard of the kingdom of God in our community. There are many other rows—gospel-preaching churches where these people can be fed and serve Christ. We need to realize that God may be leading them to another church. They are not rejecting our husband's ministry or us. They are seeking to do what is best for their families.

As we pray and ask God for comfort, thanking Him for the trial, the Holy Spirit will do His work in comforting us and assuring us of God's love and sovereignty. He has allowed this to happen for a purpose. Through His peace, which is ours on a moment-by-moment basis we are able to persevere through the trial for the honor and glory of Jesus Christ.

As a footnote, our church weathered this storm—and many others—and is a strong, growing church now. However, we must resist in any way, taking credit. It is a very dangerous situation to become prideful, taking our eyes off Jesus and putting them on the success of our ministry.

The Hurt of Criticism, Complaints, and Gossip

One pastor's wife told me that criticism is her top struggle. Maybe it's yours. She said it is especially painful when it comes from a leader in the church. If you haven't experienced this, you will. It somehow helps to keep in mind that we all experience the same trials. We have common problems (1 Corinthians 10:13). The criticism can be of our husbands, our children, our church, or us. It all hurts. Like me, you know how ungrounded criticism can sap the joy out of ministry if we allow it.

The apostle Paul experienced it when the self-styled false apostles in the Corinthian church assaulted his character. He wrote, "For even when we came into Macedonia our flesh had no rest, but we were afflicted on every side—conflicts without, fears within. But God, who comforts the humbled, comforted us by the coming of Titus (2 Corinthians 7:5-6). He received God's comfort to go on.

Our husbands are usually the ones to receive the complaints, unless they are given to us to pass on to them. The service is too long. There aren't enough hymns, or not enough choruses. The drums are too loud, we shouldn't have drums. The carpets are worn out; nobody has invited us over. There aren't enough social events, or there are too many. There is not enough political involvement, or there is too much. There is too much emphasis on giving; the pastor is too explicit in talking about sin. The pastor's wife is too involved, or not involved enough.

Being in the place of leadership is often unpopular because it is impossible to meet the desires of all the people all of the time. Tough decisions have to be made that not everyone appreciates. There will be misunderstandings.

A woman in their congregation told one dear pastor's wife that she and her husband reminded her of Barbie and Ken. Although their outward appearance always seemed to this person to be perfect, they were hurting inside. This ministry couple has a physically disabled son for whom they have cared for nearly 30 years. How could anyone who really took the time to get to know them think they have a storybook life?

My husband has chosen not to tell me most of the criticism that he receives because he doesn't want me to be hurt or take up an offense. He almost always bears it alone, but takes it right to the Lord. I have not always been happy about his decision in this area but it has been for the best.

How do we come out victorious in this trying circumstance? Let's look at some biblical principles:

Keep Loving Them

Think of the last three times that you were hurt by what you perceived to be unkind remarks. You can't think of any? If so, you passed the test!

"[Love] does not act unbecomingly, does not seek its own, is not provoked, does not take into account a wrong suffered" (1 Corinthians 13:5). There will always be people who are not content with your husband's ministry or your part as his wife. If you are sensitive to criticism from the people in your church, and you hold onto these hurts, you need to ask God for His kind of love that doesn't hold onto wrongs suffered.

When we are being criticized, we have to remind ourselves that God is the only One we have to please. Paul addressed this when he wrote the believers at Thessalonica, "so we speak, not as pleasing men, but God who examines our hearts.... nor seeking glory from men, either from you or from others" (1 Thessalonians 2:4b, 6a). If it weren't for God's grace we wouldn't be able to make any right decisions; but by His grace we can step out with confidence, knowing that He is directing. It doesn't matter if we please anybody if we are doing what is right.

As hard as it may be, we must pray for the love of Christ to flow through us so that we react in love when we're criticized. Paul wrote the believers at Corinth, some of whom had mistreated him and had been disloyal to him by not defending him against the false apostles, "our heart is opened wide" (2 Corinthians 6:11b). He let them know that he still loved them and had room for them in his heart. What an example for us!

Overcome Evil with Good

Our assignment from God is to return good for evil as Paul admonishes us to "Bless those who persecute you; bless, and do not curse… Never paying back evil for evil to anyone … If possible, so far as it depends on you, being at peace with all men … Do not be overcome by evil, but overcome evil with good" (Romans 12:14, 17a, 18, 21). We need to seek ways of doing good to those who hurt us. It may be to pray for God to bless them. It may be an act of kindness. This is what sets us apart as followers of Jesus Christ, who overcame the greatest evil that has ever been done by bringing salvation through it. When we act in love, it changes our feelings toward that person.

Forgive and Cover It Over

If you didn't pass the test of remembering wrongs suffered, ask God to help you forgive those who did the wrongs. Further, commit to not dwelling on it, nor bringing it up to them or others, unless you need to seek counsel on the matter or confront them about it.

Jesus said, "For if you forgive others for their transgressions, your heavenly Father will also forgive you. But if you do not forgive others, then your Father will not forgive your transgressions" (Matthew 6:14-15). If you want a good dose of conviction, read the parable that Jesus tells about forgiveness and how God chastises His children severely for lack of it (Matthew 18:21-35).

You have no option. You must forgive! A root of bitterness can spring up if you do not forgive (Hebrews 12:15). You must ask God to give you the grace to grant forgiveness to that person who hurt you.

You can choose to cover over the offense unless you need to confront the issue with the person in order to resolve it. "He who covers a transgression seeks love, but he who repeats a matter separates close companions" (Proverbs 17:9). "Hatred stirs up strife, but love covers all transgressions" (Proverbs 10:12). We have had all of our transgressions covered by the blood of Jesus, therefore, we can choose to cover other people's hurts against us and not even bring them up. Just as Jesus bore the cost, we can bear the pain and choose to cover it over.

Have you often been sorry you just didn't cover over an offense? I have. When in defense of myself I speak something caustic or just display a know-it-all attitude; it just requires me to seek forgiveness of the person for my wrong response to what was done to me.

Don't Be Defensive

When confronted by criticism or complaints, the best course of action is to listen to the complaint and try to understand it from the other person's perspective. If we are doing what is right before God and our consciences, we need not be defensive if it is questioned. We can seek to learn from the other person's ideas and humbly ask God to change our thinking, if that is what is needed. Most of the things that we are criticized for are unimportant matters—not moral issues.

This whole issue of differences is addressed in Romans 14 and 15. The kingdom of God is more than eating and drinking—external things, non-essentials. It has more to do with holy, obedient living. Paul urged the believers to bear the weaknesses of those without strength and not just please themselves. If Christ, the perfect Son of God, could bring sinners into His family, how much more should we as forgiven believers be willing to accept each other and lovingly overlook our differences over inconsequential matters?

If someone prefers worship without drums, that is fine and you need not insist on thinking alike on such matters. But if your church has decided to include drums in the worship, and that person feels they can't worship with drums, he or she may need to go to a church where no drums are included in the worship service.

Keep a Sense of Humor

As in most situations, a sense of humor comes in handy when dealing with criticism and gossip. Below are some examples of complaints and gossip about us and others in ministry. While it was important to address and clear up the issues, you can imagine the good laugh we had over them.

Word got back from the state committee who examines group homes that I, the pastor's wife of the Evangelical Free Will Baptist Church (the mistake with our church name was humorous in its own right), was telling the girls in my Bible study at a group home that they were adulteresses and that they had snakes in their stomachs!

A bit of gossip got back to us that a lady wouldn't go to our church because we make all the divorced people sit in the first three rows! How preposterous!

One pastor friend we know received a letter of complaint that there was no cranberry sauce at the Thanksgiving dinner at the church. As petty as that seems, it turns out that the pastor's wife had even brought a cranberry dish to the dinner.

Praise and Thank God

Even when people are saying or doing hurtful things to us we can still praise God in the midst of it. In Jesus' Sermon on the Mount He taught us how to operate in His "backwards kingdom." He said, "Blessed are you when people insult you and persecute you, and falsely say all kinds of evil against you because of Me. Rejoice and be glad, for your reward in heaven is great; for in the same way they persecuted the prophets who were before you" (Matthew 5:11-12). Add to that, "in everything give thanks, for this is God's will for you in Christ Jesus" (1 Thessalonians 5:18).

We can praise and thank God that we are counted worthy to suffer shame for Jesus! We can put our minds on what is true, dignified, right, pure, lovely, commendable, excellent, and worthy of praise (Philippians 4:8). There are plenty of people who do appreciate what our husbands are doing. We can focus our minds on the faithful ones within our church—our "joy or crown of exultation." Let's keep the negatives in perspective. They are a minority. Let us revel in the inner thrill that God is using us in spite of all the opposition, criticism, and complaining that may be going on.

If Necessary, Confront

Sometimes, for the sake of unity in the church it is necessary to confront an individual. If so, we should go to that person in the spirit of Galatians 6:1—gently and humbly—talking about the matter without judging his or her motives. If my sister or brother and I are out of sorts with each other, our first order of business is to get that straightened out before coming to worship. Jesus said, "Therefore if you are presenting your offering at the altar, and there remember that your brother has something against you, leave your offering there before the altar and go; first be reconciled to your brother, and then come and present your offering" (Matthew 5:23-24).

When do I go? This has helped me remember: If I have had my toes run over by a bicycle (i.e., have been offended), "The one with the hurt toes goes, because she's the one who knows" (quote from Jay Adams). If I have been hurt, then I go, unless I choose to cover it over. It is crucial for the health of the Body to confront someone who is spreading gossip. Like cancer, it will eat away and cause untold damage if not confronted.

You might begin by saying, "I always want to believe the best about you, _____. Could you let me know what was just said about _____? This is what I heard, _____. If this person wasn't the source of the gossip, track it down to the source.

When you have confronted and the Lord has brought about repentance on the person's part, or an understanding of what was meant and restoration of the relationship, you have brought Christ glory.

The Pain of Outright Rejection

Perhaps you and your husband have gone through outright rejection or have been rejected by a certain segment of your flock. Maybe your church has asked you to leave or the church you were planting has failed. If so, you've experienced unspeakable pain.

One of our good friends in the ministry was asked to leave a church less than a year after he had just moved his family across the country to serve there. The preceding pastor had left that same church after a short ministry because of the critical spirit of the congregation. Bob mentors pastors and has heard too many similar stories. We have known of some churches that have hurt several pastors in a row, so much so that they left the ministry. It is sad that churches can be so unloving and even cruel to their servants.

But here is a question to ponder: Just what will it take to get us to give up ministry? Rejection? Criticism? Lack of appreciation? People questioning the value of our ministry? Discouragement? At what point do we give up and say, "This is too hard, I quit!"?

Here are some biblical principles to help us know how to handle rejection victoriously and have the blessing of God on our life.

Realize That Our Lord Was Rejected

Let me draw us to the truth that will set us free from bitterness, resentment, anger, and discouragement. Jesus said of Himself, "The stone which the builders rejected, this became the chief corner stone; this came about from the Lord, and it is marvelous in our eyes" (Matthew 21:42b). In fulfillment of Scripture "He was despised and forsaken of men, a man of sorrows and acquainted with grief" (Isaiah 53:3a). He bore our sins as the rejected Son of God. Doesn't that put our rejection in perspective? The servant is not greater than his Lord. Should we expect better treatment than the perfect One?

Ask God for Perseverance

Women, we must stand by our man—encourage him to begin again. We must plead with God for perseverance—staying power. His strength is perfected in our weakness.

Perseverance is so important in any work for God. I'm learning from my husband who is so persevering. He just keeps reaching out in love and asking God, "What do you want me to learn through this?" We can learn to thank God for the trial by faith, asking Him for wisdom and seeing what we can learn from it to be more conformed to the image of His Son. "Knowing that the testing of your faith brings about perseverance" (James 1:3).

When times are tough we need not plead with our husband to leave the ministry. He has a calling from God. It would be wrong for me to have my husband leave the ministry to please me. God will give me the strength to stay the course. The grass isn't greener in another church or mission field. All ministry is hard.

It is very sad when a man who is called by God to ministry leaves because of his wife's insistence. I know of men who would fervently desire to be in ministry but their wives could not stand up under the hurts of ministry. They are missing the greater blessing of persevering together. If she becomes ill and he cannot perform his duties, or if he must step back because of family difficulties, God will honor that. Our observation and experience has been that churches benefit from the longevity of their pastors. They experience the faithful care of a shepherd who knows them over years and cares enough to persevere through trials.

When it was rough, Paul could not abandon his calling. He told the believers to "…be steadfast, immovable, always abounding in the work of the Lord, knowing that your labor is not in vain in the Lord" (1 Corinthians 15:58). May this encourage us—it's not in vain!

Paul saw himself as a clay pot—expendable and lowly but containing the wonderful treasure of the gospel, "so that the surpassing greatness of the power will be of God and not from ourselves" (2 Corinthians 4:7b). Through the power of God, dear sisters, we do not need to lose heart. We can, with hope and confidence, live for the eternal and lasting, not the temporary and fleeting. "Therefore, since we have this ministry, as we received mercy, we do not lose heart" (2 Corinthians 4:1).

Seek Help

In times of seeming failure and hurt you need not be "Lone Rangers" toughing it out. Sometimes ministers and their wives need ministering to. Ask a couple whom you respect to come alongside you to give you wise counsel and comfort from the Scriptures and the support you need.

We were never meant to go through these trials alone. Perhaps you need help in turning it over to the Lord and seeking His comfort and strength to go on. In humility, we need to accept help when we need it. In fact, God's model is to use others in the Body of Christ to spur us on to keep on keeping on for Christ.

Comfort Others with the Comfort You Receive

Right in the midst of the trial we went through when several families left our church at once, Bob had committed to be the field-conference speaker for our denomination's missionaries in Africa. He thought, "I can't even keep my own church together, how can I minister to them?" However, through his brokenness and the lessons that God was teaching him, God used him greatly. The missionaries were in hard places too. They were encouraged as we cried together over our ministries. They appreciated someone who understood what they were going through. The wives and I received mutual encouragement from one another.

The next year Bob and I were asked to minister to our missionaries in Japan. Some were ready to quit. They were experiencing tough times. They, too, were encouraged and strengthened through the comfort we were receiving from the Lord that was being passed on to them. We clearly experienced the truth of this verse: "Blessed be the God and Father of our Lord Jesus Christ, the Father of mercies and God of all comfort, who comforts us in all our affliction so that we will be able to comfort those who are in any affliction with the comfort with which we ourselves are comforted by God" (2 Corinthians 1:3-4).

If you aren't suffering, you probably know other pastors and wives who are going through the fire and who need to be encouraged and comforted. Why not get together with them, call them, or send them an email with some loving words, soon!

Be Encouraged by Great Examples of Perseverance

We can take courage from the life of Jonathan Edwards. As a key figure in America's Great Awakening in the eighteenth century, he and his wife modeled great perseverance. He pastored a church in Northampton, Massachusetts for 23 years—the largest church outside of Boston where the revival began, while his wife Sarah was the mother of their 11 children. Samuel Hopkins, a writer of the day wrote:

> It was a happy circumstance that he (Jonathan) could trust everything to the care of Mrs. Edwards with entire safety and with undoubting confidence. She was a most judicious and faithful mistress of a family, habitually industrious, a sound economist, managing her household affairs with diligence and discretion. While she uniformly paid a becoming deference to her husband and treated him with entire respect, she spared no pains in conforming to his inclination and rendering everything in the family agreeable and pleasant.[13]

Jonathan did a great deal of traveling and speaking during the revival and Sarah was left at home with the children. Then a problem started brewing in their church. In the eyes of their flock they seemed

---

13 Elisabeth D. Dodds, *Marriage to a Difficult Man: The Uncommon Union of Jonathan and Sarah Edwards*, (Douglasville, Georgia: G3 Press, 2023), 31.

to be too extravagant with their money and Sarah was asked to turn over the itemized family budget so everyone could see how they were managing and spending their money. The other problem was that pastor Edwards had decided not to accept into church membership the non-committed.

In 1750, there were problems aplenty. Sarah had just given birth to her eleventh child and two months later, physically and emotionally depleted, she was flattened by rheumatic fever. That spring, townspeople shunned the Edwards family, refusing to talk with them on the street. Church attendance was only a fraction of what it used to be. A petition was circulated and 200 church members signed it asking for Edwards's dismissal as minister. By mid-year Jonathan was unemployed. Paul Elmer said in Cambridge History of American Literature, The citizens of Northampton had ousted the greatest theologian and philosopher yet produced in this country.[14]

Jonathan then received a call to pastor a church composed of a few white families and 42 Indians on the western frontier of Massachusetts. "In primitive Stockbridge, Jonathan preached in a small stuffy room through an interpreter to a small congregation, mostly of Indians who had covered themselves in bear grease as a protection against the winter cold."[15]

Sarah continued to support her husband while probably wondering why the Lord had led a scholar like her husband to such a place or why she, who was accustomed to finer things, was to live in a log cabin surrounded by wigwams.

If Sarah could persevere under those circumstances, I think that I can!

Look for the Good That God Is Working in It

God used this situation for good in Edwards' lives and He can use your particular trial for good in your life. Jonathan had more time to write in this smaller church and his writings are treasured to this day. When the French and Indian War started heating up, his ministry there had to come to a close and he was given the call to be the president

---

14 Ibid, 94.
15 Ibid, 95.

of Princeton University which he accepted reluctantly. After just a few weeks he became ill with smallpox, before Sarah moved to New Jersey to be with him. On his deathbed he said,

> Give my kindest love to my dear wife and tell her that the uncommon union that has so long subsisted between us has been of such a nature as I trust is spiritual and therefore will continue forever. And I hope she will be supported under so great a trial and submit cheerfully to the will of God. And as to my children, you are now to be left fatherless, which I hope will be an inducement to you to seek a Father who will never fail you.[16]

Their marriage, which was characterized by harmony, love, and esteem survived all the pressures of ministry and received God's blessing on their posterity. A study of 1400 descendants of Jonathan and Sarah Edwards indicated that it produced many people in serving positions—"12 college presidents, 65 professors, 100 lawyers, 30 judges, 66 physicians, and 80 holders of public office including three senators, three governors, and a vice president of the United States."[17]

We may not always see the fruit of our suffering but by faith we know that God is working for good in our lives (Romans 8:28-29).

---

16 Ibid, 99.
17 Ibid, 75.

COPING WITH LONELINESS

"The one thing that I struggle with the most as a pastor's wife is the loneliness. I don't feel I can talk with ladies at the church though they understand that I hurt and struggle. They expect more from me than I have to give." This heartfelt expression that was shared with me is not uncommon. Another couple shared that with the husband being the only pastor of a small independent church they believed there couldn't be a more lonely position in the world. They felt that they had no one to whom they could unburden their hearts. They were especially tender having just gone through a sore trial.

Why would we as pastors' wives be lonely? We are in the middle of the action. We are aware of everyone's lives yet sometimes we experience times of deep loneliness and even feelings of sadness and despair.

I'm sure we would agree that just being alone does not cause loneliness. We all need some of that. So what does cause loneliness? It comes from the feeling of being cut off from the spirit of others, being left out, isolated or ignored.

We are actually in good company when we experience loneliness. There are numerous examples of loneliness in the Bible. David cried out, "Look to the right and see; that there is no one who regards me; a way of escape has been destroyed from me; no one cares for my soul" (Psalm 142:4). Again he says, "I lie awake, I have become like a lonely bird on a roof" (Psalm 102:7).

The prophet Jeremiah lamented, "For these things I am weeping; my eyes run down with water; because far from me is a comforter, one who restores my soul. My children are desolate because the enemy has prevailed" (Lamentations 1:16).

Isn't it amazing to think about the ways that we handle our loneliness that can become so destructive? We try to assuage our loneliness by just getting busier in a frenzy of activity. We put up our defenses to keep from being hurt. We may get involved in a hobby or sport. Some people turn to food. Some go out and splurge on a new outfit, drown themselves in chocolate, or have a pity party. The use of psychotropic drugs is at an all-time high. Many of these actions are not inherently bad, but they become destructive when we look to them to be our comfort or source of peace. As we've seen in earlier chapters, true comfort and peace are only found in Jesus Christ—and are revealed in His Word. Let's discover the antidote to loneliness through the truth of Scripture.

Make God Your Joy

What path do we take to keep loneliness from overtaking us? We must make God our joy. We have a choice when we are feeling down and lonely—go out and splurge on a new outfit, drown ourselves in chocolate, have a pity party or be radical—turn to the true source of joy—God Himself!

The Lord invites you to fellowship with Himself. You were made and redeemed for fellowship with God and your delight needs to be in Him first and foremost—to have no other gods before Him. Jesus summed it all up:

> Jesus answered, "The foremost is, 'Hear, O Israel! The Lord our God is one Lord; and you shall love the Lord your God with all your heart, and with all your soul, and with all your mind, and with all your strength.' The second is this, 'You shall love your neighbor as yourself.' There is no other commandment greater than these." (Mark 12:29-31; cf. Deuteronomy 6:4-5)

Although King David experienced loneliness, he sought to love the Lord his God with all his heart and found his source of comfort and delight in Him. He affirmed this by telling God, "Whom have I in heaven but You? And besides You, I desire nothing on earth. My flesh and my heart fail, but God is the rock of my heart and my portion forever" (Psalm 73:25-26).

When you are lonely, ask yourself, "Am I expecting others to meet my needs as only God can?" David knew where to go in his loneliness. He wrote, "Surely wait in silence for God, O my soul, for my hope is from Him" (Psalm 62:5). Loneliness can drive our hearts to the heart of God; it can be used as a spiritual alarm clock to turn us to God and in that way is used for good in our lives.

Take Delight in God's Promises

The Psalms are a comforting place to turn to get our focus where it needs to be. Open up the Psalms in your loneliness and pray that God will comfort your heart as you let them fill your heart with praises to God by faith. Set your heart on His grace and magnificence. Think on all that He is for you and has done for you. Confess the sin of putting your comfort and pleasure above everything else, including God Himself—making it the idol of your heart. He will cleanse you and give you His peace and joy in exchange for your sin and turmoil.

As we wait upon God, His Word is our solace and comfort. We must cling to those promises, meditate on them, and trust in them. He tells us that He will always be with us (Isaiah 41:10; Matthew 28:19-20). He is in us (John 14:17). In Him we live and move and exist (Acts 17:28). His thoughts of us are like the sand on the seashore and we are never out of His presence (Psalm 139). I can have His peace in this world because Christ has overcome the world (John 16:33). I can have His joy no matter what the circumstances (John 15:11).

As a new pastor's wife in an area of the country that was totally new to me and foreign to my background (we both grew up in small towns and we found ourselves in the shadow of New York City)—I often experienced feelings of loneliness and not fitting in. My husband was busy finding his way in a new career and I was doing the same. My new career was being a pastor's wife. For the three years before God blessed us with our first child, there were times of loneliness. What to do? Turn to God's promises. I remember putting them on index cards around the house. It's a battle to keep our minds on God and not to lament our circumstances. As we rely on Him and remember His goodness we are enabled to put off the feelings of self-pity and replace them with trust and satisfaction.

Go to Jesus in Prayer

Jesus understands. All His closest friends rejected Him. He was alone when He bore our sins on the cross so that we should never be totally alone. He prayed, "Eli, Eli, lama sabachthani?" that is, "My God, My God, why have You forsaken Me?"(Matthew 27:46b). Jesus must have gone to the far reaches of loneliness. He carried all of the sins of every man, woman and child, chosen in Christ, across the span of time from Adam and Eve to the end, upon Himself. Consequently, God had to turn His back upon Him and He died alone—forsaken even of the Father.

We can go to Him and pour out our hearts.

> Therefore, since we have a great high priest who has passed through the heavens, Jesus the Son of God, let us take hold of our confession. For we do not have a high priest who cannot sympathize with our weaknesses, but One who has been tempted in all things like we are, yet without sin. Therefore let us draw near with confidence to the throne of grace, so that we may receive mercy and find grace to help in time of need. (Hebrews 4:14-16)

Our prayer may sound something like this:

> Dear Lord, You know how lonely I am. I thank You that You understand. Please take this away and replace it with Your peace and joy. I want to know You better and be conscious of Your presence with me at all times and dwell on Your promises. Give me wisdom to know how to reach out and initiate friendships. I'm your humble servant. I love You and thank You. In Your Son's precious name. Amen.

Focus on Others and Initiate Friendships

As we gain new strength and comfort through the Word and prayer—casting our care upon Him—we can initiate friendships.

Loneliness can come from a focus on self. "Why am I feeling left out?" "Why is no one reaching out to me?" Real joy is found in giving our lives away for others and for the sake of the kingdom of God.

So if you are frustrated because your phone never rings to see how you are doing or for social purposes—only when there's a need—you pick up the phone and call to see how someone is doing and set up social opportunities. Jesus said, "And treat others the same way you want them to treat you" (Luke 6:31).

You may be lonely when in a group of people because you don't connect with any of them. It could be in church of all places or in a women's Bible study. You may think that you are not missed when you are not there, left out of things, or just not noticed. Then look for someone who is lonelier than you, reach out to that person, notice her, include her. As you take your eyes off of yourself, you will find yourself making friends in the most unexpected places. This is a wonderful thing to teach your children as well.

Our daughter didn't have a lot of friends going into public high school after three years of homeschooling. Because of her Christian stand, she didn't fit in. But the Lord gave her great friends who were the other newcomers or people who were in need of friends.

If you are lonely because you are new in the community or in a foreign country you're not alone. If you feel other women may not take you in because they already have their friendships made, you're not stranded. If God called you to leave behind all your familiar places, friends, and family for His kingdom, He promises others to take their place (Mark 10:30).

In the shadow of that big city God provided Ann, a dear neighbor who came to faith in Christ. When we moved across the country to our second ministry leaving family and friends behind, God again supplied me with new friends.

God's plan is for you to have the closest of friends and He expects you to seek them out. "A man of too many friends comes to ruin, but there is a friend who sticks closer than a brother" (Proverbs 18:24). Why not call and invite that woman over for lunch that you think would be a good friend? Invite her and her husband over so you can be friends as couples.

Ministry can set us apart from others unnecessarily. If we experience loneliness because we are in a separate category because our husbands are in vocational Christian service, we must break down the barriers. Many women are intimidated by our position, so we may need to make the first move.

Could it be that people think they have to be more spiritual around us? Maybe that is because we don't share our own struggles with anyone because we are trying to maintain that front or we think they just wouldn't understand. Maybe we always seem glum or down about something and not fun to be around. Some of these things can be changed.

One sure way to overcome loneliness is to choose a few faithful friends with whom we can be vulnerable. How can we bear each other's burdens if we don't have a friend? We need the prayers of our sisters, their loving support, and their counsel. I value the input of my sisters in the Lord so very much and often seek their wisdom.

Do you feel that you are too busy to develop friendships because of your other pressing responsibilities? Perhaps you are in the season of life with small children and you don't get out much. Homeschooling may place demands that preclude much contact with others.

My dear sister, if you are too busy to develop these kinds of friendships, then you are too busy. We need good friends to share our lives with. That is part of the special joys of life that we don't want to miss out on. It is also a necessity to keep us faithful in our Christian lives. The writer of Hebrews exhorts each of us to "encourage one another day after day, as long as it is still called 'Today,' so that none of you will be hardened by the deceitfulness of sin" (Hebrews 3:13).

Yes, it is impossible to be best friends with every woman in the church. But I believe that we should have at least one or two best friends. Some pastors' wives have been told not to have a "best friend" because that is showing favoritism and might cause jealousy among the other women in the church. I remember speaking on this subject in South Africa and a young pastor's wife who lived in a small, gated gold-mining community was so surprised when I encouraged the wives to seek out a close friend. She was very lonely and had been told it was wrong for her to have a best friend. This advice robbed both her and the women around her of the mutual blessings of close friendships.

David and Jonathan were best of friends. That friendship was a gift from God to David especially during his time of persecution. If we are experiencing deep friendships, that will be an example to others in the church of the relationships that they each need to be building into their lives for accountability and encouragement. That is why it is better to have a few good friends than a plethora of acquaintances. "A man of too many friends comes to ruin, but there is a friend who sticks closer than a brother" (Proverbs 18:24).

Deep friendships take time and consistency to develop. But if you make it a priority and pour into just a few, it will be attainable. My daughter invited a couple of women her age in the church to walk with her once a week. They put their babies in strollers and have great fellowship while also getting some exercise. In this way she is able to mentor some younger women spiritually and enjoy close friendships with them.

If you are homeschooling, find another homeschool mom who you can get together with once a week to share ideas or to teach a class for you in her special area of expertise. Then you can do the same for her. If another homeschool mom is not available, find a grandmother figure that you would like to learn from and ask her to get involved.

We can also take advantage of ministry partnerships to develop closer friendships. In whatever ministry you are involved in, you should have partners. If you are leading a ladies' Bible study or teaching Sunday school, have an apprentice teacher. If you are regularly visiting or counseling, have an apprentice who will be by your side. As you meet weekly to pray for your ministry and for each other; your friendship will also flourish.

There are many creative ways to blend your responsibilities and friendships. You can shop together, carpool to work, exercise together, cook together, do crafts together, have a Bible study together, take your children to the library or park together. It is possible!

If you longed for a kindred spirit to share with as Paul had in Timothy, have you considered seeking out another staff wife who may be feeling the same way? She is another one who is fighting in the trenches with you. She understands your situation and will be a great person to share with. If there are no women on your staff, you will still need to reach out and make a few close friends that you can minister to in your own church. There is nothing wrong with even reaching out beyond your church and looking for a friend from another church, or even community, who is in a similar situation as you.

We need not be in the battle alone. There must be others who are in the fight with us that we can gain mutual encouragement from. We cannot let those with whom we work languish in the trenches. We are in this together. We have to let our needs be known if we are the ones in need of fellowship and encouragement—regardless of our field of service.

If you're like me, you may be tempted to give up pursuing deep friendships because just when you get close to someone she moves away or changes churches. Suddenly you are left without a close friend and have to start all over again. This has happened to me many times. As hard as it is, it must not deter us from pursuing another friendship.

Have a Consuming Purpose

Having a consuming purpose beyond ourselves is vital to overcoming loneliness. John Piper writes:

> God created us to live with a single passion to joyfully display His supreme excellence in all the spheres of life. The wasted life is the life without this passion. God calls us to pray and think and dream and plan and work not to be made much of, but to make much of Him in every part of our lives.[18]

My consuming purpose as a mom will seem diminished if I examine my feelings of loneliness when my children are out of the home. God has ordained that our children leave us, and when that happens there is a big adjustment. But in that loneliness we can center on doing things that will magnify Christ.

A missionary to Mongolia shared about her extreme loneliness on a

---

18 John Piper, *Don't Waste Your Life* (Wheaton, Illinois: Crossway, 2003), 37.

field where they were the only believers in the area. When her children left for college her loneliness was intensified. Instead of going down in despair she poured herself into making Christ known in their needy corner of Christ's vineyard with even more fervor. I also found that my ministry to teen mothers has filled my heart as my children have moved on. Do you have a consuming purpose in your life?

Treasure Your Husband's Friendship

If you are bereft of all your friends, you are never alone because of your husband who is your "companion" (Malachi 2:14), the primary one whom God has given you to dispel loneliness. Work on making that friendship the best that it can be! How sad for our husbands to think that we are friendless when they are there for us! We can take intense pleasure in the friendship that we have in our man, and we should always seek to make it better. We can ask them to pray for us in our burdens. A key purpose of marriage is for companionship and for lifting one another up.

You may feel like the ministry has robbed you of your husband. Because your husband doesn't have a 9-to-5 job, it may seem like he is constantly too busy. He is always studying late, visiting people, or going to meetings. When he is home he is tired of talking because of interacting with people all day long, whereas you have been cooped up in the house all day with the kids and are dying to talk to someone.

If you have made sure that you are not making an idol out of your husband's friendship and you are seeking Christ first, then there may come a time when you need to talk to him. Just as we do with any other problem that we encounter, bring it to him in meekness. Husbands are to live with their wives in an understanding way, but they can't understand us unless we share with them (1 Peter 3:7). We are to go to them in private. Hopefully our husbands will listen to us as we pour out our hearts and seek to work on this area of friendship and communication.

The depth of your companionship is just as important for him as it is for you, even though he may not realize it as readily. This is so vital that we are going to take the whole next two chapters to delve into how to make the most of our marriages.

Relinquish for the Kingdom of God

Perhaps your husband has a traveling ministry that takes him away from home. In that case, you as a wife have chosen to sacrifice your husband's presence in the home for the kingdom of God and He will bless you for it.

Even if you have not decided together on this type of ministry, it is important that you relinquish your husband to ministry. For him to fulfill his calling you must make sacrifices. You may have to bear with times of loneliness for Christ's church. The only one who can meet your deepest need is Jesus. If you are not satisfied with Christ alone, then you will never be satisfied no matter how much attention your husband gives you. If you are satisfied with Christ, then you can make the most out of the time that you do get together and seek Him to help you to know how to cultivate more of it.

Sometimes, your loneliness may come due to the actions of others. Our daughter Michelle's mother-in-law wrote to her and her husband, Tim, expressing how much she missed them (they are missionaries in Africa). She then told them how she was encouraged by the life of Hannah who in return for her giving Samuel back to God, she was given a son who was mightily used to draw his own generation, and all generations after him, to the One he so faithfully served. She shared that there are surely costs, but the rewards are even greater.

Tim responded, "Yes, we are missing y'all more and more too as the time wears on. But as you said, it makes the reunions all the sweeter, and in the meantime, it offers us a tangible reminder that Christ owns us and that this is a small sacrifice of love in response to His great love for us. And it appetizes us for Heaven all the more."

Dear wife, if you are lonely, seek your solace in the One who died alone so you would never be alone. Make Him your joy. Take delight in the promises of God and go to Him in constant communion. Focus on others and initiate friendships. Reach out to others who may be lonely too. Have a consuming purpose. Make the most of your husband's friendship. Relinquish all those you love for the kingdom of God, remembering that any sacrifices you make for Christ will be richly rewarded.

LIVING BY THE MODELS FOR THE MINISTRY MARRIAGE

What is happening to many ministry marriages? They are failing. They are coming apart at the seams. It seems like people in ministry are being uniquely targeted by Satan. What does God say about it? The struggle is real.

> Put on the full armor of God, so that you will be able to stand firm against the schemes of the devil. For our struggle is not against flesh and blood, but against the rulers, against the authorities, against the world forces of this darkness, against the spiritual forces of wickedness in the heavenly places.
> (Ephesians 6:11-12)

Sadly, we're all aware of marriage casualties of couples who were devoted to serving the Lord. When the marriage of a ministry couple fails, it deals a devastating blow to the church of Jesus Christ, not to mention the family.

Sisters, it is absolutely imperative that we build strong marriages! Strong marriages mirror the unity of the Trinity, the incarnational submission and respect of Christ to His Father, and the redeeming love of Christ for His bride. Enduring marriages draw people to the source of such unsurpassable beauty.

This chapter gets to the crux of why I wrote this book—to encourage you to focus on building oneness with your husband. We'll look at four models for understanding God's design for your marriage when the two become one, based on the oneness that Jesus demonstrated with His Father.

The Mystery of Oneness

The unity of husband and wife is a mystery. Where shall we begin to search out this mystery of marital oneness? Back to the Garden of Eden. It is there that God created man and woman in innocency to be completely one with each other and Himself. They had complete unity in heart, mind, and body. What a paradise that must have been!

What was the source of that unity? It was God Himself who existed for eternity within the three distinct persons of the Godhead—the Father, Son, and Holy Spirit. This first model for the ministry marriage is found in the Trinity.

One plus one plus one does not equal one, but in God's math it does. This is a mystery of profound proportions—three distinct persons, yet one (in essence)! They are in perfect interpersonal relationship with each other. There is no competition, discord, or rivalry. There has never been a moment of anger or jealousy. There is always perfect fellowship and a unity of purpose although they have different roles.

Similarly, as being created in the image of God, we are called to reflect this oneness within the Trinity. Wayne Grudem writes,

> Just as there was fellowship and communication and sharing of glory among the members of the Trinity before the world was made (see John 17:5, 24), so God made Adam and Eve in such a way that they would share love and communication and mutual giving of honor to one another in their interpersonal relationship.[19]

Do you remember when the pastor made the proclamation at the conclusion of your wedding, "I pronounce that they are husband and

---

19 Wayne Grudem, *Systematic Theology* (Liecaster, England: InterVarsity Press, 1994), 455.

wife together, no longer two but one flesh, in the name of the Father and of the Son and of the Holy Spirit; those whom God hath joined together, let not man put asunder. Amen."? Didn't that give you a thrill? God, the very source of unity joined us as husband and wife together as we made that covenant before Him.

It is a total and irrevocable commitment. The oneness is of His making. This is how it was from the beginning. Jesus, when speaking about marriage, quotes the creation account,

> [He] said, "For this reason a man shall leave his father and mother and be joined to his wife, and the two shall become one flesh"? So they are no longer two, but one flesh. What therefore God has joined together, let no man separate. (Matthew 19:5-6; cf. Genesis 2:24)

What happened in the garden that spoiled that unity? Sin! We learned that Eve sinned and then influenced her husband for evil, then blamed the serpent for her sin. Adam followed her into sin and then shifted the blame to her and then to God Himself. He said, "The woman whom You gave to be with me, she gave to me from the tree, and I ate" (Genesis 3:12).

Have you noticed all the blame shifting that takes place when we have a sin problem? For Adam and Eve, sin brought estrangement from each other and from their loving creator God and they were cast out into a hostile world that was blighted by their sin. Sin had, and continues to have, devastating consequences.

Enter God, in love, seeking them. God was the initiator, providing for their sin problem and restoring fellowship with them. Enter Jesus Christ seeking you and your husband. Can you see that when we admit our sin and alienation from God and receive the blood sacrifice of Jesus Christ on the cross, we are at one with God? That is the atonement—at-one-ment.

My marriage is unique in that I am at one with God through Jesus Christ and that makes me uniquely one with Bob. We have a complete oneness that those outside of Christ cannot experience. We have one Savior and Lord, one name, one new family, one goal, one Word to guide us, and one focus of our lives—to glorify God.

We have the Holy Spirit living within both of us to empower us to love each other sacrificially and to help us work through all hindrances to our oneness. With Christ in our lives there is hope for any difficulty we face. By His grace we can forgive as we have been forgiven. The Spirit knits us together and gives us a new heart that desires to serve Christ and give sacrificially to one another in love.

Picture a triangle with God at the apex, your husband and you at the other two points. The closer you both grow to God and make him the top priority—the apex in both of your lives—the closer you become to each other. It's true in geometry and in human relationships.

If we desire harmony and oneness in our marriage, I believe we must understand and imitate how Jesus lived out His life in the relationship He had with His Father and use that as a model.

The Love of Christ for the Church

Not only does marriage mirror the unity within the Trinity, it reflects the mystery of the oneness between Christ and each member of His church (Ephesians 5:31-32). The oneness we have with Christ is borne of love. When you responded in faith and entered a love relationship with Christ, you became one with Him. You are His bride. Think of it, Christ, the eternal Creator and Sustainer of the universe who lived in resplendent glory for all eternity with His Father and the Spirit in heaven becomes one with you. What a staggering thought! This love of Christ is the second model for the ministry marriage.

We love Him because He first loved us. This love is exclusive. Jesus alone is to be worshiped and adored as our heavenly Bridegroom. It is permanent and relentless. Nothing can separate us from His love—not the trials and cares of this life, not differences, not independent thinking or acting, not anything else that appears to be more loveable or attractive. This same devotion is to be our model in human marriage. It is to be broken only by death.

Imagine the joy that could be ours if our foremost goal in our marriage was to mirror the kind of love that Christ demonstrated for His church. Christ loved us and gave Himself up for us (Galatians 2:20). That is the goal that is placed before our husbands in Ephesians 5:25; as wives, we should likewise exhibit sacrificial love. The older women are to "instruct the young women in sensibility: to love their husbands, to love their children" (Titus 2:4).

Have you found that marriage magnifies your own selfishness and desire for going your own way? I have. We have to learn to love sacrificially like Christ. When we were first married I memorized 1 Corinthians 13:4-8—a passage that gives God's description of love's attitudes and actions. I prayed that God would help me to exemplify those qualities in my love for the wonderful man He had given me. I have to keep returning to this passage over and over again. It convicts me and puts me on the right path. If I want to have a good dose of conviction, I will fill in my own name and see if it fits in the place of love. When I see it doesn't then I need to ask God to produce that love in me.

Love is patient, love is kind (1 Corinthians 13:4). Do I go out of my way to do kind things for my husband? Do I use the same kind, patient tone of voice with him as I do with others on the phone?

Love is not jealous, does not brag, is not puffed up (1 Corinthians 13:4). Even when he gets all the praise and thanks, do I rejoice in his accomplishments, remembering that we are one?

Love does not act unbecomingly, does not seek its own (1 Corinthians 13:5). Am I excused for being irritable and touchy at certain times of the month? Do I complain and want things the way I want them, when I want them? Do I rejoice in opportunities to sacrifice so that he can pursue his calling?

Love is not provoked, does not take into account a wrong suffered (1 Corinthians 13:5). Do I hold grudges? Do I take offense and wear my feelings on my sleeve? Do I have pity parties?

Love does not rejoice in unrighteousness, but rejoices with the truth (1 Corinthians 13:6). Do I hate evil in myself and work hard to kill sin? Do I pray for my husband's sanctification and rejoice to see God work in His life?

Love bears all things, believes all things, hopes all things, endures all things (1 Corinthians 13:7). Am I loyal even when the church shrinks or the ministry fails? Do I believe the best about my husband or grow suspicious? Do I trust that the God who allows riches or poverty, sickness or health, peace or persecution is the One who will cause all things to work together for our good as we become more than conquerors through Him who loved us?

Love never fails (1 Corinthians 13:8). Does my husband know that I will stand by his side anywhere through anything until death parts us, or our Savior returns?

With Christ-like love, marriage can be a foretaste of heaven on earth.

If you ever feel the temporary urge to give up on your marriage because your husband doesn't love you like Christ loved the church, then remember that God's love is out of His grace and not conditioned on our worthiness. He loved us while we were yet sinners (Romans 5:8). It is most important that you love him no matter what. Love is the fruit of the Spirit. His love never fails. Love is the most important thing in the world. Love is the only thing that will last forever. Everything else will pass away—faith to sight, hope to possession, but the love of Christ is stronger than death and will endure forever. It is the one thing that will never fail.

Having your ministry fail or any other severe trial can put a strain on your marriage. If that is the case, you should get help as a couple in that kind of a situation. That help should include biblical counsel and support from godly friends who will encourage you, and support you, and hold you accountable. Your marriage is more important than your ministry. If that fails, all else crumbles with it.

Christ's Dependency and Submission

If anyone who has ever lived could have been independent—it would have been Jesus Christ. But the amazing truth is, Jesus said or did nothing on His own even though He was God in the flesh. He said, "Do you not believe that I am in the Father, and the Father is in Me? The words that I say to you I do not speak from Myself, but the Father abiding in Me does His works" (John 14:10). The third model for the ministry marriage is found in this attitude by the Son of God.

Jesus totally depended on His Father. He didn't seek glory for Himself by independent actions. All He did was to glorify His Father. He said, "Whatever you ask in My name, this will I do, so that the Father may be glorified in the Son" (John 14:13). Dependency and seeking the other's glory works toward promoting oneness. Independency works against it. Dependency says, "I don't want to go my own way, do my own thing. I'll go with you. We'll go together." It says, "I need you." It doesn't indicate weakness. Jesus was omnipotent yet dependent on His Father.

Why is it that we want to do our own thing without consulting anyone including God? John Piper says it points to the root of our sinful condition.

> Independence from God is rebellion against God. At root, our sinful condition is the commitment to be our own god. I will be the final authority in my life. I will decide what is right and wrong for me; and what is good and bad; and what is true and false for me. My desires express my sovereignty, my autonomy, and though we don't usually say it—my presumed deity.[20]

In marriage we give up our independence and our autonomy. We walk together as one. Throughout the life of Christ, we see this fleshed out.

Oh that we as wives would work toward oneness with our husbands just as Christ demonstrated His dependency on and submission to His Father! As a wife, I am privileged to reflect Christ's voluntary submission. "Wives, be subject to your own husbands, as to the Lord" (Ephesians 5:22).

Submission is a military term meaning "to arrange or rank under, adapting your plans and priorities under the one over you." It means for the wife to arrange her priorities under those of her husband. It means she does not resist her husband's leadership. This is radical kingdom living!

Jesus' example of submission to His Father dispels any thought that submission indicates an inferior role or position. Jesus was equal to the Father but in submission to Him. Jesus obeyed His Father. In the garden he said, "yet not My will, but Yours be done" (Luke 22:42b). What unity this demonstrates!

Submission does not mean lack of equality before God. We are

---

20 John Piper, *Pierced by the Word* (Sisters, Oregon: Multnomah Books, 2003), 66.

joint heirs of the grace of life with our husbands (1 Peter 3:7; Galatians 3:28). Although submission does not show a hierarchy of value, it does show a chain of command. Christ submits to His Father, the church submits to Christ, husbands submit to Christ, wives submit to husbands. "For the husband is the head of the wife, as Christ also is the head of the church, He Himself being the Savior of the body. But as the church is subject to Christ, so also the wives ought to be to their husbands in everything (Ephesians 5:23-24).

As Spirit-filled wives, we are called to submit to our husbands' leadership in the home just as we submit to our Bridegroom, Jesus Christ (Colossians 3:18). Christ sacrificially purchased me with His own blood. When I received His gift of salvation and became His bride, I recognized Him as Lord of my life. He is in control. Likewise, when I, as a wife, commit myself to my husband, I am receiving a head (1 Peter 3:5-6).

When I follow Christ's example and submit to my husband I am giving him a priceless gift. Rather than merely external submission, my submission needs to be that of a willing and loving follower. Submission is not only an action but also an attitude. It is not only allowing him to lead but also encouraging him in that leadership role. It involves asking his opinion, searching for his preferences, seeking to please. Most of the submission that I am called upon to exhibit is in the everyday situations of life. These give practice for the big decisions.

You and I have the privilege of being submissive to our husbands like Christ was to His Father and the church is to Christ. God has placed the ultimate responsibility of the household on our husbands even though most of the raising of the children and household duties are delegated to us. That makes them responsible to be our providers and protectors. God made it our husbands' responsibility to love us as Christ loved the church. That's a big order!

So, is it especially easy for us as wives of men in ministry to be dependent and submissive because our husbands are so spiritual? I don't think so. Whether or not our husbands are perfectly fulfilling their role or not, we must submit and it is never easy. Everything in our culture glorifies the independent woman, and influences us against submitting to our husbands. Are we going to let the world squeeze us into its mold, or are we going to show the world a superior way?

Submission did not come easy for me in that I was a career woman before we were married. As a teacher and dean of women I was independent and used to leading. It was hard not being in complete control with myself alone to think about. I have had to learn to rank my priorities under Bob's—to make him my focus. But as I have made his success my calling, I have found the greatest joy and blessing.

We can learn from remarkable women of the past like Abigail Adams, one of my favorites—one of the most distinguished first ladies in the history of our country. She grew up in the home of a Puritan minister in a society that held its clergy in highest esteem, as they were the most highly educated and influential leaders in the community in morals, politics, and social life. Abigail was well read and was very astute in many areas. She married John, a budding lawyer, in 1764 and was called upon to support him in his many endeavors as he used his skill as a thinker and writer to shape the course of our destiny as a country. When he first began in public life by drafting the resolution opposing the British Stamp Act he knew that he was entering the fray and he asked Abigail's opinion if he should stay out of it. She replied, "No, John. We're small, we three dependents of yours, and not of much use in a fight; but we'll follow you down the trail as far as it goes."[21]

That trail led him to the Second Continental Congress where he was a delegate. He helped draft the Declaration of Independence and the Massachusetts State Constitution. It led them through many separations while he was away in Philadelphia and abroad when he served as an ambassador in France and the Netherlands. The trail led him to negotiate a peace treaty with Britain, and then to become minister to Britain, which meant more time away from family. Then the trail led him to become the first vice president of the United States and then the second president. (He is considered to be the best presidential speaker up to the present. His inaugural address on July 1, 1776 to the Continental Congress was so riveting that latecomers demanded he deliver it again and he obliged.)[22]

---

21 Irving Stone, *Those Who Love*, (Garden City, New York: Doubleday & Co, 1965), 141.
22 Allan Metcalf, *Presidential Voices* (Boston, Massachusetts: Houghton Mifflin Company, 2004).

It was a very hard trail. Abigail managed the finances and since they were poor public servants, she took up the slack and ran their farm including the care of the cows while her husband ran the ship of state. Her life was hard. She suffered the death of two of her children—one, a son who died a drunkard and a gambler. She was often ill and escaped an early death. When she had the opportunity to be with her husband, the travel was horrendous. They both suffered abuse and were misrepresented by some of the people they were the closest to, but through it all she had an indomitable spirit and a strong faith in God.

By reading her biography I saw a strong marriage bolstered by Abigail's aim to make John a success through the way she released him for service to his country during a very turbulent time. She accomplished this through her management of the home, earning extra income through their farm, caring for the children, expressing faith in her husband, reading and keeping her mind active discussing issues, and encouraging him in his position. Abigail is a model of perseverance, frugality, good taste, and hospitality. As well as entertaining heads of state and cabinet members and their wives, she also welcomed the general populace. Here was a woman who didn't hold grudges, gave wise input to her husband, and remained submissive, humble, and flexible—all qualities that I would like to emulate.

God blessed her in that not only was she married to the president thereby sharing the honor of the highest position in the land, she also had the honor of being the mother of the sixth president of the U.S. She was welcomed by King George III and his wife and the king of France into their palaces. She was privileged to be friends with and host such people as George and Martha Washington, Ben Franklin, and Thomas Jefferson into her home. She was part of a generation who shaped our republic.

I see an application to my own life. Will I seek to make his work—the ministry—a success through all means possible? It will lead through some rough places, but it is worth every sacrifice. It is shaping a far greater kingdom—the Kingdom of God.

When we were called to church planting in California, the final decision to move was my husband's to make. I let him know that I would support him whether we stayed in New Jersey or if we moved. The important thing was to follow where God was leading him even if it meant leaving extended family behind. When we were discussing moving to California, my home state, I told my husband that I would happily move anywhere in the state except to a certain, especially hot area where I had grown up. Knowing that moving would have a far-reaching impact on our family, we made it a matter of concerted prayer. He took my thoughts into consideration, pursued counsel from godly men, and then he made the final decision to move.

Wouldn't you know it, God moved us to that especially hot area! Even in that God gave me His grace to happily move. As I reflect back there are no regrets, although it has been difficult being away from our families.

Now you may be thinking, "But my husband makes some pretty unwise decisions. Do I submit when he is going to do something that I think is bad financially or in another way?"

We are responsible to let him know our thinking on the matter and we are free to make godly appeals, but then step back and allow him to make the final decision. The Bible is clear, "In the same way, you wives, be subject to your own husbands so that even if any of them are disobedient to the word, they may be won without a word by the conduct of their wives, as they observe your pure conduct with fear" (1 Peter 3:1-2). God can sovereignly work through our husband's mistakes, if they are that.

The Trinity had a plan for redeeming the world and They were one in how it should be accomplished. We know that Jesus took the submissive servant role to accomplish that plan. How amazing that Jesus, who was one with the Father, equal with God, did not consider it something to be grasped, but made Himself of no reputation, taking the form of a slave and died the death of a criminal on an ignominious cross (Philippians 2:5-11). By becoming a servant and dying our death, Jesus accomplished the purpose that He and His Father had planned before the world came into being.

With Christ-like submission and dependency in our marriage Satan doesn't have a foothold to separate us. We will be going forward under one head, accomplishing the will of God.

Christ's Respect

Are we ministry wives deficient in respecting our husbands? Perhaps there are husbands who don't live up to their wife's expectations of what they want in the relationship emotionally, spiritually, financially. The result is an erosion of respect.

Let's return to the life of Jesus Christ—the perfect example of respect, the fourth model for the ministry marriage. Out of the oneness that He enjoyed with His Father He chose to honor and esteem Him through everything He did. As we read through the Gospels this stands out clearly. He honored His Father by keeping His commands. He said, "...just as I have kept My Father's commandments and abide in His love" (John 15:10b). He taught His disciples to pray for His Father's name to be hallowed and that His kingdom would come and His will be done on earth as it is in heaven. He said, "For Yours is the kingdom and the power and the glory forever. Amen" (Matthew 6:13b). He said, "I glorified You on the earth, having finished the work which You have given Me to do" (John 17:4). Jesus respected and honored His Father to the utmost. As we emulate Christ in His relationship of oneness with His Father, we will respect our husbands.

The Apostle Paul commands you to do that. Look at how the Amplified Bible chooses to expand the idea of this verse: "Let the wife see that she respects and reverences her husband [that she notices him, regards him, honors him, prefers him, venerates, and esteems him; and that she defers to him, praises him, and loves and admires him exceedingly]" (Ephesians 5:33b, AMPC). Wow! What man wouldn't thrive under that kind of respect and admiration!

The Apostle Peter tells us that we should be adorned with the inner beauty of a "lowly and quiet spirit, which is precious in the sight of God" (1 Peter 3:4). He cites Sarah as an example who obeyed her husband, "calling him lord" and he tells us wives to not be afraid of that kind of respect.

Let's get down to some specific ways that we can respect and admire our men. We can be lavish in our praise and yet genuine. I praise Bob for the way I see him using his gifts. I tell him he is the greatest expositor of the Word in the world. I doubt that he is convinced, but I think it makes him happy that I think so.

After one exhausting day in the ministry, Bob threw himself on the bed and said, "After eight years in the ministry just what have I accomplished?" My response was, "You've made one woman the happiest woman in the world." He has remembered that and how much it meant to him. That was all he needed.

You have the privilege of being your husband's greatest admirer. He probably gets many accolades from the people he serves. Hopefully he gets the most from his lifetime companion.

It's so easy to take our spouse for granted. We need to remember to thank him for all the same things that we would thank someone else for, and more. I may work just as hard as he does, but that does not negate the need to appreciate what he does. We are to give thanks in everything (1 Thessalonians 5:18). Need I remind you that most women would give anything to have a husband who is a spiritual leader and a respected man of God? It is a real privilege to be by the side of a man committed to serving God and others.

Just think of it! You can give your husband your love, support, and encouragement in his day-to-day responsibilities as no one else can. His role is demanding, sometimes like a pressure-cooker, and you have the privilege of loving and ministering to the minister.

Focusing on your husband's positive qualities will help you to respect him. When was the last time you praised your husband for something that you admire in him? We must always keep in mind that our job is not to change our husbands or help them solve all the problems in the church—just love and respect them. I am not the voice of my husband's conscience. It is always easier to see my husband's faults rather than my own. Yet it is prideful to think that I know how he should be fulfilling his role. He needs the freedom to grow as a person and to experience failure without hurtful criticism. Nagging, suggesting, advising, or belittling has no place in the life of a respectful wife.

What if you see hypocrisy in your husband and his public image doesn't match with his private reality? What are you to do? Your husband is also your brother in the Lord. We are told in Scripture what to do when there is habitual sin. "Brothers, even if anyone is caught in any transgression, you who are spiritual, restore such a one in a spirit of gentleness, each of you looking to yourself, so that you too will not be tempted " (Galatians 6:1). It is your responsibility to restore him if you see his sin and you are "spiritual." Being spiritual means walking in the Spirit; not necessarily that you have to be a spiritual giant.

First, take the log out of your own eye (Matthew 7:1-5). If I have had any part in the sin or have responded to it in the wrong way, I need to ask for forgiveness then follow the basic process for restoration, as outlined in Matthew 18:15-20. You may need to involve other church leaders to help restore our husband. It's not right to cover up for him. If sin isn't dealt with, God won't be able to bless him. I must respect him enough to restore him.

We can learn from other ministry couples of the past, even negative examples. What could Molly Wesley have done differently to make her marriage a success instead of the miserable failure that it was? She married John who was 47 years of age and who continued his life as an itinerant preacher after they were married. He traveled the length and breadth of England, Scotland, and Ireland and his preaching became the basis of the Wesleyan Revival that changed the hearts of the English people and probably saved those countries from a blood bath similar to that across the channel known as the French Revolution.

When he died at the age of 88, Methodism had 153,000 adherents and had spread to America and Holland.

John's evangelistic missions had kept him away from home three quarters of the time, which failed to leave enough time for them as a couple. When her family commitments would allow (she had four children when they married) she would accompany him on his travels. They were separated just four years after they were married, and then were reunited several periods of time during their 20-year marriage. He wrote her love letters and tried to boost her confidence by telling her that people were asking about her and telling her that her name was precious among the people to whom he ministered. The separations and attitude toward it by Molly gradually widened the gap until their marriage reached the point of no return. In his last letter to her he bitterly wrote that if she were to live a thousand years, she could not undo the mischief she had done. Could Molly have done things differently to help make the marriage a success? Perhaps, but he could also have, if he were more committed to the marriage. He wrote in his journal, "I cannot understand how a Methodist preacher can answer it to God to preach one sermon or travel one day less in a married than in a single state."[23]

"An excellent wife is the crown of her husband, but she who causes shame is like rottenness in his bones" (Proverbs 12:4). With Christ-like love and respect our marriages will be crowned with glory!

Marriage is an amazing gift from God. With it He shows the world the unity that He has in the Godhead and that He desires with His children. As ministry couples we want to be brilliant reflections of that kind of oneness.

So, to stand strong in the trenches with people falling all around us, let's be devoted to unity. Our marriages will be strengthened as we trust God to give us a strong, sacrificial, growing love for our husbands, a voluntary submission and unconditional respect for them till death do us part.

---

23 John Wesley, *The Journal of John Wesley* (Chicago, Illinois: Moody Press), 185.

MAINTAINING THE MINISTRY MARRIAGE

In the book *The Long Winter*, the pioneer Ingalls family endures seven months of blizzards with no trains to bring supplies. When the coal runs out they have to make a plan to keep the fire alive or they will all freeze to death. Pa and Laura spend all day twisting hay into sticks that they can burn in the stove to keep their little kitchen bearably warm.

As women who are involved in ministry, we realize that there is a blizzard of distractions raging outside. Just as a fire goes out without fuel, so our marriages will become cold and lifeless, and even fail, without constant loving maintenance. In the last chapter we looked at different models for a beautiful marriage. Now we will look for ways to fuel our marriages to keep them burning brightly so that our homes are the havens that God designed them to be.

As in chapter 7, we'll look to Jesus as our example, who was completely one with His Father. This oneness was evidenced by love and respect for, dependency on, and submission to His Father. Now we will look at how He maintained that oneness throughout His time on earth. Through following His example and taking the principles from His Word, we will be able to experience incredible unity in our marriages.

Committing to Close Communication

Jesus was committed to constant communion with His Father. It didn't matter how busy His ministry schedule was, He often went alone to pray or talk to His Father, even if He had to do it in the middle of the night (Mark 6:46; Luke 9:18).

How do we have that close communion, fellowship, and communication with God and each other that we desire? We commit to coming together in mind, heart, and purpose. This has to be a priority. If Jesus needed that constant communion with His Father for the oneness He sought here on earth, so do we. In this fast-paced world where we are scattered as a family most of the time, we have to work at having time to be together and to communicate.

Sharing Ourselves

Love seeks to communicate and take the beloved into everything. Jesus said, "I have called you friends, for all things that I have heard from My Father I have made known to you" (John 15:15b). Instead of waiting to be asked or expecting your husband to know your needs out of his own sensitivity, you need to share freely—taking joy in sharing the blessings of your day as well as your burdens and desires.

If he is to live with you in understanding, as he is commanded to do (1 Peter 3:7), you need to communicate your thoughts and feelings with him. Sharing involves all areas of our lives—our innermost thoughts, our interests and concerns, our time and activities, our family goals and spiritual needs.

Perhaps your husband comes home tired from talking and counseling and dealing with situations, which require a lot of emotional and spiritual energy. Ministry marriages are frequently taxed in this area.

Consider the reformer Martin Luther, who operated in a "fishbowl atmosphere." He would often like to withdraw into himself when his wife Katie wanted to share and their rhythm of work and rest did not coincide.

> After a day with children (they had six), animals and servants, she wanted to talk with an equal; and he, after preaching four times, lecturing and conversing with students at meals, wanted to drop into a chair and sink into a book. And then Katie might

ask him a question about the Grand Master of Prussia or about predestination or why David in the Psalms bragged about his own righteousness when he really didn't have any. "All my life is patience," said Luther, who must have recognized that patience wasn't his strongest virtue. "I have to be patient with the Pope; I have to be patient with the heretics; I have to be patient with my family; and I even have to be patient with Katie." Katie had to be even more patient with her genius husband. He was a man of many moods.[24]

We need to ask for patience with our husbands and lovingly seek to share with them at the proper times. A good way to do this is to plan for a "huddle time" when your husband gets home—to "call the plays" for the rest of the day. It could be just ten minutes. My daughter and son-in-law like to go for a walk so that they can put the toddlers in the stroller and talk uninterrupted. We are letting our children know that our relationship is important as they see us make time for each other. As we involve our children in this, they will learn to be good spouses in the future.

Listening

We can show our husbands that we are really interested in them by working at being good listeners—attentive, without interrupting. I tend to jump in with my comments and reaction before I have heard the whole story. Proverbs says, "He who responds with a word before he hears, it is folly and shame to him" (Proverbs 18:13).

The kind of communicating that Scripture commends is given to us by James: "Know this, my beloved brothers. But everyone must be quick to hear, slow to speak and slow to anger; for the anger of man does not achieve the righteousness of God" (James 1:19-20).

Do I listen to my husband and discern when he is discouraged or weighed down in need of an extra dose of encouragement through my words and other creative ways that I can think of to build him up?

Timing is important in communication. Our edifying words are to be spoken "...for building up what is needed..." (Ephesians 4:29b).

---

24 William J. Petersen, *Martin Luther Had a Wife*, (Wheaton, Illinois: Tyndale House Publishers, 1963), 28.

Rather than dumping all the tragedies of the day on him the minute he comes home it's best to concentrate on the good things. What was the best thing that happened to each of you today? Save the hard things until later, when we are out of earshot of the children and we can share and pray about issues.

Have you also found that it is important to plan times to talk about sensitive issues at the right time? For us, it is usually not right before bed. Emotional issues can best be handled in the light of day when our sleep is not being robbed from us.

Early on in our ministry we found that I needed to wait until Tuesday to make suggestions regarding Bob's message the previous Sunday morning. He is not ready to hear those things before then. Most of the time, after waiting a day, only the good things come out and the minor things, which I thought could be improved upon, are forgotten. We are our husband's greatest critics because we want them to be the best. But if we are constantly criticizing them in an effort to help them improve, it can actually tear down their confidence.

Do you constantly catch yourself evaluating your husband as a speaker instead of seeking to have God speak to your heart through His Word? This is something that I struggle with constantly. I shouldn't be thinking about how people are responding to his preaching rather than concentrating on my own life in relation to the Word of God. Just think of how much more our husbands will be built up when we share how his preaching impacted our lives!

Building Him Up

We are admonished, "Let no unwholesome word proceed from your mouth, but only such a word as is good for building up what is needed, so that it will give grace to those who hear" (Ephesians 4:29). If we are quick to hear and slow to speak, then we will have time to think about our words, whether they will build up our husbands or pull them down. Women, we must speak words that will strengthen and encourage our husbands, whether or not they deserve it. That's imparting grace.

If we are constantly criticizing or tearing our husband down with our words, that will diminish the sharing and the closeness emotionally and physically that we desire. Rather, we need to constantly be saying loving words to nurture our husbands and assure them of our love. Tell him he is tough and tender, rugged and romantic, serious and silly. Don't you love it when your husband opens up to you and pours out his heart? He needs to know that you are his place of emotional safety where he can be himself and be completely accepted. The only way our husbands will share the deeper things with us is in an atmosphere of acceptance and unconditional love.

We can minister grace to our husbands when they come home to us—"love builds up" (cf. 1 Corinthians 8:1). It is up to us to make home a welcoming place for our husbands. Maybe your children are like mine were; welcoming your husband home from the office, joining you at the door with, "Daddy's home! Daddy's home!" That is just a memory now for me, but Bob still gets a warm welcome when he enters our home after a busy day of kingdom work. There's nothing like a welcome home! There was a saying that Martin Luther liked to quote: "Let the wife make her husband glad to come home and let him make her sorry to see him leave."[25]

Maintaining good communication will be the glue that cements you strongly together as a couple. It will facilitate submission as you listen to your husband to see where you can pull together to accomplish what God is leading him to do. It will portray respect to your husband as you listen to him and use edifying words. It will demonstrate love to your husband as you initiate and share with him as his best friend.

Keeping Confidences

My husband needs to know that I'm not telling anyone else about the private things that he shares, even with my best friend or sister. This is so important! "He who goes about as a slanderer reveals secrets, but he who is faithful in spirit conceals a matter" (Proverbs 11:13). "But he who repeats a matter separates close companions" (Proverbs 17:9b). Paul lays out the basic principle of marriage when he says that each is seeking to please the other (cf. 1 Corinthians 7:34). It certainly would not please my husband to know that I was sharing intimate details of our marriage or confidential information with others.

---

25 Ibid, 37.

Building a Flourishing Friendship

How is the friendship element of your marriage? Do you have a growing friendship with your husband? As your communication deepens, the friendship aspect of your relationship will flourish also. You will see your husband as your best friend, taking everything to him first, enjoying his company in all kinds of circumstances—whether good or bad. That is what marriage is all about, but it takes work to achieve.

Jesus called His disciples His friends (John 15:15). What a privilege to be Jesus' friend! A friend is a confidant—someone with whom you confide or entrust a secret to. You have faith in him. You are sympathetic toward him in his need; you feel with him and just love to be together. You have affection for your friend.

My husband is my best friend. I treasure his friendship above all others on this earth. What a blessing! I trust that you, too, have a wonderful friend in your husband. Growing our friendship with our husband is so important. In order to help the friendship grow, we must work at spending time together and sharing interests.

The principle that Jesus laid down in His Sermon on the Mount holds true here—"for where your treasure is, there your heart will be also" (Matthew 6:21). As you invest your time and effort into times with your husband, sharing the children and their interests, working and playing, your friendship will flourish.

When we share common interests and hobbies, our friendship grows. We can make it our aim to think of ways to enter more enthusiastically into our husbands' lives—their interests and passions. For example, I have gone to Bob's softball games every season for the past 24 years, not because the games are especially exciting to watch but because it lets him know my interest in him.

If we are able to, we also set aside quality time together weekly. Bob and I have kept a "date night" for most of our marriage. We may stay at home or go out. It is a time in the week we look forward to, when we can relax and take pleasure in each other's company. It's especially enjoyable to take turns planning these times and surprising each other.

Favorite dates for us include lingering over our meal at our favorite Italian restaurant, attending a high school or college musical, and taking in a concert or the local symphony. One memorable date included Bob surprising me by renting a convertible for the day and taking a drive exploring a new area in the mountains. We sometimes double date by going to a sporting event or community play or simply going out to dinner together. Our date may consist of playing games with another couple after the children are in bed, and having a simple dessert. An occasional good movie is also an ideal date option. While we have been blessed greatly by keeping a "date night" throughout the years, you should be careful not to feel unnecessarily guilty if you are in an especially busy season where you are unable to keep a "date night". The most important thing is consistently building a deep friendship in the Lord with your husband—whatever that might look like in every season of your marriage. Now that we are "empty nesters" we might decide to relax at home and read a good book aloud to each other that we really enjoy. These times together, however, only happen when we set aside the children , household, and church tasks so we focus on our own friendship and love affair.

Fanning the Flames of Romance

Are ministry marriages always what they should be in the area of physical oneness? I think we all have our share of challenges. If this is a challenging area of your life, I want you to know that by God's grace it can be all that He intended it to be.

What does the Lord have to say about your physical oneness with your husband—with your sex life? Scripture has many insights into this important aspect of our marriages. We are told that when God remedied Adam's loneliness and brought Eve to him, Adam said, "This one finally is bone of my bones, and flesh of my flesh" (Genesis 2:23). Or to paraphrase it, "Wow, there she is!" He was overjoyed!

Here was someone with whom he could have intimate communion. They were one in two senses—she had come from him and she was to come back to him in the marriage relationship. They were made to cleave to one another—come together sexually. God ordained the leaving and cleaving that involves establishing a new relationship, taking precedence over all others, which is sometimes difficult but so very necessary.

It is a joy to realize that it is God who designed the physical, sexual union when our two bodies are joined together as one in a physical, mystical union! Children are a rich blessing derived from that union, but not the only reason for it. God was so gracious in making the sexual act for more than procreation; we know this because of the way it promotes such oneness and gives us such pleasure. He has made the sexual act the most intimate of all human relationships.

This union is holy and such an important aspect of the marriage relationship. Paul sets the physical aspect of marriage in the context of the pure and sacrificial love of Christ for His church (Ephesians 5:31-32). The bed is a holy place (Hebrews 13:4). There you exchange gifts—your body with your husband's body. This gift-giving has the wonderful effect of bringing oneness and the spiritual and emotional well-being that comes from feeling loved and accepted. This is one of the good and perfect gifts coming down from the Father for our joy and delight (James 1:17).

If you want to be encouraged to pour out your love on your husband more extravagantly, read the Song of Songs, in which the highest, purest, and most wonderful elements of romantic love in marriage are portrayed. Its eight chapters of beautiful poetry picturing the love relationship in marriage should help you be bolder in expressing your admiration for your lover. Better yet, read it together with your husband.

Your body is to be given to your husband willingly to please him and to bring him sexual satisfaction (1 Corinthians 7:3-5). It is a guard against unfaithfulness. If you are withholding affection, or sexually depriving your husband, that is sin. We may abstain temporarily from sexual activity, but only when it is mutually agreed upon for prayer and fasting. Satan can get a foothold when we are vulnerable from not coming together.

Women, do we make time for those intimate times together and let our husbands know how important they are to us? If you are frequently too tired, it would be wise to see what other activities could be cut out of your schedule or attempt to rest to prepare yourself for this most unifying and pleasurable part of the day of coming together with your husband. Praying for God's strength is also appropriate. He will give you His strength and energy for this sacred aspect of your marriage.

Do you make it a special time? Your marriage should have a deeply satisfying and free sexual aspect. Christ has taken away the shame of nakedness that is our sin. As you give yourself unreservedly to minister to your husband sexually, you will find deep fulfillment and satisfaction.

Ministry is emotionally draining, and there are times when the concerns add an emotional burden that is hard to overcome. Your husband is called upon to comfort those who are suffering. He needs your comfort and attention to his inner needs that he cannot always express. You need to tell him how much you love him for who he is—your lover and friend.

Closeness through physical contact, tender touching and the sexual union, is an opportunity for a husband and wife to bask in each other's love and forget for a time the burdens that press in. It provides feelings of support, tenderness, and comfort, which are truly wonderful. What a joy it is to be your husband's source of physical affection and pleasure!

During a severe trial in ministry, at the peak of our grief, when we were both devastated and wondering if our fledgling church would survive, I arranged an evening at home alone without the children. I even planned it around a theme complete with romantic music, appropriate attire, and a special meal by candlelight. It was just what Bob needed. We found that in each other we could weather the storm. By God's grace, we came through it with much prayer, soul-searching, and waiting on God—and loving and supporting each other. That evening demonstrated that I could step outside my own pain to comfort him. It is always more blessed to give than to receive.

As a wife, you can set up the conditions—provide the closeness, touching, eye contact, the right emotional climate—for your husband to experience romantic feelings, which will draw you together in the wonderful union that God has ordained in marriage. When you come together you are acting out the oneness that you are as husband and wife.

You need to fervently love your husband. Ask God to give you a renewed passion for your man if your delight in him has waned. Constantly think of ways to say, "I love you." We dare not be indifferent in this area, but devotedly committed to loving our men passionately.

Committing to Faithfulness

We must not let our hearts be drawn away from oneness with our husbands. We must fight to remain faithful. Let's not forget that we can be tempted and unfaithful in our thoughts as well as actions. We are called to purity. As you are devoted to loving God and your husband, that is your strong defense. Any kind of sexual sin or any other kind of sin is a hindrance to your oneness in marriage.

We see this from the very beginning. When Adam and Eve sinned it affected their relationship with each other and their Creator-Friend. Hiding and blame-shifting took place. Their transparency and oneness were destroyed. As we have noted, God gave them a covering that involved the shed blood of an animal. How wonderful that God always makes provision for our sin!

Can you see how our sin is just the same—a hindrance to marital oneness? Our sin may be immoral thoughts, pride, selfishness, stubbornness, anger, bitterness, lack of love, harshness, impatience, or many others. Women, we must kill sin in our lives. Any wandering or lustful thought—lusting after another man, fantasizing through movies, novels, or television shows, must be taken captive to Christ (2 Corinthians 10:5).

Our weapons against sin are mighty through God to the pulling down of strongholds. Think about the cost of your salvation. Jesus suffered and died to set you free from your sin. Don't indulge it for a second! We have been bought with a price; our bodies are not our own. They belong to Christ and are the dwelling place of the Holy Spirit (1 Corinthians 6:20).

When you realize that your own sin has disrupted your marriage you can call out for the forgiveness found in Christ's atoning death and His power to overcome (1 John 1:9). Don't try to excuse or defend yourself, instead be quick to ask forgiveness from God and your husband and reopen lines of communication.

If your husband has committed sexual sin against you by committing adultery or engaging in pornography or any other kind of perversion, you have a responsibility to confront it biblically (Matthew 18:15-20). First you go to him. If unsuccessful, you go to him with the elders of your church or organization. If he is truly repentant, there are steps to take for healing your marriage. It will probably mean his stepping back from ministry, even if he is repentant, for a time to gain a reputation of being the husband of one wife—a one-woman man (1 Timothy 3:2, 12). Depending on the severity of the sin, godly elders will need to discern whether his sin has biblically disqualified him from pastoral ministry since he may no longer be "above reproach" (1 Timothy 3:2). God will give you His grace to forgive as you have been forgiven in Christ. If he is repentant, you can rebuild a solid marriage.

Sometimes even a potential sin can disrupt your unity as a couple. If you sense that your husband's heart is being drawn away from you through a relationship he has with another woman, you definitely need to talk to him about it. If he assures you that there is nothing there, do not be drawn into sin by becoming suspicious and distrustful. If you sense that another woman is seeking your husband's attention, protect your husband from temptation by talking to him about it.

My husband never counsels a woman alone, to guard against being drawn away in the helping role. Bob wants to be sensitive to me in this area and welcomes my input. We must take every precaution to guard our marriages. We are not exempt from being led into sin either and should not put ourselves in a position of temptation with another man, even if it is ministry related.

Resolving Conflict Lovingly

Sometimes there is conflict in a marriage that is not necessarily because of sin, but just because we have differences. These differences can cause sin if we do not know how to resolve them properly.

One evening as Bob and I were having a heated discussion over an issue that we were working through our son called from the bedroom and asked us to stop arguing. Bob responded, "We aren't arguing, we're discussing." To which Daniel retorted, "Then can you discuss a little quieter?" We had to admit that we needed to solve things in a manner glorifying to Christ.

Since Martin Luther and his wife Katie had quick tongues, their home was not exempt from arguments.

> "But," said Martin, "think of all the squabbles Adam and Eve must have had in the course of their 900 years. Eve would say,

'You ate the apple' and Adam would retort, 'You gave it to me.'"
With all the bantering, the Luthers had a good marriage. To
have peace and love in marriage is a gift which is next to the
knowledge of the Gospel, he once said. And no one could deny
that the Luthers had that gift.[26]

A little humor often helps a tense situation.
In the heat of conflict we need to remember God's recipe for unity.

> Fulfill my joy, that you think the same way, by maintaining the
> same love, being united in spirit, thinking on one purpose, doing
> nothing from selfish ambition or vain glory, but with humility of
> mind regarding one another as more important than yourselves,
> not merely looking out for your own personal interests, but also
> for the interests of others.
> (Philippians 2:2-4)

If I would only obey this command and have a humble spirit to fully listen to my husband's ideas—and consider them as more important
than my own—how much sooner we would be able to work through
our differences. If I would do nothing out of selfishness, looking out
for his interests, as if they were my own, we would not even get into
half of the conflicts that we find ourselves in. Why not begin the day
by asking God to help you obey this powerful passage?

When a difference arises, we can resolve it without sinning if we
are committed to this Christ-like attitude and the good communication that we discussed in the previous section. "Iron sharpens iron, so
one man sharpens another" (Proverbs 27:17). A good marriage is not
one where there are no conflicts but one where the couple is committed to working through conflicts God's way.

My husband and I have been so thankful that we have made it
our rule to never go to sleep angry. This is inspired by Ephesians 4:26
that says, "...do not let the sun go down on your anger." While it is not
always possible to come to an agreement before one goes to sleep, it is
possible for each of you to be committed to confessing and asking for
forgiveness for any unresolved anger in your heart as soon as possible.

---

26 Ibid, 34.

The issue itself can be worked out at a later time with love and prayer. The result will be more often enjoying a peaceful night's rest.

My dear sisters, rather than being quick to lose patience and give up, let's be committed to forging strong relationships that work through sin and differences. With God's help we can resolve conflicts in ways that will bring us closer.

Total intimacy is a life-long process. It involves intentionally working on unity—as we have seen—by committing to close communication, seeking to edify with our words, keeping confidences, building a flourishing friendship, fanning the flames of romance, seeking to be faithful to our husband, dealing with sin, and resolving conflict in a loving manner. It involves sharing everything, our hopes and dreams, our failures, our successes, our sufferings and joys, our possessions and our bodies. What each does is for the other. It does not mean total uniformity, because God has created us to be different. Our differences must not hinder our unity; their existence is designed to enhance our lives as one.

It takes time and work to build a good marriage that fulfills God's design and meets the deepest desires of our hearts. Through His enabling we can leave our father and mother, cleave to our spouse, and become one flesh for the glory of God.

BEING THE MINISTRY MOM

I can't tell you how grateful I was to become a mother after waiting to become one till I was well into my 30s. I was exuberant! I felt like I would just burst with the love I was feeling for our precious daughter Michelle, our firstborn child. Then when our delightful son Daniel was born, it was love at first sight all over again.

If you're a mother, you likely experienced this same euphoria; maybe it was mixed with a kind of postpartum depression. Either way, I imagine you would lay down your life for your child in an instant. In a sense, God calls us to do that very thing on a daily basis for the rest of our lives. As pastors' wives, our mothering comes under greater scrutiny. This is an overwhelming task because the flock is watching our example.

My goal in this chapter is to renew your purpose as a mother through the Word. I will share some of the things I have learned from other mothers in the past and as a mom through my years in the "thick of it." My hope is that you will be encouraged and strengthened to be the most God-honoring mother you can be. Despite all the pressures and challenges, I have found that there is no greater, more fulfilling investment of my life, no richer calling than that of a pastor's wife and mother.

Let's plunge into how we can perform our role of ministry mom with excellence.

Expressing Love, Affection, and Affirmation

We spent the last two chapters noting the importance of expressing love and affection to our husbands. Keeping your relationship with your husband strong and growing is the best thing that you can do for your child. Likewise, you need to demonstrably show your love to your children.

Our talk with our children should be constantly seasoned with words that build up (Ephesians 4:29). They flourish through our expressions of love, affection, and affirmation. Recently, one of my grandchildren, Titus, when asked what his favorite thing about the day was, responded by saying, "Having you tell me I did a good job." We should be our children's best encouragers. "Well done, son!" "Good going, Honey!" "You did great!" "It couldn't be better!" "Way to go!" "I can't get over it!" "You came through with God's help!" And of course you cannot say those most precious words, "I love you," too much. Honest praise excites a child to do his best.

There is no doubt that children become affectionate as we show affection to them. Family hugs, cuddling in bed, snuggling under a blanket in front of the fireplace—these times of closeness are a vital part of their nurturing! In my journal I have this poignant entry when our son was six years old, "Last night Daniel called me into his room and said, 'Do you know what I've got for you?' I said no and he asked me to get down on his level and he said, 'A kiss!' as he planted one on my cheek. He then said, 'You know what else I have for you?' Then he gave me a hug! What a loving boy!" Let's treat them the way that we want to be treated.

It is so important to demonstrate sincere thanks for all the giving that takes place in the home. You will find that thankfulness is contagious. Daniel, in mimicking his dad, was known for his thankful spirit, and he inspired others to give thanks. There was hardly a meal that he did not thank me for, even through his teenage years and into adulthood.

Love may be expressed tangibly in many special ways. Over the years I've given little gifts and notes of encouragement on different occasions to those in our congregations and I've tried not to forget our children in the process, knowing that they need these special reminders of our love as well.

Training in the Word of God

We know God's first and greatest command is, "You shall love Yahweh your God with all your heart and with all your soul and with all your might. These words, which I am commanding you today, shall be on your heart. You shall teach them diligently to your sons and shall speak of them when you sit in your house and when you walk by the way and when you lie down and when you rise up" (Deuteronomy 6:5-7). It is helpful to ask ourselves if our children are being treated as our foremost disciples. If we aren't careful they can get lost in the shuffle. The cultivation of the deepest and most long-term relationships with our children can be sacrificed for the maintenance of many temporary and fleeting ones.

How can you and I teach our children to love God with all their hearts, souls, and strength? Like Moses, who taught God's chosen people all that He had commanded him to teach them, our most important task is to teach our children to love the Lord. This training takes place as we go about our day and at special times set aside for teaching.

"We love, because He first loved us" (1 John 4:19). The more we teach our children about God and His love for them, the more they will love Him. God has revealed Himself to us in every page of His Word. It is good to have a plan for regularly reading through the Bible with your children, either through Bible picture books or the actual text. It is amazing how much you can read if you just set aside a family worship time each day.

It is good to teach through the Bible chronologically for many reasons. One reason is that children love stories. God knew what He was doing when He made most of the Bible narrative. Don't try to teach bare doctrine. Let the stories show them who God is. Then let the Bible unfold. Our children need to know that they were created by God before they will see that they should obey Him. Our children need to see what God thinks of their sin in order to be convicted and see how precious the mercy and love of God is. For them to value the cross, they need to know their desperate condition in light of God's holiness. God's great love shines more brightly against the black backdrop of our sin.

Children learn about God through the Old Testament stories that show God's righteous character and the way He works with sinners and His people. They learn by precept and example that God is holy and hates sin. He is just and punishes sin. The Ten Commandments and other Old Testament laws show them what sin is. They begin to realize that they break God's law every day, especially if you teach them that we can even break the law in our hearts as Jesus taught. They learn that God is just and punishes sin. He is also gracious and forgiving and provides a way for the sinner to come to Him through an atoning sacrifice.

Then as we read the Bible stories of Jesus' life, death, and resurrection over and over to our children, they will see how God took care of that sin problem through the sacrifice of His own sinless Son. Our prayers are that our children will come to know and love Him and desire to give Him their hearts and lives.

The new birth changes rebellious hearts into hearts that love God. Even a young child can understand that a new, clean heart is needed to be with God in heaven. Our grandson recognized this when he was talking to his mommy while taking a bath. His mother asked what they would do upon arriving in heaven. Evan jumped in and said; "First we'll thank God for giving us new hearts!"

If your husband has a plan for family worship, that is wonderful. Encourage him in it. When he is tied up, carry on without him.

Scripture memorization is also important so that our children can love God. As they hide God's Word in their hearts, it will be there for the rest of their lives for God to bring to mind for guidance in all the challenges they will face. It will keep them from idolatrous living. The Israelites were taught about the one living, eternal God—holy, omnipotent, merciful, and loving. This truth would help keep them from worshiping the false gods of the heathen around them. Isn't that comforting when evil seems to be so strong in our society!

One way to help children memorize Scripture is through catechism questions. Our daughter has made it her goal to catechize, or drill, her children with doctrinal questions from a book designed for small children.[27] When Evan had completed learning all the answers, she gave

---

27 Carine MacKenzie, *My First Book of Questions and Answers* (Fearn, Ross-shire, Great Britain: Christian Focus Publications, 2001).

him a party to celebrate with his surrogate South African grandparents. Now she is working on the memory verses that go with each answer in the catechism. The goal is for them to have verses memorized on all of the major Bible doctrines.

Another way to memorize Bible verses is according to the character qualities that you want your children to work on. For example, one of the traits we worked on was attentiveness so we memorized Hebrews 2:1. "For this reason we must pay much closer attention to what we have heard, lest we drift away." Then we acted out Samuel's listening to God and discussed it. See *Appendix B* for a listing of character qualities to work on with related verses.

Our grown children noticed that their son might need some work on humility when Daddy asked, "Evan are you being proud?" Immediately he defended himself saying, "It's not bad to be proud." Daddy replied, "But Satan fell from heaven because he was proud and God won't share His glory with another." The humble little four year old corrected him, "No, he didn't fall, he was thrown out." Then he asked, "Can't we ask God for some of the glory that He doesn't need?" Seize the teachable moment. Take time to discuss and grapple with the questions that concern them.

We heard the progress he was making later when we asked Evan what verse he was learning and he said in his little voice, "God is opposed to the proud but He gives grace to the humble." His mommy asked, "Evan, are you proud or humble?" He answered, "I'm asking God to make me humble." Imagine that a young child could begin to learn the character quality of humility by asking God to help him obey His Word! It will be a life-long process, but how good to begin early!

Family devotions should be geared to our children's level so they never become wearisome. They should be fresh and interesting and applicable to life. Ask them questions and let them ask you questions. It is through asking questions and wrestling with answers, even at a very young age, that children grow in their understanding of God. Dramatizing a passage using members of the family is a great way to bring the Scripture to life. There are great books to use for family devotions that have real-life stories a child can relate to illustrating particular biblical principles. Often they contain further questions for discussion or you can make up your own.

When our children were young we instituted a "Family Night" to get a consistent focused time together. This was a night committed to the family; church needs did not interfere. These times were often planned with a theme, a Bible story, and included an activity and snack. If we are to have time reserved for family, our first ministry, then we must set the time aside on our calendars. It's okay to not answer the phone and to have uninterrupted time. Do you have at least one night in the week completely devoted to your family?

Training in Prayer

We can do nothing well as parents without prayer. Jesus said, "I am the vine, you are the branches; he who abides in Me and I in him, he bears much fruit, for apart from Me you can do nothing" (John 15:5). Jesus, the perfect Son of God needed to commune with His Father in prayer, how much more do we? It is there that we find mercy and grace to help in our times of need (Hebrews 4:16). It is through prayer that we ask God for the wisdom we need for this task of parenting (James 1:5). In prayer we beg God for our children's salvation and daily needs.

Our children need to learn that they also cannot live without prayer. Without prayer they cannot love God or be forgiven by Him or see Him work in their lives or the lives of others.

Children can learn to pray at an early age. We can start teaching them to pray even before we know for sure if they are saved. All people are born knowing that there is a God. It is when they refuse to honor Him and give Him thanks that they become fools (Romans 1:18-21). As we teach them to honor God as their Creator, we are softening their hearts to love Him as their Savior and Lord.

Children start learning to pray just by listening to our prayers. Then they can start memorizing Scripture prayers or repeating after us. We can encourage them to pray on their own by thanking God for who He is and what he has done for us. Children love to list to God all of the things that they are thankful for that we often overlook. One of Evan's very first prayers at breakfast was, "God, thank you for this food, and this wonderful day with Daddy and...and...with you God, and Jesus." What times of joy, hearing their heartfelt prayers to our Lord and Savior!

The best time to teach our children to confess their sins and ask for God's forgiveness through prayer is when we are disciplining them. We didn't force our children to pray for forgiveness. But each time we disciplined them we asked them if they wanted to pray or have us pray for them. If they chose the latter, we would pray that God would give them repentant hearts and help them to turn to Jesus for forgiveness of their sins. This process brought about a real turning point for our grandson Evan. He finally realized that he couldn't be forgiven unless he himself prayed and asked God to forgive Him through Jesus. Now he usually chooses to pray for God's forgiveness and goes out of the discipline session rejoicing that God has answered his prayer and forgiven him. It is these kinds of prayers that give assurance of salvation.

Little ones can even learn to pray for the difficult things. When Michelle was only three, we as a family were working on the principle of thanking God for our trials. We were so touched to hear her pray, "Thank You God for my "boo-boo." She got it!

It is good to have a regular time of prayer each day with our children. We did this each night as we put them to bed. These were some of our most meaningful times as we tucked them in and talked to them individually about their days. I want to encourage you, along with your husband, to make bedtime prayers a priority in your family, even when your children are older. We often did this through high school. There is so much to talk and pray about at the end of the day. My cousin John Coulombe, who is a pastor, faithfully took his guitar in and sang and prayed with his boys as part of their bedtime routine. They are following in the footsteps of their dad who took the time for them in his busy life.

We also must pray with our children throughout the day as needs arise. If they scrape their knees, we pray for them. If they find a baby bird out of its nest, we pray for it. If there is an accident on the road, we pray for the people involved. If they are having trouble getting along, we stop and pray together. If they have big exams coming up, we pray for them. If they are trying out for a team, we pray for them. Pray without ceasing!

Then we look for answers to prayer and thank God for them. In helping our children recognize answers to prayer and God's providential working we played "I Spy." We asked at the dinner table, "Did anyone have an 'I Spy' today?" An "I Spy" is an answer to prayer or another providential happening that others might term a "coincidence." This gives an opportunity to "see" with the eyes of faith and share what God has done that day.

Talking to God is one of the highest privileges we have as Christians. Let's teach our children to come with confidence to the throne of grace, that they may receive mercy and may find grace to help in time of need (Hebrews 4:16).

Walking Our Talk

How important that we practice what we preach! Since our children see us telling others almost every day of our lives how to live out the Christian faith, how important it is for us to demonstrate that faith in our homes! This will do more than anything to bring our children to Christ and to keep them on the path of holiness. My parents were not in vocational ministry but I observed their faith at work in the home. This molded my life. My husband's life was molded the same way by parents who genuinely loved the Lord.

Children sense hypocrisy. It is helpful to pray daily that the fruit of the Spirit would be produced in your lives as you yield to the Spirit. If your inner life or home life doesn't measure up to your profession— your children sense that this doesn't ring true and it may turn them away from Christ. We want to discipline ourselves for the purpose of godliness (1 Timothy 4:7). Our children will either see us living disciplined lives that they can follow or they will see that we are undisciplined and follow that. We need discipline in every area of our lives.

We don't have to be perfect parents. We just need to be willing to admit our mistakes to our children and ask for forgiveness when we are wrong. This shows them the genuineness of our walk with God. We may sin against our children by disciplining them in anger or unfairly. We may set a bad example in a certain area. We can confess that to them and ask them to pray for us. They will be happy to help keep us accountable. One of our grandchildren was riding with his daddy to pick up the babysitter for the evening. Along the way, Tim told him that Mommy and he wanted to have some special time to talk with each other. Applying his recent memory verse from Proverbs 10:19, Evan warned, "But Daddy, the more you talk, the more you sin!"

If we are walking our talk, our children will want to grow up and be just like us. One Sunday morning Evan requested, "Daddy please also pray that God will make me a preacher when I grow up. Only God can make me a preacher."

Disciplining Consistently

We find out early on that pastors' children are no different from the other children, expectations notwithstanding. They do things that embarrass us, like throwing temper tantrums at church or throwing rocks that hit other children. We have to recognize these times as worthwhile for others in our church as they get to observe us handling these situations that every parent faces. We have to ask God for the wisdom to handle the situation fairly and as God would have us. It is tempting to over-react. Many times we are grieved more over hurt pride than over what our child did. God has His ways of humbling us, doesn't He?

There is much written on child discipline. Some "experts" advise behavior modification techniques—merely using reward and punishment. Is this a biblical approach? Our children are made in God's image and are not to be controlled like mere animals by external stimulus. God does reward good behavior, but it is offered for meaningful effort on our part as the result of thoughtful appeal of the one in authority.

Other child-rearing experts say that we should never use corporal punishment but merely reason with our children. They assume that all children are born innocent and we just need to cultivate the good. We know that the Scriptures are in direct opposition to that theory. Every bit of advice needs to be evaluated by biblical standards.

The Word says, "The rod and reproof give wisdom, but a child left to himself brings shame to his mother" (Proverbs 29:15). The rod (physical discipline) is to be given along with reproof. Through reproof you explain how what they did was sin. You also explain how the sin can be handled God's way through confession, being forgiven, and making restitution. This method teaches children that there are consequences for sin, and it also points out the heart attitudes, which must be dealt with if they are to achieve victory over the sin.

Susanna Wesley explained her views on child rearing in a letter dated July 24, 1732. Her advice is straightforwardly biblical and validated by the fact that her family of 19 children whom she educated herself, was considered to be the most loving family in the shire. Two of her sons, John and Charles Wesley, helped to shape the church significantly. She wrote,

> In order to form the minds of children, the first thing to be done is to conquer their will, and bring them to an obedient temper. To inform the understanding is a work of time, and must, with children, proceed by slow degrees, as they are able to bear it; but the subjecting of the will is a thing that must be done at once, and the sooner the better; for by neglecting timely correction, they will correct a stubbornness and obstinacy which are hardly ever after conquered, and never without using such severity as would be as painful to me as to the child. In the esteem of the world, they pass for kind and indulgent, whom I call cruel parents; who permit their children to get habits, which they know must afterward be broken.[28]

Another woman of Wesley's time who raised 11 children, also was spoken well of by the writer Samuel Hopkins. He writes of Sarah Edwards,

> She had an excellent way of governing her children. She knew how to make them regard and obey her cheerfully, without loud, angry words, much less heavy blows...if any correction was necessary, she did not administer it in a passion... In her directions in matters of importance, she would address herself to the reason of her children, that they might not only know her will, but at the same time be convinced of the reasonableness of it... Her system of discipline was begun at a very early age and it was her rule to resist the first as well as every subsequent

---

28 Jabez Burns, *Mothers of the Wise and Good*, (Box 61232, Vestavia Hills, Alabama 35266: Solid Ground Christian Books, 2001), 52-54.

exhibition of temper or disobedience in the child... wisely re-
flecting that until a child will obey his parents, he can never be
brought to obey God.[29]

What an incentive for us to bring our children's wills into subjection
at an early age! We must train our children to deny themselves and
obey us and thus obey God.

During the early formative years it seems like you are constantly
disciplining your children and often feel like you aren't accomplishing very much in a day. Michelle wrote of some discipline issues that
seemed to consume most of her time. We encouraged her with the fact
that every time she must stop to discipline her sons she is discipling
them. It should not be looked upon as an interruption to her day, but a
purposeful part of it since her children are her first disciples.

The wonderful news is, as your child learns to respect and obey you,
he will also learn to respect and obey God and share in His holiness
(Hebrews 12:3-11). So if we want our children to share in His holiness
and carry on the work of the gospel, we must discipline them earnestly.

We can learn from Amy Carmichael, who as a missionary to India
raised hundreds of children in her orphanage. Many years later, one of
her children recalled that when they were very small they "lived on the
wings of her love." The biographer then points out that nearly all her
children spoke of her love, but many mentioned their fear of her as well.
She was strict. Out of that strict upbringing came selfless individuals
who continued to carry on her work.

As we subject our children's wills we must be careful not to crush
them. Let's look at Paul's words, "Fathers, do not provoke your children
to anger; but bring them up in the discipline and instruction of the
Lord" (Ephesians 6:4). Discipline flows out of a relationship of love
with our children. If they know that we love them fervently, they will
accept discipline. Love is always the guide. If we love our children, we
will have a united plan and discipline them consistently.

There are many ways that we can provoke our children to anger.
One way that we may do this is by making unreasonable demands.
Some things happen because of their immaturity, like spilt milk. Adapt

---

29 Dodds, *Marriage to a Difficult Man*, 32.

your expectations to fit each child at each stage of life. Discipline for sin. Disobedience and disrespect are sin (Ephesians 6:1-2). An unloving attitude or action is sin. Lying is sin. Stealing is sin. Discipline consistently. The rod and reproof must come after the first offense or you are tempting your child to keep testing the limits.

Another thing that can turn a child off is to single him out for special behavior because he is a pastor's kid (P.K.). They sense the hypocrisy in this. Behavior is either right or wrong for anyone. My husband and I committed ourselves to avoid putting this kind of pressure of false motivations on our children. We didn't want to make them hate being P.K.s. We are not to provoke our children to anger but to positively bring them up in the discipline and instruction of the Lord.

Some people are afraid that if they are strict with their children, their children will rebel. On the contrary, consistent use of the rod and reproof brings wisdom. Through discipline our children will learn how to wisely restore relationships. When we discipline our children we teach them to ask forgiveness of the person offended. This brings such relief to both parties. It need not be brought up ever again. The situation is over and dealt with. It brings real joy! When our grandson Evan was disciplined and asked for forgiveness of a playmate, he went running to his mother calling, "Mommy, she forgave me!" Learning how to restore relationships will serve them well for the rest of their lives.

As we discipline our children faithfully, they will gain the wisdom of self-control and submission to authority. If our children are helped to deny themselves and do right in the course of their day, the habit of right doing will help them later when they face bigger and harder temptations such as alcohol, sex, and drugs. In working with our children consistently they will grow in their ability to obey and respect those in authority over them and bring joy to their employers, church leaders, and government. Like Jesus they will "keep increasing in wisdom and stature, and in favor with God and men" (Luke 2:52). This will bring us joy as we see them succeed.

If you use the Scriptures to reprove your child, your discipline should lead to the greatest wisdom, the wisdom that leads to his salvation. This seems to have been the case for the apostle Paul's disciple, Timothy, who had a faithful mother and grandmother. Paul told him:

> But you, continue in the things you learned and became convinced of, knowing from whom you learned them, and that from childhood you have known the sacred writings which are able to make you wise unto salvation through faith which is in Christ Jesus. (2 Timothy 3:14-15)

This was also the case in my own life. The Lord brought me to faith in Christ through my disobedience to my mother. She pointed out my sin and led me to faith in the Savior. Isn't it wonderful that the gospel is so simple that even a small child can recognize his sin, find forgiveness in Jesus Christ, and be saved!

Some children may not be able to identify a particular time of salvation but consistent discipline can be the tool that God uses to show them their need for salvation. Proper response to discipline may be one fruit that helps give them assurance of salvation. What a priceless privilege to lead our children to faith in Christ! Let's not neglect the tools that God has given us to till the soil.

As mothers we are called upon to pick up the slack and keep things consistent in the home, as our husbands are so busy in ministry. It is easy to let up on discipline when Dad is not around. If we do, we will learn from experience that a child without discipline will bring us to shame. There are many church ministries to become involved with, but nothing is more important than training our own children.

I would like to encourage you to read *A Plan for Disciplining a Young Child* in *Appendix C*. As a young pastor and father, my husband read all he could find on biblical parenting. Then he made this simple list that we agreed upon as a guideline for disciplining our children. We practiced it to the best of our imperfect ability and passed it on to many parents. As you read through this list you may see some areas where you need to strengthen your resolve. You may want to make your own simple list like this to put up in your home or pass on to others.

Our children are no different than any others. At times, you may even be accused of having the worst children in the church. Good, don't give up. Persevere with God's simple method of the rod and reproof, given in love. Then you will be able to show those who are watching that even the worst sinners can be trained by discipline and saved by grace.

Being Active in Education

Biblical wisdom leads to skillful living in every area of life. Our children need to know that the Bible applies to history, math, science, the arts, and every field. It applies to how they will conduct themselves in their careers and community. We must be involved in their education to make sure that they develop a Christian worldview. We can do this in many ways. We can delegate to the public school, a Christian school, or do it ourselves. Homeschooling is a major commitment. Our two children had all three experiences. The key to their success is our involvement. We must teach them to think critically about what they read and hear to determine if it matches up to the grid of Scripture. We must know what they are reading and listening to if we are going to do this faithfully.

Our involvement in our children's education should include encouraging them to obey this command, "Whatever you do, do your work heartily, as for the Lord rather than for men" (Colossians 3:23). Because something is done for the Lord and heartily, means it must be done with excellence. How do we get our children to pursue excellence in all that they do for God's honor and glory?

We can set the example through our life-long love for learning. Are we constantly studying and thinking through issues? Are there meaningful discussions in the home? If we aren't setting the standard, we can't expect the results we want.

Then, we need to come alongside to help them do their work with excellence, pointing out for whom they are working—the Lord. Excellence can become a habit, no matter what the ability. The Lord deserves nothing less than their best. The grades are not as important as the motivation and the effort that was put into it. We should reward excellence with appropriate praise.

Along with helping our children with their education comes our responsibility as they get older to talk about sensitive subjects like sex, dating, homosexuality, transgenderism, LGBTQ+ issues, and drug use, even though we might think our children know a lot about these things. They may have a lot of misinformation and these things need to be approached from a biblical perspective. Our kids need to know that we care deeply about these issues, and we need to give them the support they need in dealing with them.

Encouraging Physical Activities

How does a pastor's family find the time to spend with their children in physical activities? They make the time! Sadly, studies have shown that in the majority of homes in America, parents spend just an hour or less a week in some type of physical activity with their children such as taking a walk or playing catch. They claim that the primary obstacle is work but I would imagine that they spend more than an hour a week watching T.V. together.

We all need exercise. Why not make it a family event? Rather than going to the gym, you can jog around the neighborhood pushing your stroller or take a family bike ride. Children can then continue these activities on their own. When they enjoy the beauty in nature through having hours free to climb trees, walk or skate, and play with their friends, we are giving them glimpses into the goodness of God. These are the joys of life! This spills over to our church family as we share what we're doing.

If we make time to join them in their play, these times of physical exercise can also draw us closer. One such time when Daniel was in kindergarten I recorded in my journal: "Daniel and I went on a bike ride today around the block and through an orchard. While we were on the way he asked if turtles would go to heaven. When I said, "Probably not," he argued that his friend Alex was sure they would and especially his pet turtle Speedy. At that point Daniel pointed out Speedy's grave marked by a cross. It was then I could enter into his world and express sorrow over the death of his friend's pet.

Bob and Dan drew closer as father and son as Bob coached his baseball and basketball teams for about 10 years. We enjoyed watching both Dan and Michelle play on teams through high school. Someone has pointed out that one of the best things we can do for our children, apart from playing with them, is to watch them. One parent we know of, who is the president of a large ministry, has watched his sons play 200 football games! That type of involvement is a huge encouragement to them!

As much as we desire our children to learn different skills and play various sports to prepare them for this competitive world, we have to be wise in the use of our time. Our children don't need to take swimming, ice-skating, horseback riding, and harp lessons as one child did, all before she was five years old. Help them to choose one or two activities in which to truly pursue excellence and then support them.

Making Family Traditions

Because we are in ministry, things can be pretty serious much of the time. That is why we need to consciously make the effort to have happy, light-hearted times together. We are told that in God's house He gives us to drink from the river of His pleasures (Psalm 26:8). Home is to be a pleasurable place in which to enjoy His goodness—a place where we can enjoy and appreciate one another; where laughter and good times abound; where everyone is loved and secure.

It is our joy as moms to initiate family traditions and ways of celebrating special occasions. Our families will have blessed memories to cherish for the rest of their lives—of birthday parties, sporting events, church picnics, bedtime stories, popcorn and games as a family, slumber parties, riding bikes together, and exploring God's creation.

Holidays are wonderful opportunities to make family traditions—ways of celebrating that bind us together. They can also be times to include others who need a family. At holidays we always make an effort to invite people who might be lonely. Michelle caught on and brought many out-of-state college friends home with her to join us for Thanksgiving dinners. One of those guests became our son-in-law five years later.

We love decorating the table for the occasion and making special place cards with each person's name and a Scripture to read after the meal. The decorations and special foods can really set the stage for great times of family sharing. At Thanksgiving we always go around the table after the meal and share what we are most thankful for that year.

On Christmas Eve we love to quietly sit around the living room and enjoy the luster of the Christmas tree lights as we read the Christmas story from the Bible. Then we open just one gift each.

We looked forward to Easter each year as Resurrection Day. The highlight of the day in our home was not Easter baskets with lots of sweets, but enjoying one of the most festive days at church—with beautiful music and great preaching. We always invited people to come to church on that day and one of Michelle's best high school friends was saved at an Easter service.

Our holidays and traditions have to be examined from a Christian perspective. God gave the Passover to Israel so that the children would ask why they were eating the unleavened bread and bitter herbs and so be reminded of their deliverance from Egypt. Our children will ask questions. Our curious 4 year-old grandson asked, "Why do they call these things Easter Bunny eggs? Bunnies don't lay eggs." His insightful two-year-old brother, Titus, replied, "No, bunnies lay chocolates!" So what will we answer them? What about the Easter Bunny and Santa Claus? What about Halloween? If some people want to have fun with these man-centered substitutes, we don't necessarily need to put a damper on it. But we need to make sure that our children have much more fun celebrating Jesus and the deeper meaning of the holidays.

Having good times together as a family builds into our children's lives for the future and opens lines of communication. It builds strong ties of love and trust and causes them to appreciate the One who gives us richly all things to enjoy, being careful not to look down on those less fortunate (1 Timothy 6:17).

Promoting the Arts and a Christian Worldview

"By wisdom a house is built, and by discernment it is firmly established; and by knowledge the rooms are filled with all precious and pleasant riches" (Proverbs 24:3-4). As moms who fervently love God, we can make our homes places of art and beauty and discernment.

If God's praises fill our hearts, they will also fill our homes. We can have glorious Christian music come into our home by way of radio or the internet. We can set the mood for the family through the music that accompanies our day. I have fond memories of the praise music being turned up extra loudly during family chore times when our children were in the home, each doing his own particular job. It helped us all do our work with greater joy.

Children can gain an appreciation for fine music in the home—music that glorifies God. Classical music certainly fits into that category. As children are exposed to great music, they gain an appreciation for it. As they go to concerts and hear great musicians, they are inspired to practice and develop their own talents. The instrumental and vocal lessons our children received are benefiting them for a lifetime.

Art is another treasure that should fill our homes. Mankind has been relating to the world and God through art for ages because we are made in God's image and are made to create. We can learn so much about the peoples of different time periods by studying their art. We can take our children to art museums. We can hang reprints of the masters on our walls. We can teach them biblical standards of beauty so that they can create art that will stand out in their generation. We can give them many opportunities to work in different mediums as they are growing up. Both of our children have an artistic bent and we have relished the way that has developed over the years.

Literature will also bring a great deal of pleasure into our homes. We can read to the children in the evening before bed—tales that have inspired millions over the years such as *Pilgrim's Progress*, *Robinson Crusoe*, *The Chronicles of Narnia*, the *Little House on the Prairie* books, *Little Men*, *Little Women*, and missionary biographies. Our children will gain an appreciation for reading that will be a blessing their whole lives.

This is an effort that continues with the next generation. Our children are passing on the joy of reading to their children now. We received this note: "A few nights ago, we were finishing our latest book in *The Chronicles of Narnia*—*The Silver Chair*. Titus, who is two (in a rare moment of actually caring what was being read) asked, "Where are the pictures?" So Michelle replied, "There aren't any pictures. You must make them in your head—picture the lions in your head." So Titus proceeded to examine his skull very thoroughly with both hands. We asked him why and he said he was trying to open up his head and find the lions!"

Historical novels and biographies provide my husband and I with hours of enjoyment. Bob reads book after book to us so we can enjoy them together.

The most common art form of our day is the movie. If you are discerning, you can enjoy some good family entertainment and even education through movies. Look for movies that promote positive character qualities. We didn't let our children watch movies on their own. We watched with them and then we could discuss the values and message of the movie. It is important to teach your children to be critical viewers.

If we fill our homes with music, art, literature, and a few good movies, our children will be saved from the black hole of the T.V. In his book, *Don't Waste Your Life*, John Piper makes this point very forcefully,

> Television is one of the greatest life-wasters of the modern age. And, of course, the Internet is running to catch up, and may have caught up. You can be more selective on the Internet, but you can also select worse things with only the Judge of the universe watching. TV still reigns as the great life-waster. The main problem with TV is not how much smut is available, though that is a problem. Just the ads are enough to sow fertile seeds of greed and lust, no matter what program you're watching. The greater problem is banality. A mind fed daily on TV diminishes. Your mind was made to know and love God. Its facility for this great calling is ruined by excessive TV. The content is so trivial and so shallow that the capacity of the mind to think worthy thoughts withers, and the capacity of the heart to feel deep emotions shrivels.[30]

Hasn't Christ saved us to impact our world, not to be conformed to it? Therefore, we must protect our children from uncritically drinking in the world's philosophies. Yet, at the same time we must expose them to the media and teach them to evaluate what they hear and see. We want to raise thinking children who grapple with the issues of the day. We want to raise world Christians who care about what is happening in other places. We must carefully expose them to local, national, and world news. We can discuss current events with our children and help them to understand them from a Christian worldview. Teach them to

---

30 Piper, *Don't Waste Your Life*, 128.

ask questions. How will this happening affect the progress of the gospel? How does this war measure up to the just war theory? How can we show mercy and help these people who are suffering? They learn from how we react to the news and national emergencies and times of crisis. By the time they get to high school, they should be able to take a biblical stand in debating topics such as welfare, abortion, euthanasia, and war.

It takes time, planning, and sometimes finances to teach our children to enjoy the finer things in life. But true peace and pleasure comes from thinking on "...whatever is true, whatever is dignified, whatever is right, whatever is pure, whatever is lovely, whatever is commendable..." (Philippians 4:8). Let's feed the hearts and minds of our children so that they are trained to recognize what is good and cultivate it in their own lives. As we fill our homes with the treasures of music, art, literature, and discernment, our congregations will be blessed by our example.

Having a Zeal for Serving and Evangelism

As wives of men in ministry, we know that our homes are not only for our enjoyment and for the raising of godly children, but it is a base out of which to minister to others. When our children are truly being trained in the Word of God, they will not just have full heads but full hearts. They will be ready and eager to serve. As they learn how Jesus laid down His life for them, they will desire to lay down their lives for others. If we try to isolate them or shelter them completely from the world, we are robbing them of opportunities to practice what they are learning. Instead, we must make them a vital part of our ministry.

Ministry homes usually have no trouble finding opportunities for good works, as that is part of the texture of our lives. We fulfill this admonition by "not lagging behind in diligence, being fervent in spirit, serving the Lord" (Romans 12:11). But it is also easy to focus all our energies on people within the church and forget about the world around us. We often have to go out of our way to actually make friends who are not already a part of the church. With a little extra effort we can take advantage of opportunities such as giving to the children of prisoners at Christmas, befriending a child who has no father, ministering to an unwed teen mom and her child, and bringing neighborhood children to Sunday school.

We can have our children pray continually for the salvation of our neighbors. They can see us reaching out across the fences to help meet their practical needs. They can participate in taking Christmas goodies to their homes. They can help bake hot cross buns for them at Easter. We can have evangelistic Bible clubs in our homes for the children. When our children see the deeds of kindness we show to the lost and hurting, they also see the joy that is involved in seeking to meet those needs.

An incident that stands out in my mind was when Daniel was in the first grade. One day he asked me if he would be able to play in heaven. It was a set-up question. I said that I thought so. He responded that he wanted to tell Pedro how he could go to heaven too so they could play together. A guest speaker had just spoken at our church on motivations for witnessing so Bob wrote and told him to add that one to his sermon notes. He wrote back and said that he would pray for Pedro. A couple of months later when Pedro was visiting in our home Daniel explained the gospel to him and prayed with him to receive the Lord as his Savior. What a blessing to see our son putting his understanding of evangelism into action.

Let's pray that as our children grow and mature in their understanding of sin and salvation, they also grow in their fervency to share the good news with their friends. By our own attitudes and actions we can demonstrate to our children that the most important business that we could be about as a family is sharing the love of Christ. Our teenagers especially need to see this great purpose for their lives. Will we allow the world to drive them or will we as parents show them the way of the Master who came to seek and to save the lost?

> Who confronts them (our children) with urgency and tears? Who pleads with them not to waste their lives? Who takes them by the collar, so to speak, and loves them enough to show them a life so radical and so real and so costly and Christ-saturated that they feel the emptiness and triviality of their music collection and their pointless conversations about passing celebrities? Who will waken what lies latent in their souls, untapped—a longing not to waste their lives?[31]

---

31 Ibid, 120.

Training Them for Missions

What greater goal could we have for our children than that they would give their lives for missions? How do we go about raising world Christians with an excitement for foreign missions? We can be sure that our church has a strong missions emphasis. Children can be involved in mission conferences. A junior worship hour each week can even be devoted to education about, and prayer for, missions as it is at our church. We can use the book *Operation World* to pray for different countries and their needs. We can visit mission fields and host missionaries in our home so they come to know them personally and continue to pray for them. We can give them great missionary biographies to read.

By God's grace, ministry homes can be a place where children thrive on ministry and go as straight arrows for the Lord all the way through. Some arrows fly to the ends of the earth. From the time our daughter Michelle was 12 years old, her goal was to be a teacher, missionary wife, and mother. Through high school she devoted herself to excellence in her studies, being active in school activities, learning a foreign language, and being a witness on campus.

Then came college. On the very first day she met Tim Cantrell. Here was her kindred spirit! Seeing his love for the Lord and for missions (not to mention his tall athletic frame and Texan charm), she thought that she would be thrilled if this was the one for her.

But the Lord had a lot to teach her about waiting on Him. They were friends for four and a half years, both being focused on their studies and college-related ministries. We were, all the while, praying that God would bring them together if this young man was the right choice for our daughter. One summer they even went on a mission trip to Ethiopia together where they were both further confirmed in their calling toward missions. Yet Tim didn't seem interested in Michelle.

Just when we had finally given up hope, God reminded this lonely seminary student of Michelle. He wrote us a letter saying that he would like to pursue his relationship with our daughter to see if this godly and beautiful young woman could become his best friend for life. With a little cultivation, it didn't take long for the friendship to blossom into romance. Four months later, after receiving Bob's blessing, they were engaged and five weeks later they were married. Michelle taught school for a year and Tim graduated from seminary. After that, he was ordained and then he took his wife to the mission field. A year later they presented us with our first grandson! Thus in His time, God fulfilled the desire of Michelle's heart to become a teacher, missionary wife, and mother.

I relate this to you because it is a wonderful story of God's grace and faithfulness. He is faithful to give our children the desire to serve Him. He is faithful to fulfill their desires. He is also faithful to empower us as parents to support them.

To say that it was easy to release Michelle and Tim for ministry overseas would be untrue. It was hard! Even though we had many, many years to prepare ourselves for this, it was hard. But it was not as hard as it could have been in earlier times. We received this email from Tim: "You've made such a sacrifice, letting me steal your daughter away to foreign lands for the cause of Christ. But at least I didn't ask for her hand in marriage the way that Adoniram Judson asked for his bride's hand." This was his letter to Ann's father:

> I have now to ask, whether you can consent to part with your daughter early next spring, to see her no more in this world; whether you can consent to her departure, and her subjection to the hardships and sufferings of missionary life; whether you can consent to her exposure to the dangers of the ocean, to the fatal influence of the southern climate of India; to every kind of want and distress; to degradation, insult, persecution, and perhaps a violent death. Can you consent to all this, for the sake of Him who left His heavenly home, and died for her and for you; for the sake of perishing, immortal souls; for the sake of Zion, and the glory of God? Can you consent to all this, in hope of soon meeting your daughter in the world of glory, with the crown of righteousness, brightened with the acclamations of praise which shall redound to her Savior from heathens saved, through her means, from eternal woe and despair?[32]

Ann's father let her decide and she accepted Adoniram's marriage proposal.

---

32 Francis Wayland, *A Memoir of the Life and Labors of the Rev. Adoniram Judson, DD.*, Vol 1 (Boston: Phillips, Sampson, and Company, 1854), 24-25.

How do we handle the pain of separation? We rely on God's grace. We shed tears at times when missing them wells up within us, and we ask for His comfort. We keep in touch. Email is a wonderful blessing as well as our phone apps where we can see each other and talk face to face. It has been a special blessing to be able to visit them, see the great work they are doing, and be able to participate in it several times. We thank God for calling our children into His service.

Tim has a wonderful ministry pastoring Antioch Bible Church in Johannesburg, South Africa and is the president of Shepherd Seminary training up men to serve the church in Africa. The only hope for that country, which is suffering through the AIDS plague, is turning hearts and lives to Jesus Christ. What a blessing to know that God is using them! We thank God for the opportunity to sacrifice for the sake of the gospel by supporting our children.

Releasing Them

We all have to release our children, whether it is to missions or to go away to college or just to get married and move across town. It is so easy to idolize our children, to let them control us and be the center of our lives. We can have an inordinate affection for them. If you are like me, you find yourself having to constantly give your children up to God. He would have us hold them on the open palm of our hands, letting Him work with them and mold them. We do not own our children. They are loaned to us for a while. How important it is to realize that they belong to the Lord first and foremost for His purposes—not ours, not to live out our dreams but to be what God wants them to be.

As our children grow and mature we can expect them to be able to make wise decisions based on their training, and we must release them to do that. Sometimes they will make wrong decisions, but that is how they learn. If we never give them the opportunity of making decisions, they won't grow. Many times the teen years are the time for them to find out if this faith that they grew up with is their faith or merely their parents' faith. It is hard to watch that struggle take place, but God gives us His grace to step back and allow Him to work. This brings us to the topic of our next chapter, when that happens.

ATTACKING THE PROBLEM OF REBELLIOUS CHILDREN

Sometimes the ministry home can stoke the fires of rebellion in a child's heart. Even though you may saturate your family with all the resources you have in Christ, you may see your child make wrong choices and take the path of rebellion. This is the hardest thing for parents to go through! It is agonizing to see the one for whom you've prayed, delighted in, and given your life to, turn away from Christ.

Dear friend, I want to look at this issue with you from a very personal perspective. I pray you'll be encouraged through the wisdom found in God's Word and by seeing God's faithfulness to our family.

I have our son's permission to relate his story.

Daniel's rebellion began in junior high school. We saw our son, who had formerly had a tender heart toward the Lord, become completely cold. There was no one at church with whom he connected so he wasn't interested in going. He felt that people were still looking at him as a little boy. He was not sure that the faith that he had as a child was valid for a young person seeking his independence.

Daniel's rebellion heightened in high school and the gulf widened between us. His non-Christian friends took precedence over the family; their influence dominated his behavior. He had no interest in studying and his grades went down. He pretended to respect authority but did his best to get away from it. His lifestyle could only be characterized as a person without God in his life.

He worked very hard at a part-time job, which provided him with money. This had positive and negative consequences. One negative was the ability to buy marijuana. We knew that our son was using marijuana, as we saw the symptoms. Of course, we warned him about the physical consequences of the drug and appealed to his conscience, but to no avail. We told him that if we ever found it in his room we would call the police. One day we had to follow through. He was taken away in handcuffs for possession of marijuana. How heart-breaking to see him headed down the path of destruction and death! In all of his inner rebellion, he never spoke unkindly to us. It was a quiet rebellion. Those were the darkest days of our married life. They lasted five years.

God used a hard experience to bring Daniel to see where his life was headed and to show him that God does discipline His children. These are his own words:

> When I truly began to fear the Lord was when I had been disciplined by Him, and only Him, and had been reading through the Old Testament (an assignment in a college class) at the same time. The Israelites did what was right in their own eyes and God killed thousands. I knew that I was doing much worse things than grumbling and complaining. I knew that if God didn't discipline me or if I didn't respond, then I wasn't His. So I decided to seek out Jesus because I knew He was giving me a second chance.

It was hard to see him disciplined, but we had to let God do His work that brought him to repentance. It was then that Daniel turned his life completely over to Jesus Christ, to serve Him with all of his heart and soul. Soon, he began sharing the good news with others.

In looking back, Daniel says he knows God is now using his past rebellion for good. He says, "It gives me an opportunity to relate to those going through similar struggles. I am able to give God the glory and credit for everything that I do. I am able to worship God and give Him my life, which is the most I can offer." He said, "I learned that all is vanity except to glorify the Lord."

Upon his graduation from a Christian college he wrote us the following note:

> Dear Parents,
>
> I am so grateful for what you have both sacrificed to send me to college. It was the best choice I have made in my life besides marriage to Tiffany. I have grown in the four years I have been here more than you will ever know. I have changed into a different person and wish I could take out or delete five years of my life. But God is good and He works all things to His glory, even our sin. Praise God!
>
> I just wanted to say a huge thanks to you both for staying strong in Christ and helping me in my walk. So many believers stray from the faith, but you both remind me of the tree, a great oak, firmly planted by streams of water.
>
> I love you Mom and Dad, and am so glad that you could share in my joy.
>
> Love, Dan

Daniel now teaches Bible and history in a Christian school. He and his wife Tiffany are a great team, both teachers and serving the Lord. We have fully forgiven him and our love for him never abated. We love our children just the same and thank God for what He taught us in raising both of them. I relate this story because I want you to rejoice with us in His faithfulness, and to have hope if you are going through this in your life right now. I want to share some principles from God's Word that we clung to during this trial that helped us persevere.

God is sovereign and He can even use rebellion for His own glory. Daniel got it right, "God is good and He works all things to His glory, even our sin." He can testify to his students of the emptiness of a life bent on pleasure and devoid of God. It is easier to see it at the end rather than in the middle of it. While we are in the battle, we must keep our minds on the sovereignty of God.

Consider how God used the rebellion of our first parents for good in the Garden of Eden. He did so to demonstrate His glorious grace through the cross. We raise our children by faith in the One who entrusted them to us for a time. If you are in the middle of a rebellion, take heart. God has handpicked this trial to come into your life for His own purpose. He will sovereignly work in answer to your prayers for His own glory.

God is in control even though you may wonder how He could be when your child is so out of control. God still loves your child and is at work in that child's life to bring him to repentance. It is not our job to convict of sin. That is the work of the Holy Spirit. Our job is to teach the child God's law and show him God's love. Beyond that, we must pray, trust God, and wait patiently for Him to work.

Rebellion is not your fault. You do not necessarily need to blame yourself if your child is rebellious. His actions are revealing an unconverted heart or the heart of a wandering child of God. Where did all this rebellion come from? As we know it originated in the Garden when our first parents chose to disobey God. That act infused sin into all of mankind. It isn't anything that we do or do not do that makes our children sin. Each person is responsible before God for the choices he or she makes. Scripture makes this very clear, "The soul who sins will die. The son will not bear the iniquity of the father, nor will the father bear the iniquity of the son; the righteousness of the righteous will be upon himself, and the wickedness of the wicked will be upon himself" (Ezekiel 18:20).

We see in the Old Testament books of Kings and Chronicles that Israel sometimes had good kings with bad children and bad kings with good children. Children can have the best homes possible in which to grow up and still choose to rebel and go their own way. Even if you could be the perfect parent, that would be no guarantee that your children would follow Christ.

However, a godly home does make a difference. The Scriptures make it clear that God's usual pattern is to bless faithful parents with faithful children. "You shall know therefore that Yahweh your God, He is God, the faithful God, who keeps His covenant and His lovingkindness to a thousand generations with those who love Him and keep His commandments" (Deuteronomy 7:9).

There are many temptations in our world today, even in Christian schools that a teenager faces that can draw them away from the Lord. Some of the main ones are seeking to fit in with the world, addiction to social media apps like Instagram, TikTok, Snapchat, etc., premarital sex, pornography, drugs and alcohol (which could also be tied in to wanting to fit in). They are vulnerable to all of these and some succumb.

If it happens that you have a rebellious child, it is natural to evaluate your parenting. None of us can claim perfection, and there is always much to learn. But Satan will have a heyday if we wallow in self-incrimination for any perceived failures in parenting. We must not get caught in a trap of hopelessness, discouragement, or depression that comes from dwelling on guilt and failures on our part as parents. Do not fall into the hole of self-pity, grumbling, or complaining that God allowed this to happen. We can become bitter and angry with God. Worry is counter-productive. It dishonors God, who has allowed this to happen in our lives. Instead attack the problem through:

◊   Self-evaluation and Forgiveness
◊   Staying United
◊   Stepping Back from Ministry, if Necessary
◊   Crying out to God
◊   Thanking God for this Trial

Self-evaluation and Forgiveness

As God's children, we have hope that the world does not even dream of. We do not have to be devastated by our failures or try to hide them and move on as if nothing had happened. We can drag them out into the light, confess them and forsake them, and begin afresh. If, after evaluating your parenting before God, you think you may have contributed to your child's rebellion due to your failure as a parent, take heart! That is the part that you can fix by the power of the Holy Spirit. Ask God to show you any sin in your life so that you can seek forgiveness for it.

Solomon exhorts us, "Discipline your son while there is hope, and do not direct your soul to put him to death" (Proverbs 19:18). Ask yourself, "Have we wisely disciplined our child? Could any of his foolishness be due to our failure to discipline consistently?"

Eli was a priest who held a place of great spiritual privilege. But God judged him for his permissive parenting. He had to see both of his sons die in their rebellion because he had honored his sons above God. Eli did not like their sin and he reprimanded them. But God made it clear that he became a part of their sin when he did not rebuke them effectively (1 Samuel 2:29; 3:13).

Is gaining my child's approval or friendship an idol of my heart? Am I seeking to please my child above God through overlooking behavior that needs to be disciplined? Do I faithfully set standards and carry out discipline, or am I permissive? These are questions that parents should ask themselves. It is never too late to ask for forgiveness and start over with proper expectations and consistent follow through. "Discipline your son, and he will give you rest; and he will give delight to your soul" (Proverbs 29:17).

Evaluate Your House Rules

Let me remind you to draw the lines of acceptable behavior biblically not arbitrarily. Examine your house rules. Are you exasperating your teens with too many unbiblical requirements? The more mature your child becomes, the more you can relax the authority structure and become a counselor or guide. Teenagers need to learn to make their own decisions, especially in gray areas. Our daughter was walking with the Lord during high school so we had very few rules for her. She had no set curfew, but our son was always pushing the limits. Therefore, we wrote out certain guidelines for him, along with the consequences for disobeying them. Scripture references were given for the guidelines.

Part of successful parenting is choosing your battles. Not every fad is worth a fight. Issues of the heart are what God is looking at, and so should we. Focus on the root of the problems facing your child. However, if there are certain cultural fads that you do not want your child to go along with, help him or her to see the faulty value system that underlies that fad. As they see how that value system conflicts with Scripture, they will understand that your rules are not arbitrary. On negotiable issues allow your teenager to make his or her own decisions.

A father or mother can't legislate righteousness. It comes from within. But it is sometimes necessary to put the forms in place so that the habits are there when the heart is right. It is often necessary to require our children to do what they do not want to do simply because it is good for them. That is not teaching hypocrisy, but duty. We required Dan to attend one church service a week as long as he was living in our home. He chose the morning worship service. That was a great choice because he heard the Word of God that does not return void. Tiffany came with him and it was there that she committed her life to faith in Christ as her Lord and Savior.

As Christian parents we must not endorse or sponsor ungodly or immoral behavior in our homes. If you are giving a rebellious child an empty house for the weekend while you're away, or giving them a car, or money, or permission to pursue immorality, then you are sponsoring their wickedness. Lines must be drawn, and consequences must be enforced, severely if need be. We must fear God more than we fear our children's disapproval—otherwise, we will become like Eli. The answers are not easy. It involves much prayer, heartache, and effort in evangelizing them through our example and words.

If the child is a believer, you must help him apply Romans 12:1-2. We are to offer ourselves as a living sacrifice to God, and we are not to be conformed to the world's mold. Anything that contributes to the deeds of the flesh would fit into the world's mold (Galatians 5:19-21). Ask your child, "Do the lyrics of this song contribute to dissension and despair or do they contribute to peace and joy?" The ultimate test for any activity is, Can I do this for God's glory? Can I watch this movie or program on television; read this magazine; have this poster on my wall or listen to this music for God's glory (1 Corinthians 10:31)? You can help your children evaluate their lifestyle by asking them good questions. You could list out 10-15 questions of this nature. You must explain to your child that if he doesn't make wise choices, you will have to make them for him because it is your conviction that the things going on in your home must all be to God's glory—even in his bedroom. Eli can be cited as an example, who was guilty and judged by God for not restraining his children. You don't want God to have to judge you.

Evaluate Your Example

Consider what kind of example you have set and are setting for your child. There is nothing that teenagers see through more quickly than hypocrisy. We need to ask ourselves, Have I modeled a vital relationship with Jesus Christ for our child? Am I seeking to be what God wants me to be in the home? Do I discipline myself for the purpose of godliness? Do I share what God is doing in my life?

Ask yourself, "Have I spent enough time with my child or have I been too busy with other activities or ministries? Do I have time for play as well as serious activity? Am I available to merely watch or listen to my child?

When our son was going through his time of rebellion we sought ways to spend time with him even though he was retreating. We turned down any speaking engagements that would cause us to leave him alone on the weekends. We tried to make our house the place where he would want to bring his friends to hang out. We continued to have our meals together as a family. Bob had breakfast with Dan and read from the Bible and prayed for his day.

Examine your attitude and not just your actions. Ask yourself, Do I evidence the love of Christ in my home, seeking to be a servant, showing kindness and patience, or am I easily provoked? Am I approachable or do I portray a proud attitude of never having to struggle with anything? Am I a loving leader in the home, respecting my child and giving him room to fail? Do I preach and nag, or do I calmly seek to open lines of communication? Is confrontation given in the spirit of gentleness, and is discipline administered in the same way? When a child is rebelling, acting in love is usually difficult. But love is from God and we can draw upon His supernatural love for the rebel.

Am I humble in asking for forgiveness when I'm at fault? If there have been areas of failure in parenting, these can be admitted and corrected, and forgiveness can be sought from the Lord and your child. You can ask your child for forgiveness for being too harsh or too permissive. Name your failures specifically. Don't worry that you will be pointing out something that he has not already noticed. Your child may not want to forgive you right away for any of the sins mentioned above.

You can wait and just seek to be what God would have you to be and pray for the softening of his heart while at the same time modeling a forgiving attitude. Your child may need to see this new attitude or behavior over a period of time.

As your child sees you changing in some of these areas, God can use that in a mighty way to soften his or her heart. However, these changes need to be made first and foremost to please God, not to get your child to change. As we learned from Eli, it is God who we are first dishonoring when we fail in our parenting. He is the One who can forgive us and He is the One who can draw our children to repentance as well.

Staying United

Satan would use this heart-breaking situation to destroy your marriage. So here is a question for you. Would you jeopardize your marriage in seeking to get your child back? Yet sometimes we feel like attacking our husbands for the way they are dealing with the situation. Watch that you don't cater to the rebellious child rather than submitting to your husband's leadership in the home, which might be requiring a tougher stance than we would take. God has placed our husband at the head of the home and it is his responsibility to lead in this very emotional and trying circumstance.

It is appropriate to share your thoughts and insights but then step back and allow him to direct your child, giving your wholehearted support. The rebel needs to see a united front. If we negate our husband's discipline or directive, a rebel will use this to avoid further correction or to draw the attention off of him and onto the problem you are having with each other. If as a couple you argue over these matters, you are aiding the enemy.

You must never let your wayward child come before your husband. In some situations, the child can sap all your emotional energy and response leaving nothing for your husband—your first priority.

It is so easy for a trial like this to take the joy from your life and marriage. If that happens, it is crucial that you turn to Christ and then to your husband. It's important to let the rebellious one see your joy in the Lord and love again for your husband.

Stepping Back from Ministry if Necessary

God gives a high standard for the homes of the men who lead His church. A man is only qualified if he is "beyond reproach, the husband of one wife, having faithful children, who are not accused of dissipation, or rebellious" (Titus 1:6). As we saw in the previous chapter, a leader must be, "leading his own household well, having his children in submission with all dignity (but if a man does not know how to lead his own household, how will he take care of the church of God) (1 Timothy 3:4-5)?" Have you and your husband wrestled with these passages?

Are you willing to support your husband if in his conscience he knows that he is not ruling his household well and must step down from ministry? Encourage him to seek the wisdom of the elders of your church or supervisors of your ministry to know if he is still above reproach and able to lead. When Daniel was in rebellion, Bob told Daniel that he was ready to step back from ministry if he did not come back to Christ. He then went to the elders and told them that in obedience to the Scriptures just quoted, he would step back from his role as their pastor-teacher if they would so direct him. After discussing the matter and seeking God's will, they came to the conclusion that Bob was doing all in his power to have his child in submission under him. He was setting godly standards in the home and carrying out discipline when those standards were violated. Daniel was considered to be an adult who was making his own decisions and was responsible for his actions. As far as they were concerned, Bob was above reproach. But if Daniel had a reputation for overt rebellion and dissipation (Titus 1:6), and there was any doubt about Bob's commitment to parenting, it would have been better for Bob to step back rather than discredit the church in any way. The honor of the church and the souls of our children are worth the loss of any career.

Hiding the rebellion of your child is no way to escape from this possibility of having to step down. Every child is born a rebel. It is our responsibility to keep them in submission and keep administering the gospel to their troubled hearts. We need close friends and others in the church to be praying with us for our children. They need to see us struggling for the faith of our children just as they must struggle the same for theirs. But these passages would indicate that there may be a time when rebellion crosses the line and a man cannot focus on broader ministry because he has more work to do in his home.

In this case, it may be best for a man to step back for a time from ministry. If our board had decided that our son's rebellion necessitated such measures, we were ready to comply. This is a drastic consequence of the child's behavior and may cause the young person to evaluate his life seriously. When your child sees that his or her soul is more important to you than your ministry or career, he or she will be brought face-to-face with the sacrificial love of Christ.

A parent must not support and enable his child to continue in unrepentant sin. When our son turned 18 we told him that we could no longer support his lifestyle and that he would need to move out. At that point he decided to go away to college. Since he was willing to go to a Christian college where he would be away from his former friends and temptations, we did continue to help him financially. We hoped that the godly environment would help bring him to repentance, which it did.

Crying Out to God

Women, we need to cry out to the Lord. He says,

> Now return to Yahweh your God, for He is gracious and compassionate, slow to anger, abounding in lovingkindness, and relenting concerning evil. Who knows whether He will not turn and relent and leave a blessing behind Him, even a grain offering and a drink offering for Yahweh your God?
> (Joel 2:13-14)

Be broken before Him, seeking humbly for Him to do a purifying work in your own life and that of your precious child. While in the midst of our son's rebellion we shed many tears. I have never wept so much in my whole life!

We cried out to the Lord together as a couple. God can do "far more abundantly beyond all that we ask or understand, according to the power that works within us" (Ephesians 3:20). As we passionately, and ardently bring our child before the Lord, He works on the heart, mind, will, and the ability to act.

My husband made a list of 40 verses from Proverbs that he prayed for Daniel over the years of his rebellion. We have seen many, many specific answers to those prayers. Let me encourage you to pray according to the Scriptures. As we pray according to His will, He promises to answer (1 John 5:14-15).

As you and your husband pray together for wisdom in dealing with this trial, God will give you insights on how best to love and discipline this child whom you love so dearly and are so concerned for. This will draw you and your husband closer to the Lord and to each other. Never lose heart nor give up on your child; keep praying and beseeching God to work. "Weeping may last for the night, but a shout of joy comes in the morning" (Psalm 30:5b).

Monica, the devout mother of Augustine, persisted in prayer while her son followed an evil and deluded lifestyle for over 30 years. Augustine writes of his mother,

> While I was yet walking in sin, often attempting to rise, and sinking still deeper, my dear mother in vigorous hope, persisted in earnest prayer for me. There was a time coming, when Thou wouldst wipe away my mother's tears, with which she watered the earth and forgive this my base undutifulness.[33]

Augustine wasn't the only one who noticed her tears. A certain bishop assured her, "it is impossible that the child of such tears should perish."[34]

Augustine was dramatically saved and greatly used by God as a bishop in the early church for forty years.

Whether or not your child comes back to God in repentance and faith, God is still worthy of all your love and devotion. As Job said, "Though He slay me, I will hope in Him" (Job 13:15a). God is not obligated to answer our prayers. We have to pray, "Your will be done," and leave the answers with Him.

Thanking God for this Trial

From a human perspective, this sounds ridiculous. Yet, God is in this trial and He is in it for good, to bring glory to Himself. As you

---

33 Burns, *Mothers of the Wise and Good*, 15-16.
34 Ibid, 17.

and I thank Him by faith—that brings glory to Him. Look at James, chapter one:

> Consider it all joy, my brothers, when you encounter various trials, knowing that the testing of your faith brings about perseverance. And let perseverance have its perfect work, so that you may be perfect and complete, lacking in nothing. But if any of you lacks wisdom, let him ask of God, who gives to all generously and without reproach, and it will be given to him.
> (James 1:2-5)

When you thank God for this trial, it releases the trying circumstance to God for Him to work. God wants to mold you more into the likeness of His Son through this trial (Romans 8:29). He wants to produce the fruit of the Spirit in you to make you more like Christ. Examine your life in that light. How can you learn more love, joy, peace, patience, kindness, goodness, faithfulness, gentleness, and self-control through this trial? Think about each thing that happens.

What will my son's lack of interest in spiritual things help me to learn? I can learn patience to trust God to work in his heart. What fruit can God produce in my life through my response to my teen daughter's pregnancy? I can experience and show love, self-control, and peace which passes understanding in the face of a terribly hard situation. What can my son's use of drugs teach me? I can learn peace in the midst of a heartbreaking situation. What can my daughter's unkindness to me produce in my life as I rely on the Holy Spirit? It can produce kindness and gentleness.

God puts us through the crucible to produce the best fruit in our lives. When things are going smoothly it is easy to be kind and loving and gentle. In those times we don't grow as much as when we suffer. This process of sanctification is painful. It hurts to have our rough edges sanded away, but as we yield to the Holy Spirit, He will supernaturally produce the fruit in our life. Therefore we can thank God for the fruits of our suffering.

I have been amazed at how God has used the trial of our son's rebellion to enhance our ministry. One woman in our church said that they loved our daughter, but they were more thankful that we had a rebellious son because that gave us empathy of what they were going through and knowledge of how to minister to them in their daughter's rebellion.

As we live in the midst of a sinful world system, we are constantly fighting the world, the flesh, and the devil. Our children can be drawn away from Christ and the life He came to give. But God has not left us without spiritual weapons to join Him in the fight for their souls. First, we allow the sword of the Spirit to cut to the quick and deliver us from any sinful habits in our parenting. Then as forgiveness is granted, we step out with renewed strength and unity as a couple to wage war for the souls of our children. There is no cost too great. We are willing to give up our ministry and career. We cry out to God with specific, persevering prayer. We give thanks, knowing that our sovereign God who can bring the dead to life can also bring a harvest of joy from the tears that we have sown.

BEING ONE IN PURPOSE

"One in Christ" are the words that we had engraved on the inside of our wedding bands. For more than three decades we have been living out that oneness. The marvelous fact is that we are more one now than we were on that glorious day that we first became one. Our oneness has deepened as we have lived it out united for one purpose.

In an earlier chapter I related the encouraging example of Mary Moffet, a great pioneer missionary wife to South Africa. Her biographer states,

> ...the early missionaries were not saints; they were men and women of strong convictions with the courage to go out and tell others of Christ. What was astonishing in them was the firmness of purpose which overcame not only physical hardship but human weakness and error from which none of us are immune. These were generally very ordinary men and women made extraordinary by the Faith in which they believed.[35]

Similarly, do we have a firm purpose and faith in an all-sufficient God to carry us through in ministry? I believe that if we have a full understanding of our husbands' calling, that of shepherding God's flock, it will aid us in being one in purpose with them. United for one goal, we will be made extraordinary for God's glory.

---

35 Mora Dickson, *Beloved Partner*, 221.

Our husbands study shepherding in seminary, they read books and articles about it, they attend conferences to sharpen their skills in it, and we are often left wondering where we fit in and how we can support and encourage our men in their tremendous task of shepherding the flock. It is so much more popular in our society to encourage wives to pursue their own interests and passions than to make it their aim to help their husband with his calling.

We see from the creation account that "Yahweh God said, 'It is not good for the man to be alone; I will make him a helper suitable for him.'" (Genesis 2:18). This account of man and woman, who were created in the image of the triune God, shows they have different roles, just as the Father, Son and Holy Spirit have different roles. The wife is to be a helper for her husband. She is to assist him in his task. By helping, it assumes a subordinate position. Her help is necessary and crucial, but the responsibility is his.

If we see our role as wives to be helpers for our husbands—to make being a pastor's wife our career—we can find real fulfillment in this meaningful and purposeful role. In fact, that is to be the role of any wife, whether or not her husband is in ministry. In whatever line of work your husband is in whether he is an astronaut, a soldier, a farmer or a CEO—there are challenges. Life in the twenty-first century is not easy.

In this chapter we'll examine what our husbands' role is as a shepherd. I hope you'll be encouraged to see your supportive role as important in your husband's effectiveness and a chief way in which you can glorify God.

Hopefully you will gain a deeper appreciation of your husband's calling as you read this chapter, and think about all that is involved in shepherding, and that it will spur you on to enter into supporting and encouraging him to an even greater extent. Please don't think of yourself as the co-pastor. I wouldn't want to overwhelm or frustrate you through adding to your burden. Remember, you are a wife first and foremost.

The Shepherd's Role Demands Sacrifice

David, the Shepherd King of Israel, wrote the twenty-third Psalm extolling the shepherd from the perspective of a sheep. His shepherd is the Lord—His Creator and Redeemer. The Shepherd cares for him and manages his life. Throughout the poem, David explains how the Shepherd meets all his needs.

Jesus Christ, our Chief Shepherd who is one with the Father, fulfilled that picture. He laid down His life for the sheep providing for their greatest need—salvation (John 10:11). He bought His church with His own blood on the cross. Then He provided for the church's growth and protection by giving it pastor-teachers—under-shepherds to care for it. To think that our husbands are called to lead, just as Jesus leads His blood-bought sheep, and to care for the needs of Christ's very own! What a privilege!

The chief end of the shepherd is to give his life for his flock. The shepherd takes the sheep from the green pastures and still waters of their home ranch, through the valleys of the shadow of death and onto the high tablelands of rich pasturelands during the summer. He then returns them back home for the long cold winter. His care is paramount for their safety and welfare.

In Phillip Keller's book, *A Shepherd Looks at Psalm 23*, he describes the life of a shepherd as a life totally devoted to meeting the needs of the sheep. The shepherd literally lays down his life for the sheep on a daily basis. The sheep cannot take care of themselves—they are incapable. He says that they require endless attention and meticulous care.[36]

That is true of God's flock. They need constant care. The life of the pastor or shepherd is a life totally devoted to meeting the needs of the sheep. We must be one with that purpose as wives. We need not be surprised that it is a life of sacrifice.

Keller says that it is no accident that God uses the analogy of sheep to describe us as human beings as we are similar in many ways. Having been a shepherd for many years he knows the similarities—"our mass mind (or mob instincts), our fears and timidity, our stubbornness and stupidity, our perverse habits are all parallels of profound importance."[37] Like sheep, we had all gone astray; we had each turned to our own way (Isaiah 53:6).

---

36 Phillip Keller, *A Shepherd Looks at Psalm 23* (Grand Rapids, Michigan: Zondervan, 1970), 7.
37 Ibid.

It is all of His mercy and grace that the Good Shepherd rescues us at the cost of His own life, makes us His own, calls us by name, and lovingly provides for us all our lifetime through and forever! It is out of love for Him and gratitude for the grace that has been given to us that we willingly give ourselves to this task.

Many times our husbands are called upon to sacrifice themselves for the sake of the flock. Pastor Richard Wurmbrand was strongly encouraged by his wife Sabina to stand up for the truth in 1944 in Romania when most of the other religious leaders were embracing the ideology that Christianity and Communism could coexist. He obeyed his Lord and stood up and addressed a large convention that resulted in fourteen years of imprisonment and torture. But God used him to be a strong witness and the founder of a ministry to the persecuted church.

Our husbands' sacrifices usually come in smaller ways but they are nevertheless important.

The Shepherd Needs Our Prayers

Prayer is important in making our marriages lasting and God-honoring—and important if our husbands' ministries are to be fruitful. Our love for our husbands should motivate us to be their most faithful prayer supporter.

William Carey, a pioneer missionary to India said, "Expect great things from God, attempt great things for God."[38] He did incredible things for the kingdom of God: translated the New Testament and Pentateuch into Bengali, led people to faith in Jesus Christ (the first convert after seven years of work), and was instrumental in bringing about societal reforms (e.g., the saving of infants, stopping the burning of Hindu widows on the funeral pyre of their dead husbands (10,000 in one year), and establishing a college. Just imagine what God will do through our husbands in ministry as we pray expectantly!

Below are some directions from Scripture as you pray for your husband:

- That he will be a man after God's own heart with an intimate relationship with the Savior (Matthew 22:37)

---

38 Deaville Walker, *William Carey Father of Modern Missions* (Chicago, Illinois: Moody Press, 1980), 150.

- That the fruit of the Spirit be produced in his life (Galatians 5:22-23)
- That he would yield to the Spirit and live through His power (Ephesians 5:18)
- That your love for each other will grow (Ephesians 5:25)
- That he remains faithful to you in thought and action and you to him (Proverbs 6-7)
- For the blessing of safety, health and strength (Proverbs 10:22)
- For wisdom as he leads the family spiritually and in all the decisions he makes (Psalm 1)
- That he would have the qualities given in 1 Timothy 3:1-7 and Titus 1:6-9

The Shepherd Leads by Example

The shepherds are to lead and guide by example. Peter writes,

> Therefore, I exhort the elders among you, as your fellow elder and witness of the sufferings of Christ, and a partaker also of the glory that is to be revealed, shepherd the flock of God among you, overseeing not under compulsion, but willingly, according to God; and not for dishonest gain, but with eagerness; nor yet as lording it over those allotted to you, but being examples to the flock. And when the Chief Shepherd appears, you will receive the unfading crown of glory.
> (1 Peter 5:1-4)

Peter exhorts the leaders of the church to be humble, hard-working in the oversight of the flock, not seeking honor for themselves nor material gain or power. They are to shepherd eagerly, not dominating those in their charge but serving as examples that they can follow.

Jesus is the supreme example of the One who became poor that we through His poverty might become rich. He came from heaven to show us how to live life and to pour out His life for the sheep. His example was that of a servant-leader. He took the form of a slave and humbled Himself by becoming obedient to the death of a common criminal (Philippians 2:3-10). That is as low as one could go. What an example we have to follow!

When Bob was called to leave our well-established church on the East Coast to plant a church on the other side of the country, we felt that we were being called primarily to live out our lives with the eight couples who had extended the call. They needed leadership in organizing a congregation of believers to worship and serve God. To an equal degree, they needed a pastor and his wife to lead them in their roles as husbands and wives and fathers and mothers; to model how to handle trials, how to witness to neighbors, and how to care for one another—in short, how to glorify God on a daily basis. That is shepherding by example. That is what our husbands and our families are called to do. What a vital role this is!

How can you support your husband in leading by example?

- Refrain from pushing him for the plaudits of men.
- Pray for your husband to be humble and encourage him in humble leadership.
- Follow his leadership, as any other sheep should within the flock. "Obey your leaders and submit to them—for they keep watch over your souls as those who will give an account—so that they will do this with joy and not with groaning, for this would be unprofitable for you" (Hebrews 13:17).
- Follow his example and also have an attitude of servanthood.
- Realize that you are an example as you flesh out what a godly wife and mother is to be.
- Be encouraged that neither your husband nor you are perfect.
- Seek to grow in Christ and have your outer life match up with your inner life.

The Shepherd Organizes the Flock

Not every pastor assists the church in establishing its constitution and bylaws and vision for ministry. However, every pastor casts a vision for the church or area of ministry of which he has oversight, and must keep the flock together for one purpose.

Sheep are safe as they are together. Jesus lamented because the people were like "sheep without a shepherd" (Matthew 9:36). The shepherd is needed for cohesiveness. Sheep left to themselves will wander off.

They do not flock together on their own. So, one of the major responsibilities of the shepherd is to get the sheep together into a flock and be their protector and leader. This takes organization.

My husband had specific goals in mind that he wanted to see accomplished when he came to plant the church. He helped establish the purpose, vision, and mission of the church. He had four main purposes.

- To preach God's Word powerfully for application
- To disciple the believers through small groups
- To have a strong emphasis on caring for one another
- To have an emphasis on world missions

Our vision statement is: "To produce disciple-making followers of the Lord Jesus Christ who will be devoted to loving God, one another, and the world."

This has become a reality as all the elders, which includes associate pastors, work together to shepherd the flock. It is so important that they work together as one. The most cohesive force in this effort has been meeting together for prayer as leaders every Wednesday morning at 6 a.m. They have done this for years. They also have an annual elders' planning retreat, which draws them together.

Our elders have worked on the necessity of unanimity from the beginning. In order for this oneness, there needs to be understanding and trust which develops as men work together and know each other.

Without the relationship of respect and trust, your husband will not be able to lead in ways in which he believes God wants. Your husband needs to know his fellow elders individually and corporately.

The pastor exerts leadership in encouraging the use of different elders' particular gifts for the benefit of the church. For this he needs to get to know them. My husband seeks to meet individually with each of them on a regular basis to encourage and pray with them in regard to their ministries.

One seasoned pastor says,

> It is not enough to get to know your elders in the regular elders' meetings. They must come to know you and you must come to

know them in a greater variety of contexts. And they need to come to know one another fully as persons too. If the eldership is to become a smoothly functioning body, exerting a powerful force for good in the congregation, its members will have to be molded together into a cohesive entity by effective pastoral leadership.[39]

How can you help your husband as he leads?

- Pray that he will be able to keep the flock united, keeping them from theological tangents as he faithfully lifts up Jesus Christ.

- Help provide social opportunities for the elders and their wives to spend time getting to know each other. I host a once-a-month breakfast for the wives of our pastors for fellowship and accountability. This is invaluable in developing oneness. We plan social opportunities for us as couples.

- Seek to encourage him in this vital role, and thank him for this behind-the-scenes aspect of his ministry.

The Shepherd Feeds the Flock

The shepherd must feed his flock for it to survive and thrive. The flock grows on the unadulterated Word of God. Paul charged Timothy,

> I solemnly charge you in the presence of God and of Christ Jesus, who is to judge the living and the dead, and by His appearing and His kingdom: preach the word; be ready in season and out of season; reprove, rebuke, exhort, with great patience and teaching. For the time will come when they will not endure sound doctrine, but wanting to have their ears tickled, they will accumulate for themselves teachers in accordance to their own desires. (2 Timothy 4:1-3)

Our husbands have the awesome privilege and responsibility of weekly feeding the flock through their sermons. They also feed the sheep through leading in worship, teaching the youth, equipping leaders, visiting the sick, counseling members, and many other avenues of ministry.

The Word of God is thoroughly adequate to equip the saints for

---

39 Jay Adams, *Shepherding God's Flock* (Phillipsburg, New Jersey, P&R Publishing, 1975), 45-47.

every good work (2 Timothy 3:16-17). Our husbands have God's powerful Word to study, seek to interpret, and apply to the hungry sheep. That is a huge task which carries with it a heavy burden! But we know that the One who called them will accomplish the work through them as they seek Him (1 Thessalonians 5:24). Seeing and hearing my husband teach God's Word is something I never tire of. I seek to pray each time he teaches that the Lord will speak to my heart and help me to apply it to my life. I have grown in my walk with Christ and thank God for his ministry in my life. I feel so blessed!

How can you help your husband as he feeds God's flock?

- Pray for wisdom as he sets goals for the maturity of the flock in what to teach (where the green pastures and still waters are).

- Pray for wisdom as he organizes the use of his time studying Scripture and equipping the saints for the work of the ministry.

- Pray for him to gain great insights into God's Word, and that he will present those without equivocation, authoritatively, and with application—that which has passed through his own life first. (One of the things which people tell me they appreciate about Bob the most is that he is "real" in his sermons—letting us know where he struggles as well. He is on the journey of being sanctified along with every other member of our flock.)

- Pray that he will not get side-tracked by bringing psychology or humanistic philosophies into his teachings to satisfy the palates of churchgoers who want to leave feeling good about themselves.

- Pray that God fills him with His Holy Spirit as he proclaims God's Word so that it accomplishes that for which it is sent.

- Pray that you will have a growing hunger for the Word.

- Look for opportunities to ask your husband about the message that he is preparing, and seek to interact with it both before and after he delivers it. Give him positive feedback.

The Shepherd Equips for Service

Our husbands could not possibly do all that is necessary to shepherd a flock of even eight families. That is why the Chief Shepherd, Jesus Christ, designed the shepherds to be equippers for others to do the work of the ministry. He gave "...some as pastors and teachers, for the equipping of the saints for the work of service, to the building up of the body of Christ" (Ephesians 4:11b-12). The purpose of this equipping is so that the whole body might be built up in love (v. 16). Jesus said, "By this all will know that you are My disciples, if you have love for one another" (John 13:35).

Men in our church were equipped to serve in biblical counseling, youth ministry, worship and missions, Christian education and family ministries and took those positions. We then had five equippers instead of one. The body is being ministered to by one another, and the body is reaching out to the community.

How can you help your husband in this aspect of shepherding?

- Encourage him to train others and release them for ministry.
- Follow his example by seeking to disciple and equip other women.
- Pray for him to be effective in this area, even if there are just a few who would be considered capable of leading.
- Pray that your flock will be trained to reach their "world" for Jesus Christ.
- Pray that all the needs of the flock will be met as the whole church serves one another.

The Shepherd Counsels for Life Application

As the shepherd seeks to feed the flock the Word of God, certain sheep demand more attention. That is when he applies the truth of Scripture to certain situations in the life of the individual or family. This is the ministry of counseling. It is in-depth discipleship. Paul wrote the believers in Rome, "But I myself am also convinced about you, my brothers, that you yourselves are full of goodness, having been filled with all knowledge and being able also to admonish one another" (Romans 15:14).

A shepherd's job is to use his staff to bring the sheep who have wandered off back to himself. Keller says,

> Again and again I have seen a shepherd use his staff to guide his sheep gently into a new path or through some gate or along

dangerous, difficult routes. He does not use it actually to beat the beast. Rather, the tip of the long slender stick is laid gently against the animal's side and the pressure applied guides the sheep in the way the owner wants it to go. Thus the sheep is reassured of its proper path...

Being stubborn creatures sheep often get into the most ridiculous and preposterous dilemmas. I have seen my own sheep, greedy for one more mouthful of green grass, climb down steep cliffs where they slipped and fell into the sea. Only my long shepherd's staff could lift them out of the water back onto solid ground again.[40]

What beautiful pictures here of the Great Shepherd who guards and protects His own from danger. The under-shepherds are to do the same. This portrays counseling individuals or couples who need that special attention of the shepherd. That is the role of the pastor—to shepherd the flock in the problems and difficulties of life with which they are dealing. That is what counseling is all about—shepherding. Many of the messes and scrapes we get into as sheep are of our own making. But in tenderness and compassion the shepherd comes to us, lifts us up, and draws us close to the Chief Shepherd. God's Word assures of the proper path. What a comfort!

When my husband began in the ministry, he was driven by the needs of one of his sheep to study biblical counseling and receive a doctor of ministry in it so that it could be a strength of his ministry instead of a weakness. Out of that he has had a vital ministry helping hundreds of people apply God's Word to their lives and teaching others to counsel as well.

How can you help your husband in this aspect of shepherding?

- Pray that he will have wisdom to gently guide those who come for counsel to walk in the path of righteousness.
- Encourage your husband in his efforts to get better prepared to counsel biblically.
- Seek to better prepare yourself to do in-depth discipleship with women.

---

40 Keller, *A Shepherd Looks*, 87.

- Keep confidences guardedly.
- Cast all our concerns on the Lord.

The Shepherd Guards the Flock

In David's shepherd psalm he says, "Your rod and Your staff, they comfort me" (Psalm 23:4b). What do the rod and staff portray that is so comforting? Protection! The shepherd was responsible to see that his sheep were not lost, killed, or injured.

It is a comfort to the sheep for his shepherd to have his rod—weapon of power, defense, and authority—with him, to guard and protect the sheep in every situation. With the rod, the shepherd protects his sheep from the danger of many predators like stray dogs, wolves, coyotes, lions, or bears.

Satan is described as a roaring lion seeking to destroy the children of God (1 Peter 5:8). The pastor is to protect the sheep against Satan's attacks. That is accomplished through the consistent preaching and teaching of God's Word—the feeding of the flock. The best protection for the sheep is to know God's Word and have it applied to their life situations in the context of the culture.

The shepherd must warn the flock of the philosophical dangers prevalent in our society, some of which are all the "isms" of our day—pluralism, humanism, relativism, materialism, secularism, hedonism, and pragmatism. This requires a great deal of study. Our husbands must be continually reading and digesting the Word—becoming practical theologians. It is part and parcel of ministry.

Our husbands' role is to warn against false doctrine. Paul taught the believers at Ephesus everything that was profitable for their faith. He then told the overseers, who shepherd the church of God, to be on the alert for the wolves that would come in among them, not sparing the flock (Acts 20:20-30). The wolves were teaching a false doctrine.

Paul also wrote Timothy that as a pastor-teacher it was his responsibility to correct, with gentleness, those who are in opposition to the truth in the hopes that God may grant them repentance leading to the knowledge of the truth and escape the snare of the devil (2 Timothy 2:25-26).

Jude encouraged his readers:

> ...contend earnestly for the faith which was once for all handed down to the saints. For certain persons have crept in unnoticed, those who were long beforehand marked out for this condemnation, ungodly persons who turn the grace of our God into sensuality and deny our only Master and Lord, Jesus Christ (Jude 1:3-4).

It is not man's wisdom, plans, programs, mission statements, worship styles, or psychology that will change lives. It is the power of the risen Jesus Christ, and His Word preached and appropriated. The Good Shepherd vanquished all our spiritual enemies—sin, Satan, death, and hell. Our reliance is on Him and on the Holy Spirit.

What can you as a wife do to help your husband guard the flock?

- Pray that your husband will have the wisdom and discernment to preach the Word faithfully, which protects the flock from the spiritual wolves that would ravish the flock, so that they will have their senses trained by solid food and practice to discern good and evil (Hebrews 5:14).
- Pray for boldness for your husband to confront error in the power of the Holy Spirit.
- As time allows, read and be ready to discuss issues with your husband, which the church is grappling with. You have wisdom to contribute.

The Shepherd Disciplines the Flock

The shepherd's rod is used for discipline. Keller says that this is the purpose for which it is used the most. He tells about observing how often the east African herders would hurl their rods at their recalcitrant sheep when they misbehaved. If they were to see a sheep wandering off on its own or getting into poisonous weeds or coming too close to danger of one kind or another, the rod would go whistling through the air to send the wayward sheep back to the flock.

The shepherd protects the flock by leading it through the process of church discipline if it is required. Discipline is for the purpose of restoration and for the health of the flock (Galatians 6). It is not optional, but must be carried out in obedience to Jesus' teaching (Matthew 18:15-20). It is the wonderful opportunity of the shepherd to help those who have fallen—not only to come to repentance and discipline, but also to see them through the process of getting to the other side in knowing the joy of forgiveness and restoration. Sometimes that is a process. God specializes in taking broken people, and turning them into His mighty leaders such as Moses, David, and Peter.

As the shepherd guards and protects his flock in these ways, there is great comfort in the knowledge that we are each in the care of the Chief Shepherd, who has graciously provided for the welfare of all of His sheep.

What can you do to help your husband discipline the flock?

- Pray that he has the grace to seek the ones who have gone astray.
- Pray that he will meet the attacks of Satan in his own life with prayer and devotion to God's Word.
- Pray for the strength and discernment he needs to carry out the process of church discipline if it is needed.
- Don't dwell on the sheep that have wandered or the ones who have been disciplined by the church; rather consider all the wonderful things that God is doing in the lives of the ones who are following the Shepherd.

The Shepherd Goes after the Lost Sheep

When Jesus was accused of receiving and eating with sinners, He told the parable about the shepherd who had 100 sheep. He asks them, if one were to get lost, wouldn't the shepherd leave the 99 and go after the lost one? Of course! He pictures the great joy over one lost sheep that is found (Luke 15:1-7). Jesus' whole purpose was to seek and to save that which was lost (Luke 19:10).

So it is with the shepherd-pastor. He must follow Jesus' example and go after the lost ones who need the Savior. He must build relationships with those who are in need of Christ and seek to share the "good news." He must train others to do the same.

Paul told Timothy, "But you, be sober in all things, endure hardship, do the work of an evangelist, fulfill your ministry" (2 Timothy 4:5).

How can you help your husband in this area?

- Pray for him to have a burden for the lost and to take opportunities to boldly proclaim the gospel.
- Pray together for God to use you as a family to communicate the love of Christ through hospitality, to those you come in contact with, such as neighbors and the parents of your children's friends.

The Shepherd Cares for the Hurting

Those sheep that are hurting elicit a special care by the shepherd. He is alert to their needs. He will seek to be there and spare nothing to see that their needs are cared for in every detail. Perhaps one is ill or hurt. He has a sympathetic eye to see if they are able to go out on their own. So it is with the pastors of the church. They must be on the alert for the needs of the hurting ones within their flocks, just as the Chief Shepherd does as we call out to Him.

Making Visits

There are many situations that warrant a visit from the pastor either in the home or in the hospital. Visits are often made when a person or family is seeking counsel about a particular decision or just out of the desire to merely get to know those in the congregation. Then there are opportunities to follow up on church visitors to present the way of salvation. There are chances to share in celebration over the birth of a child or graduation or birthday. There are strengthening visits during a severe illness or impending death. When death and mourning come, the pastor can be an invaluable help in arranging for the necessary funeral details and giving comfort.

The Word of God is the basis for all the advice offered and comfort given. God is always sought through prayer. It is an opportunity for the pastor to rejoice with the flock in the good times and to weep with them in the bad.

By visiting in the homes of the members of his flock, the pastor shows deeper concern for shepherding than could take place anywhere else. Some churches have visitation pastors to do visitation. Elders, deacons, and others in the congregation often take part in this ministry as well. This is where the love of Christ is demonstrated in a very practical way.

When visiting a family who is going through a severe trial, we have made it our practice for some years to give them a framed picture of a sketch of an artist's portrayal of Jesus, the Good Shepherd, holding a little lamb in His nail-scarred hand close to Himself.[41] The artist has captured the look of peace and contentment on the little lamb's face. It says, "He loves me! I'm in His care and I'm safe." It has been very meaningful and comforting to so many. Scriptures relating to the Good Shepherd are given with the picture (Isaiah 40:11; John 10:11; Psalm 23).

Calling on the Phone

Since our churches are no longer ministering to people confined to a small area, sometimes it is more possible and practical to give a phone call to a homebound member or one who is going in for surgery. This is not as comforting, but it is better than not being able to make contact at all.

My husband also has a vital ministry mentoring other pastors who are out of the area. This is done by phone, once a month. I have done this as well with pastors' wives.

Writing

Another means of shepherding is to write notes of encouragement to members who are going through a trial or experiencing a blessing. When our elders meet on Wednesday morning for prayer, afterwards each elder writes one or two notes to the person or family whom he prayed for, letting them know that they were brought before the Father.

Another means of providing counsel and encouragement is through email. Bob uses this means with missionaries a great deal who have counseling questions. This is an inexpensive and fast way to keep in touch and has been invaluable in keeping up with our families that are at a distance.

---

41 Some Christians believe images of Jesus are prohibited by the Second Commandment (Exodus 20:4–6). You may want to talk through your convictions on this topic with your husband.

How can you be one with your husband in this aspect of shepherding?

- Willingly release him when he gets called out at any time of day or night to the hospital or home of an especially needy member of the flock, and pray that he will be used by the Lord to give the comfort and/or counsel needed.

- Accompany him when possible. Before we had children, I often accompanied my husband on visits, or would visit women on my own. Now that our children are grown, I'm able to participate more in this rewarding ministry. What a blessing it is to hold the hand of a dear saint who will soon to be in Christ's presence, or to shed tears with a family as they endure a trial. It is a sacred privilege to minister alongside my husband in that way.

- Make phone calls and write notes to those with special needs to keep in touch with the women and families within the church who need that special interest.

The Shepherd Is Hospitable

This important duty of the shepherd of God's flock will be covered in the next chapter (1 Timothy 3:2).

The Shepherd Is Important

God's flock in the Old Testament became prey to deceivers who drew them into idolatry. God's preferred method of judging and restoring them was subjecting them to captivity. The shepherds were not doing their job. Ezekiel has a stern condemnation of them. He said that God had pronounced woe upon them.

> Those who are sickly you have not strengthened, and the diseased you have not healed, and the broken you have not bound up, and the scattered you have not brought back, nor have you searched for the lost; but with strength and with severity you have dominated them. They were scattered for lack of a shepherd, and they became food for every beast of the field and were scattered.
> (Ezekiel 34:4-5)

The shepherds were held accountable for those under their care. What a responsibility!

And what a high privilege to be one with Christ's shepherd in this demanding and very rewarding calling; to be able to help and encourage him in many more ways than I have been able to mention. May God give us His strength.

EXERCISING HOSPITALITY

"Thank you so much for having us for dinner as well as the counseling. It really was special for you both to spend time with us today." These were the parting words of the newly married couple that came for their post-marriage session with Bob. They had their check-up time with Bob while I prepared the meal and then we were able to talk together over dinner about their marriage and the "surprise package" on the way. What a privilege to have a significant part in the life of this young couple!

The shepherd of Christ's flock is to be hospitable (1 Timothy 3:2; Titus 1:8). Although this is also required of all believers (Romans 12:13; Hebrews 13:1-2), the shepherd is to lead the flock in this as in other character qualities and good works. He is to be hospitable in spirit and practice. Hospitality would be hard for him to practice alone, because most of it takes place in the home. This joint effort builds unity as a couple, serving God together in this uniquely personal ministry.

Do you consider it a joy and privilege to make it possible for your husband to carry out this part of his ministry, or do you struggle in this area? There is no question about it—hospitality involves a lot of work that often leaves us exhausted. Sometimes it seems like ninety percent of our time is spent in the kitchen. Is it worth it?

In this chapter I want to show you the importance of hospitality, and some ways to practically improve in hospitality so that you will be motivated and enabled to keep on striving in this essential realm of your ministry. I want to encourage you to put your heart and soul into it!

Why is hospitality so important to the ministry couple?

The Shepherd and Sheep Must Know Each Other

Where would Jesus have stayed if it hadn't been for the hospitality of His friends? He had no home to call His own. The home of Lazarus, Mary, and Martha was probably a favorite place to receive refreshment in His busy life and ministry. It was a place for them to get to know Him better and vice versa. Jesus showed His love for people by living with them, walking with them, celebrating with them, mourning with them, and eating meals with them. Why were the Pharisees so scandalized when Jesus ate with tax collectors and sinners? It was because it showed His love for them. Breaking bread with sinners brought salvation to their house as they came to know and trust Him. It must have been such an experience of pure joy.

We know that Mary on one occasion took full advantage of getting to know Jesus better while her sister was "distracted with all her preparations." Jesus told Martha that her sister had chosen the good part, which would not be taken away from her (Luke 10:40-42). She had chosen to sit at Jesus' feet.

Are you using hospitality to truly get to know the people in your ministry? You and I, as pastors' wives, have a unique entrée into people's lives. We can call people out of the blue and have a connection. We can drop by for a visit. We can invite someone over with no prior relationship other than that they visited church. Church members usually welcome any contact outside of church by the pastor and his wife. Hospitality is a sacred privilege and should be used to the fullest extent to give the care a shepherd would give his sheep.

Our aim should be to make our home a hospitable place where any of our church family is welcome. Our homes have been given to us as a tool for ministry. When we invite people into our home we are inviting them to have a more personal relationship with us. We are demonstrating the desire to encourage them and strengthen them in a special way. As we share over food, a time of being nourished physically, conversation takes place and friendships are strengthened. People share their joys and burdens, their families, their history, their work, and their passions including their walk with the Lord. Without hospitality relationships can remain superficial.

Martin Luther's wife is a wonderful example of hospitality.

> Katherine had not only her own children to care for—six of them—but also (at various times) her own niece and nephew, eleven of Martin's nieces and nephews, various students who boarded with them, and ever-present guests who came to confer with her famous husband.[42]

Katie's patient hospitality actually made possible one of Luther's finest books, *The Table Talk of Martin Luther*. It records the sparkling conversations that took place while the food grew cold. At one such dinner Katie gave her husband a gentle nudge, "'Doctor, why don't you stop talking and eat?' Luther knew that she was right, but he still snapped back, 'I wish that women would repeat the Lord's Prayer before opening their mouths!'"[43]

It is not easy being married to a witty theologian. Yet her hospitality enabled her husband to know his sheep and impact their world.

The World Is Watching

Jesus said, "By this all will know that you are My disciples, if you have love for one another" (John 13:35). If we are disciples of Christ, then we will be like our Master. He loved us enough to die for us. So what is a little sacrifice in order to show hospitality to each other?

Don't you enjoy being invited for a meal and fellowship? Someone cares about you enough to plan and provide food, and whatever else, just for you. You are made to feel loved—cared for. If you are like me, you probably think, it would be awfully nice to experience a little more of that. It seems in our fast-paced society there is less hospitality taking place. However, we are to do unto others, as we would have them do

---

42 Warren Wiersbe, *Victorious Christians You Should Know*, (Grand Rapids, Michigan: Baker Book House, 1984), 98.
43 Ibid, 99.

unto us. Jesus said that this summed up all the Law and the prophets. It is the golden rule (Matthew 7:12). We should practice hospitality whether or not it is ever returned.

As we shower love on one another, the world will see that Christ's love is real. Barriers to the gospel may be broken down. Our Christian fellowship should be obvious and undeniable to those around us, as it was to the pagan world surrounding the early church. Lucian, a Roman writer of satire against Christians said: "It is incredible to see the ardor with which the people of that religion help each other in their wants. They spare nothing. Their first legislator (Jesus) has put into their heads that they are all brethren."

Do you have a neighbor who is hard to establish a friendly relationship with? Give them a taste of Christian hospitality. Reach out with an invitation for dessert or dinner or simply a plate of cookies. It opens the door to friendship and to ultimately sharing the message of the love of Christ with those who may not know Him.

Taking a meal to a neighbor who is going through a trial can let them know of your love and concern. When our neighbors were undergoing a tremendous trial we did just that, along with some other efforts to bring comfort. It was received with much appreciation and the words, "You are just the best neighbors anyone could ever have, and if we ever go to church, we will go to yours!"

I related this to a young woman that I was meeting with for discipleship. We decided to make a game over it. She said, "If they do not come to church in the next two weeks you will wear an outfit that I make to church the next Sunday." I said, "Okay, if they do, you will make them four meals" (which she suggested). One week went by and I began to be nervous about that outfit she was making for me, so I casually mentioned it to them. Being that they wouldn't want me embarrassed in front of the whole church, they came. Bob was speaking on trials that Sunday. After the message our neighbor said with emotion, "I want you to tell Bob that was a hell of a talk!" It had really spoken to her heart. Once a week for the next month they received a delicious meal from my friend, delivered to them with a lot of laughter and joy. They never came back to church, but they can't say that they never saw true Christian disciples who loved them.

Our Sheep Are Following

The leaders in the church must demonstrate hospitality. It is one of the qualifications for an elder. It is also given as one of the qualifications for a widow to be put on the list for support from the church. She deserves honor "if she has shown hospitality to strangers, if she has washed the saints' feet" (1 Timothy 5:10). If the shepherd and his wife lead the way, the sheep will follow.

Although Bob and I don't always get invited to homes, we know hospitality is going on within our church family. Others are ministering to people within the body through hospitality. In fact, invitations are given in front of us without a thought. They know that we are pleased when hospitality is taking place whether or not we are included.

The principle of, "Give, and it will be given to you. They will pour into your lap a good measure—pressed down, shaken together, running over…" is true in this area of hospitality (Luke 6:38). All the love and hospitality we had poured into our church family came pouring back to us as our congregation took part in our two children's weddings, which took place on the same weekend. They attended and helped with wedding festivities almost non-stop for three days. We couldn't have done it without the help we received. A couple hosted a rehearsal brunch. One man, with the help of many others, catered the delightful dinner for our daughter's reception. Twelve homes were opened for out-of-town guests. Our children started out their marriages with everything you could possibly need and then some. This was such an unusual happening that it made the front page of our city's newspaper with pictures of both weddings. The world was watching as our church body followed and exceeded our example, and what a picture of Jesus' love that weekend was!

When we are hospitable it is a model for our children to follow as well. Our children's lives are enriched as people come into our home. They get to know neighbors, church members, missionaries from all over the world, and strangers. It becomes a natural part of their lives.

When we have experienced the blessings of hospitality in our homes growing up, we follow the same pattern. My dear mother modeled hospitality. She had an open heart and open home. I learned most of my homemaking skills from her.

It was so rewarding to experience the hospitality of our daughter Michelle and her husband Tim as we recently visited them on the mission field. She entertained us, and many others, in their home while we were there—complete with centerpiece and candlelight just as she had set the table so many times in our home. Our son Dan and his wife Tiffany are also hospitable. Not long ago Tiffany called me for a recipe to make for a couple whose child was very ill. It is a joy to have passed the baton on to the next generation.

Good modeling impacted us when we were moving to California from the east coast. We stopped to see some good friends on our way. They graciously invited us to stay for dinner and overnight in their mill house. The next day was Bob's birthday, which they just happened to find out about. In the morning Bob got up and went downstairs, he was promptly told to get back in bed. That was a strange way to be treated as a guest, but he complied.

In a few minutes the whole family knocked and entered our bedroom with a tray holding a delicious breakfast with a lighted candle, singing happy birthday to Bob. That was their family tradition and they were letting us be family. We enjoyed it so much that it became our family tradition and continues now in our children's families.

What kind of legacy of hospitality do we want to leave with those who are following us?

Angels May Be Visiting

You never know what personal blessings your hospitality may bring you.

> "Let love of the brothers continue. Do not neglect to show hospitality to strangers, for by this some have entertained angels without knowing it"
> (Hebrews 13:1-2).

Entertaining angels is a strange occurrence, but it actually happened several times in the Old Testament. Angels visited Abraham and Sarah who received the promise of a son (Genesis 18:1-15), Lot who was saved with his family from destruction (Genesis 19), Gideon who was told how to save his people from their enemies (Judges 6:11-24), and Manoah and his wife who were promised a son, Samson, who would be a deliverer (Judges 13:6-20). These people were generous to strangers—angels and the pre-incarnate Son of God. Look how God blessed them! What examples to follow!

In the book of Acts we read another example of unexpected blessings from hospitality. Publius entertained Paul and his companions (who were perfect strangers) in his home for three days after they had been shipwrecked on the island of Malta. In return, he was blessed by having Paul heal his father (Acts 28:1-8).

My husband and I entertained a stranger when we were new in the ministry before we had children. Bob brought home a bedraggled young man who had recently been released from prison. Richard had come to the church office seeking help. He said that he wanted to turn his life around. We gave him our guest room, and after showering he had a meal with us. Since we had a meeting at church that night and Richard didn't want to go, we left him home alone. Upon returning home we found that he had taken everything that he could fit into a suitcase of ours and left. We reported it to the police and he was picked up and put in jail. Subsequently, Bob visited him and took him a pair of shoes that he needed. Not only did Bob share the gospel of forgiveness with him, he acted it out. When Richard got out of jail he came right back to our house for money and a ride which Bob gave him. I shudder to think about the danger we put ourselves in, but in our naiveté God protected us. We don't know whatever happened to him. Hopefully, our hospitality showed him God's merciful redeeming love. We haven't seen him since, but perhaps he has come to know the Savior who sent him our way.

If God blesses us for caring for strangers, how much more will He bless us as we minister to the family of God? Paul admonishes believers to "...not lose heart in doing good, for in due time we will reap if we do not grow weary. So then, while we have opportunity, let us do good to all people, and especially to those who are of the household of the faith" (Galatians 6:9-10).

Paul must have known the weariness, the exhaustion—physically and every other way—that doing good can cause. He tells us not to lose heart but to remember the reward that is coming. Those hours spent preparing food and making beds and cleaning toilets are not lost. They are an investment into knowing our flock, reaching the lost, leading the sheep, and reaping personal blessings.

How Do We Improve Our Hospitality?

Prayerfully Evaluate

Now that we have looked at the importance of hospitality, let's evaluate the hospitality that takes place in our own homes and find ways to improve it. I would imagine that many of us struggle in this area. You may not be good at cooking, housekeeping, or entertaining. You may have been raised in a home where it was not modeled. You may be just plain shy. You may have had no interest in getting involved in this form of ministry because you wanted to keep your home a sanctuary for your family alone. There may be other obstacles such as health constraints. But all of these obstacles can be overcome if we realize the importance of hospitality and are willing to stretch ourselves.

You need to seek your husband's input and talk over any changes that you may want to make. What kinds of things do you want to add to your schedule in order to reach out through hospitality? What do you need to cut back on so that you have time to practice hospitality?

Let me encourage you to pray about it together and seek God's wisdom for ministering in this area, without overloading your schedules and lives. Pray for joy as you sense God's presence and favor in this special work that you are doing for His glory.

Practical Ideas

Here are some ways that we practice hospitality in our ministry home. I'm sure you could add to the list from your own ideas. We do so many of these things without really thinking about it. As you read through these ideas, see if there are any that you want to add to your lifestyle. If you are already doing these things, think about how you can keep them focused on the main goal, which is loving and knowing your guests.

Dinners. This meal affords the evening to spend together. It is important to mix people from different walks of life, generations, and backgrounds. It makes for good conversation and contributes to everyone's awareness of the variety of people in the family of God—couples, singles, and families. When our children were in the home, we invited more couples with children and the kids could play and get to know each other also. It is so good to invite new people to the church along with the old friends. This helps the new friends feel welcomed.

Sunday Dinner. This has been a traditional time for guests—right after church. However, we have chosen to do less of it now than when we were younger. Bob preaches twice on Sunday morning so he is not too eager to have guests over right after church. Now, we like to take visitors out to lunch at a restaurant. We can spend time together but still get some rest in the afternoon. We host a membership class every other month at our home, which includes dinner. This gives new people a chance to experience our hospitality.

Lunch. This meal affords me an opportunity to invite women who are new to the church or who I just want to get to know better. It's also a good opportunity to encourage a woman who may be experiencing a particular trial.

Breakfast. This is when I host the pastors' wives for our monthly get-together, when their husbands are home and can babysit before work. Bob also uses this time for men's Bible studies or elders' meetings.

Snacks. Having our friends or our children's friends over always involves serving snacks.

Teas or Coffees. Hosting ladies teas—formal or informal—is a delightful way to entertain. A nice variation of this is a mother-daughter tea. Holding these events with coffee is another alternative.

Celebrations. These opportunities to practice hospitality can include birthday parties, anniversary parties, and graduation parties. Family gatherings provide a natural setting for inviting church members, relatives, and neighbors into the fabric of our lives. Jesus showed His approval of these kinds of occasions by performing His first miracle at a wedding feast, saving the groom great embarrassment (John 2:1-11). What a celebration that must have been with the Son of God there to sanctify and bless it!

Bible Studies. Hosting weekly Bible studies has been a great blessing to us over the years. I've also hosted an afternoon Bible study for teen mothers.

Good News Clubs. Following my mother's example, I led an afternoon club for the children in our neighborhood, and then our daughter led it when she was in high school.

Meetings. Once a month, I host a meeting for the mentors involved in the ministry that I direct. Our home has been the setting for many committee meetings, mission prayer meetings, and even the Sunday-evening service when we were just starting the church.

Mentoring or Counseling Individuals. We have always invited people to our home to mentor or counsel them. It provides a welcoming atmosphere.

Block Parties. These gatherings are great for getting neighbors together.

Pool Parties. Hosting young people around the swimming pool is great in the summer.

Outreach Parties. These can be centered around an event like the Super Bowl. This provides a bridge to proclaim the gospel to unbelievers.

Open House. Especially at Christmas, people enjoy coming into your home; this type of event allows for more people to come at once.

Fellowship Dinners. Using different homes each month, couples and/or singles sign up and are assigned to a group for a meal and fellowship. We have always participated in this.

Young Life Club. When our children were in high school, it was a privilege to host this club, which reaches out to unchurched kids.

Do It without Complaint

"Be hospitable to one another without grumbling" (1 Peter 4:9). We can be doing all of these things and still not be pleasing God with our hospitality unless it is done in His way.

Have you ever felt like the ragged housewife who slaved all day preparing a meal for a large group of guests? When she sat down to the meal she asked her little daughter to pray. Her daughter delayed, "But I don't know what to say." Eager to begin the meal, she replied, "Just say what Mommy prays," only to hear her daughter begin, "Lord, why did I invite so many people?"

Our complaining hearts can undo all of the good that we are trying to do by our diligent preparations. Our preparation must begin with cleaning out the selfishness from our own hearts. Peter exhorts us, "Above all, keep fervent in your love for one another…"(1 Peter 4:8). Then his first illustration of this kind of sold-out love is hospitality without complaint.

Keep It Simple

One way to avoid complaining is to keep it simple. Be sure that you are not overextending yourself. You don't have to be a gourmet cook and try to impress people. The goal of your entertaining is not to impress people but to show love and concern for your guests. Like Jesus in the home of Mary and Martha, your guests would rather have the time with you than a fancy spread, if it is a choice between the two. Don't be like Martha—worried and distracted by so many things. It is not necessary to make things so elaborate that you can't enjoy your guests.

The purpose of hospitality is to open your lives and home for God's use in ministering to other people. Do this in a way that fits your personality. Develop your own style of entertaining. Where we live in California, the style is very informal. Cookouts, poolside gatherings, and buffets are the most common ways to entertain. Remember; don't allow the "how" of entertaining to interfere with the "why."

Let Others Help

Another way to avoid complaining is to use teamwork. Like Martha we are often tempted to complain if we think that we are bearing the burden alone. We need to avoid the self-pity that demands help. But after examining our own hearts, it is very legitimate to call others to join us in the work and blessings of hospitality.

Since our husbands are admonished to be hospitable, maybe we need to enlist their help more. Some men enjoy barbequing or helping in the kitchen. They can often help with the set-up for company and definitely help with the clean-up. My husband is a wiz at this.

Teach your children to enjoy preparing for guests. My daughter actually got excited about giving up her room and having a slumber party with her brother whenever we had guests. Now her boys think it is a great treat to take the sleeping bags in Daddy and Mommy's room so the guests can have their rooms. They pick flowers from the garden to put on the bedside tables. They enjoy helping to set the special dinner table and carry in extra chairs. Having guests makes it a festive time, whether they are strangers or family or church family.

If your goal is to make people feel at home, why not let them help with the last-minute preparations or clean-up? I remember the first time we had a gentleman who was a nationally known author in our home for dinner and he insisted on helping with the dishes. This was a moment of discovery for me when I allowed him to help. What a blessing to get to know him even better as we worked in the kitchen!

If you are so concerned about being the perfect hostess, getting everything done ahead and forbidding anyone to help, your guests can feel more like a spectator and less like a guest. Relax so that your guests will be more comfortable and the process will be more easily reciprocated. Families need to see the least stressful way to throw a dinner party so they will follow suit. Potlucks are a great way to enjoy a reciprocal feast with little work.

If we are always trying to put our best foot forward, we can sometimes stub our toes. One such Easter dinner stands out in my mind. I really wanted to make everything as special as possible for some very special guests. We had just moved into our new house and I wasn't used to our new stove. The salmon overcooked, the herb and sour cream mashed potatoes burned, as did the homemade rolls. The asparagus was the only thing that turned out, and the salad that the guests had brought. To top it off, the strawberry cream pie was runny. Not only was the meal a disaster, but the mechanic who came in the middle of dinner to fix our son's car interrupted us. Immediately following dinner while we were giving them a tour of the house, we discovered that the pipe behind the washing machine had broken and water had gone through the wall and soaked the carpet in the adjoining bedroom.

If my goal had been to impress these people, I would have utterly failed and my heart would have been full of complaints. But because it was done in love, thank the Lord, we could laugh at our flop rather than get upset about it. We certainly made a memory with these people and they were very gracious.

Be Flexible

A final tool that I want to discuss in our battle against complaining is flexibility. Sometimes an opportunity for hospitality arises and it is impossible for your husband to give you advance notice. As a general rule, my husband is good about checking with me before inviting guests over and I check with him before planning something. But when there are exceptions, we both need to be flexible.

Do you complain when inconvenienced or are you lovingly flexible? Are you willing to bend your will and change your plans in order to serve others? You can do your husband a great service if he knows that you will happily (not begrudgingly) make a meal stretch for spontaneous hospitality. Add some water to the soup and another loaf of bread. Add some beans to the ground beef. Keep a big batch of spaghetti sauce in the freezer or cupboard. Pull out the sleeping bags for the children if they need a place to stay for the night.

Do you know how to cook African style? In other words, do you know how to cook so that there is always enough for a few unexpected guests? Where my missionary daughter lives in Africa, visitors are supposed to drop in unannounced. It is your duty and joy to serve them as they would serve you. If you showed up unexpectedly in their village, they would happily kill their only chicken and stay up until midnight to prepare your dinner.

If you are flexible in this way, then you are showing fervent love. The Greek word for "fervent" describes an athlete's muscle that is fully extended, stretched out, striving to win the race. Hospitality takes work but it can be done with joy if we keep it simple, work together, maintain flexibility, and do it all out of love.

Do It in a Manner Worthy of God

One man, Gaius by name, had a whole book of the Bible addressed solely to him because of the way that he faithfully upheld the standard of Christian hospitality. His reputation for love had spread far and wide because he received the itinerant ministers of the Word and sent them on their way "in a manner worthy of God" (3 John 5-8). As the apostle John commended him, he was probably recalling what Jesus had said when he had first sent John and the other disciples out, "Truly, truly,

I say to you, he who receives anyone I send receives Me; and he who receives Me receives Him who sent Me" (John 13:20; cf. Matthew 10:40-42).

So how do we treat our guests in a manner worthy of God? We must not be anxious about the details, but we must think about the details. Give your guests your best. You will find it so enjoyable to make your home an inviting place for guests. Consider setting out fresh flowers from the garden during the warm months and lighting a fire in the fireplace during the cool months. Light candles; set a nice table; play beautiful music in the background. Food made from scratch is a treat with many people resorting to packaged foods. Learn from other women in the church who have this gift of hospitality. Pick up tips on table settings, and recipes, and ways to make people feel at home.

Think of things that you would like to know about your guests and be ready to ask leading questions. This is a time to enjoy the fellowship of believers. How did they come to know Christ? What is He teaching them? In what ways can you be praying for them? What was the most enjoyable part of their week? How did they get into their career? Share yourself with them. Relax and enjoy your guests.

It will make you well up inside with satisfaction when people leave refreshed and you know that you as a couple have brought them pleasure and met their need for Christian fellowship—especially when your husband raved about your pie! Send them out in a manner worthy of God.

Sometimes it may seem extravagant and put a strain on the budget to entertain, but it is worth the sacrifice. We may need to cut other places to have enough with which to give to others.

When Bob and I were in seminary, the pastor of the church we were attending, and his wife, had us over for dinner. It gave us a glimpse into their lives and made us realize how important hospitality is before we even entered the ministry. I can still remember it clearly—even to what she served us and that was over 30 years ago. More importantly, Jesus remembers it. He remembers forever even a cup of cold water given in His name (Mark 9:41).

Sometimes the people we shower the most with hospitality do not reciprocate. They may even choose to attend another church or drop out of church altogether. In some way or another, they may "bite the hand that fed them." A friend who was going through a divorce was in our home for a meal about once a week while she was going through the worst emotions of the ordeal. It was a way to let her know how much we cared and to give her support and encouragement. When she got on her feet again she decided to marry an unbeliever, against our counsel and without our support. From then on she treated us like enemies, turning others against us as well. Do we regret showing her Jesus' love while we had the chance? No. Our hospitality, though rejected in the end, had eternal significance.

When Jesus comes in His glory, He will separate the sheep from the goats and,

> "…Then the King will say to those on His right, 'Come, you who are blessed of My Father, inherit the kingdom, which has been prepared for you from the foundation of the world. For I was hungry, and you gave Me something to eat; I was thirsty, and you gave Me something to drink; I was a stranger, and you invited Me in; naked, and you clothed Me; I was sick, and you visited Me; I was in prison, and you came to Me." [Jesus defines that by saying,] "Truly I say to you, to the extent that you did it to one of these brothers of Mine, even the least of them, you did it to Me" (Matthew 25:34-36, 40, clarifying brackets mine).

Those entering the kingdom with Christ would be known as having exercised hospitality. Do you wish that you could host Jesus in your home like Mary and Martha were able to? You can. Hosting even the least in the kingdom is the same as hosting the Son of God. What a powerful picture! It leaves me all the more motivated to keep using my home for God's purposes and His glory.

13

MANAGING THE MONEY

How would you pass this test as a new ministry wife? Put yourself in Mary's shoes. Two weeks ago she had just married George Muller, a Prussian missionary to London. She had happily spent the whole day polishing and cleaning and unpacking her few treasured possessions. She can't wait for George to get home and see his tiny bachelor-row house transformed into a cozy home with the help of her family silverware, her mother's china, and tapestries that had been in her family for generations. But she did not get the reaction that she expected when her new husband arrived home to see her improvements. He soberly sat down in the chair and told her with a sigh that it all had to go. He was convinced that everything that was not "necessary" was an encumbrance to being able to preach true discipleship.

What would you do? If you were like me you would probably argue and pout until he realized that he was being ridiculous to expect his wife to give up everything that makes a house a home. But Mary was different. Once she understood his convictions, she did not try to weaken them. The very next day she willingly parted with all of her family heirlooms and in their place gave George a stack of pound notes saying, "Do what you think best with it, George, and may God help us both."[44]

God did help them both. Because George and Mary had given up

---

44 Janet & Geoff Benge, *George Muller: The Guardian of Bristol's Orphans*, (Seattle, Washington: YWAM Publishing, 1999), 78.

all their own possessions, and even their fixed salary, others were willing to follow their example and give generously to the Mullers' ministries. "In his lifetime, nearly one and one half million pounds passed through George Muller's hands."[45] He invested all of this money into the kingdom through running orphanages and Sunday schools, printing Bibles and supporting missionaries. He died at the age of 89 with only one hundred sixty pounds to his estate but 10,000 orphans who called him father. He was fabulously wealthy!

Being in ministry involves constant attention to financial matters, not only for our own needs, but also for the needs of the church. It can sap attention from other concerns and many times leaves us feeling stretched and exhausted trying to figure out where the funds will come from. It can cause serious marital tensions. Or it can bind a couple together in dependence upon God and give them a platform like the Mullers had for showing the church and the world that God is real.

How did Mary do it? How was she able to trust God so much that she enabled her husband to have a world-renowned ministry? She acted on scriptural principles that can likewise help you as a ministry wife turn financial pitfalls into a platform.

Let's look at these vital financial principles one by one.

God Owns It All

The first overriding understanding of our finances that we must agree upon is that everything belongs to God. God owns all we have. "The earth is Yahweh's, as well as its fullness, the world, and those who dwell in it" (Psalm 24:1). Jesus' words put a further claim upon us, "So then, none of you can be My disciple who does not give up all his own possessions" (Luke 14:33). Everything we have, including our children, belongs to God.

God promises to provide our needs for food, clothing, and shelter. But sometimes we want more. We take our eyes off of the eternal kingdom and we want more on this earth. We are like the Israelites who got tired of just barely having enough with their daily supply of manna. They had the Promised Land ahead of them but they wanted

---

45 Ibid, 196.

to go back to the land of slavery where they had cucumbers, melons, leeks, and meat (Numbers 11:4-6).

It is up to God how much He gives us over which to be stewards. He may give us abundance, or just enough. But however much we have, it is first His. He can take it away if He chooses. This truth takes the pressure off to guard and keep what we have. If God allows the ministry to fail through lack of finances, our marriages need not fail. Are you ready to say with Job, "Yahweh gave, and Yahweh has taken away. Blessed be the name of Yahweh" (Job 1:21b)?

God Will Provide: All We Need

The God who owns everything has promised to supply all our needs according to His glorious riches in Christ Jesus (Philippians 4:19). What further security could we wish for?

God provides for His servants. Remember how He fed the Israelites with manna for forty years in the wilderness? It may not always have been their preferred menu, but it was all that they needed. Remember how God fed Elijah by the brook Cherith with the bread and meat that the ravens brought him in the morning and evening (1 Kings 17:4-6)? When the brook dried up God sent him to the most unlikely candidate to provide for him—a penniless Gentile widow. After she gave the prophet her last meal, God provided through a bottomless bowl of flour and jar of oil that never ran out (1 Kings 17:7-16).

God Will Provide: Just as He Always Has

It strengthens our faith to look back at how the Lord has provided for His people. It also strengthens our faith to recount His blessings in our own lives. I have a friend who keeps a rock jar to remind her of God's faithfulness. The stones are a modern version of the altars of remembrance that the Israelites built. On each stone she writes with a permanent marker the story of God's provision and the date and then puts it carefully in the jar. The children love to look through the stones and remember God's faithfulness.

Let me share my story of God's provision for us during our early years in the ministry as an encouragement that God will continue to provide for you just as He always has for each of His servants.

"We will pay for moving your furniture," was the generous offer of our first church. We replied, "That won't be too expensive, as we have a stereo and a couple of lamps." But by the time we arrived at the parsonage we had acquired a lot of used furniture, having scavenged anything that we thought would fit into our rustic "early attic" style. Our cozy look fit well into the colonial house in the beautiful old neighborhood where the trees met in the middle of the street just six miles from New York City.

We would never forget the welcome we received when we moved into the parsonage on that first day of October. Our cupboards and refrigerator were stocked with food, there was a new set of sheets, there were new tools for Bob, and the house had been newly painted throughout. A floral arrangement was delivered to our door. That same delivery was made on the first of October for the next 10 years while we served that church. Mrs. Strickland, a former pastor's wife in our church, sent it. We also received a welcome-offering for us to buy some furniture as well. We were off to a great start at seeing how God would provide for our material needs. Would He ever fail us? Would He always provide? There wasn't a doubt!

We served that small church for 10 years and the salary was small but our needs were lovingly met. Every Christmas they took a love offering for us which was very generous and let us know how much we were appreciated. There were many side benefits, which included funds to attend conferences, honorariums when Bob spoke at camps, as well as personal gifts. There were hand-me-downs for the children. Everyone looked out for our needs and then some.

When we left that secure position and moved across the country to plant a church, we had no money with which to buy a home. On the advice of a respected mission executive, we borrowed funds from friends and relatives in thousand dollar increments for a down payment. This was done with the plan of my teaching for two years and paying these people back with interest in three years.

The first year I did not have to work as my salary for two years would be enough to pay the loans back. At the end of the first year, two of the ones who loaned us a thousand dollars needed their money back. We just did not have any money to pay them back. First we prayed and then Bob shared the need with his "Company of the Committed"—men he met with for prayer and accountability. They prayed with him about the need. The next week we received an envelope with a collage with these words on it: "It must remain a secret who this gift is from. All praise goes to the Father, from whom all good gifts come." It was signed "Stretch." * A crisp $100 bill was enclosed. This continued for 20 more days—the envelope in the mail with a copy of the collage and a crisp $100 bill. We went out to the mailbox and rejoiced together as a family as God met that need. We do not know who did that to this day but it is part of our story of God's faithfulness in our lives.

The rest of the story is that we put our house up for sale rather than my having to work outside the home. We were here to plant a church, not to buy a home. The house did not sell after six months of being on the market. What now? We received an inheritance early; loved ones donated; one lady who loaned us a significant amount asked that we repay it over time to missions. We ultimately were able to keep the house, which was our center of ministry for 20 years.

With the memories of God's abundant provision etched in our minds and hearts, does that mean that we have been free from financial concerns for our entire ministry? Certainly not. But when we remember that God owns it all and will provide all that we need just as He always has, we are encouraged to trust Him for the next hurdle. We must all remember His blessings and tell them as Asaph instructed. "But recount to the generation to come the praises of Yahweh, and His strength and His wondrous deeds that He has done... That they should set their confidence in God and not forget the deeds of God, but observe His commandments..." (Psalm 78:4b, 7).

God Will Provide: As We Pray and Trust Him

If we believe that God is the One who will provide (not the bank, not the relatives, not even the supporters or the congregation), then it only makes sense that we go to Him first with our needs. Praying replaces worry. "Be anxious for nothing, but in everything by prayer and petition with thanksgiving let your requests be made known to God" (Philippians 4:6). God will give wisdom and He will provide as we pray.

Are you and your husband too busy in ministry to spend much time in prayer? You need to make time to pray together regularly and faithfully. Praying over your big and little financial decisions and trusting God together for material needs binds you together as a couple.

Let's never forget what Jesus said,

> For this reason I say to you, do not be worried about your life, as to what you will eat or what you will drink; nor for your body, as to what you will put on. Is not life more than food, and the body more than clothing? Look at the birds of the air, that they do not sow, nor reap nor gather into barns, and yet your heavenly Father feeds them. Are you not worth much more than they? ... But if God so clothes the grass of the field, which is alive today and tomorrow is thrown into the furnace, will He not much more clothe you? You of little faith! (Matthew 6:25-26, 30)

Are you a person of faith or worry? Let's look again at George Muller, a man who refused to worry because he knew the power of prayer. One morning it finally happened, the children were all ready for breakfast and there was nothing in the house to eat. George was eager to see how God would supply. He simply prayed, "Dear God, we thank you for what you are going to give us to eat. Amen." Then he told the three hundred hungry orphans to be seated in front of their empty plates. Just as the din from the scuffing of chairs subsided, there was a knock on the door. In the doorway stood the baker, holding a huge tray of delicious smelling bread. He explained that he couldn't sleep that night so he had gotten up at 2:00 A.M. to bake for them. While the children were enjoying their fresh-baked bread, there was another knock on the door. This time it was the milkman. His cart had broken down right outside and he needed someone to lighten his load so that he could fix the wheel. There was enough milk for each child to have a mug full for breakfast and enough left over for them all to have some in their tea at lunch.[46] God delights in meeting the needs of his children when they ask.

In ministry, we are tested over and over. People in our congregations

---

46 Ibid, 166-168.

are looking at us like those 300 hungry orphans. Will we set an example of childlike faith in a big God who answers prayer? Or will we worry and make God look small and far away?

God Will Provide: As We Seek First His Kingdom

Sometimes I am amazed at the lack of "worry" that my husband shows for the financial needs of the church. I think that if I were in his place, I would be concerned about the large amount of money, which needs to come in each month to support the five pastors and all the missionaries, who are depending on our church for support. This is one area in which he has found God to be faithful and he just goes about seeking first His kingdom and depending on Him to supply the funds to do it. That is His promise, "But seek first His kingdom and His righteousness, and all these things will be added to you" (Matthew 6:33). This verse helps me put things in perspective—His kingdom comes first and then He will provide my needs.

Jesus said that He would build His church and the gates of hell would not prevail against it. It is His church—not ours. It is His "worry"—not ours.

Every year since we began as a church plant, except for one year, we have wondered where the money would come from to end the year in the black. There were always big deficits. But for those 24 years, the last month of the year the Lord brought in the funds. There was a couple in our church that gave very generously at the end of each year according to how God had blessed them. It was my custom to bake them an apple pie because they were elderly and she wasn't able to bake. I didn't know until later that several times he would return the pie plate to my husband with a check for the church for not less than $10,000. (Bob brags on my pies, but I didn't know they were worth that much!) The generous husband is now reaping his reward in glory.

That year was an exceptional time. There was no deficit to be made up. The year-end giving went over and above our needs because we have paid off our church buildings and are debt-free. We were able to then have the joy of giving some large gifts to missions.

But what do you do when the church is in financial trouble? These times test us to see whether we are truly seeking God's kingdom first and not any sort of financial gain. Paul actually warns elders that they must not shepherd the flock for "dishonest gain," but voluntarily and eagerly (1 Peter 5:2).

Those who work hard at preaching and teaching have a right to get their living from the gospel (1 Timothy 5:17-18). But they must also be willing to forgo that right for the sake of the gospel. Paul would have preferred to die rather than have anyone think he ministered for financial reasons (1 Corinthians 9:15). Therefore he was willing to work with his own hands as a tent-maker to provide for himself and those with him so as not to be a burden on the infant church (2 Thessalonians 3:7-10, 1 Thessalonians 2:9; Acts 20:34-35).

If the church cannot fully support you for a time, it would not be wrong for your husband to seek other employment. Especially in a church-planting situation, secular employment may be the best way to gain respect in the community and set an example for the fledgling flock. God gives wisdom and grace to handle each situation that comes up.

When ten families left our small church all at once, we had to take a cut in pay to bring on the youth pastor. We make our sacrifices and trust the Lord to provide if it is His will for the work to continue. Hudson Taylor put it this way, "God's work done in God's way will never lack God's supply."

God Will Provide: As We Exercise Contentment

Whether in plenty or in want, God can give us the grace to learn contentment. Paul said,

> ...I learned to be content in whatever circumstances I am. I know how to get along with humble means, and I also know how to live in abundance; in any and all things I have learned the secret of being filled and going hungry, both of having abundance and suffering need. I can do all things through Him who strengthens me. (Philippians 4:11b-13)

God will provide contentment if we are truly seeking first His kingdom and His righteousness. Can we say with Paul, "I have coveted no one's silver or gold or clothes" (Acts 20:33)? He mentioned this because covetousness is a temptation for those in ministry. It is a temptation that we must gain victory over. Paul repeats himself three times warning that the overseer or deacon must be free from the love of money or he is unqualified for leadership (1 Timothy 3:8; Titus 1:7). Are we, as wives, free from the love of money, or are we putting an extra strain on our husbands with our lack of contentment in what they are able to provide?

Contentment does not imply that properly motivated ambition is wrong. We know that God wants us to work hard and to excel at what we do. Laziness, complacency, or apathy is not what God wants, but rather that we be faithful stewards of the talents and possessions that He has entrusted to us. Biblical contentment is an inner peace based on the belief that God is in control of our present station in life and our financial situation.

Our society constantly holds out everything from fancy doorknobs to new SUVs to lure us into more possessions. New and better computers and cell phones are coming out every few months. Affluence is the goal. If we have lots of money and things, and novel experiences that money can buy, that's the "good life"—or what brings fulfillment and security.

I hate to admit it, but it is a constant struggle to be thankful for what I have and not be greedy. Seeing the nice things that I could have for the home or wanting the best for our children has caused me not to give as cheerfully as I should at times. It's easy for us to look around to pastors of other churches or people within our congregations and want what they have.

Jesus said, "Watch out and be on your guard against every form of greed, for not even when one has an abundance does his life consist of his possessions" (Luke 12:15). What does our life consist of if not possessions? God's kingdom!

> But seek His kingdom, and these things will be added to you. Do not fear, little flock, for your Father is well pleased to give you the kingdom. "Sell your possessions and give it as charity; make yourselves money belts which do not wear out, an unfailing treasure in heaven, where no thief comes near nor moth destroys. For where your treasure is, there your heart will be also. (Luke 12:31-34)

A desire for the things of this world can crowd out the passion for ministry, and hinder giving generously to Christ, and for the advancement of His kingdom. Conversely, a desire for Christ and His glory will crowd out greed. The world is passing away and everything in it so I must not become attached to things. I must keep my mind on things above, not on things on the earth for my life is hid with Christ in God (Colossians 3:2). I recognize that all I have is a gift from my heavenly Father and it is to be put to kingdom use. I must constantly hold it in the open palm of my hand.

Dear sister, this focus on Christ's kingdom, holding loosely to worldly goods, is how we will win the battle against greed. It is especially important that we conquer this temptation or our husbands will be accused of being wolves rather than eager, voluntary shepherds.

We have been reminded that God will provide as He always has, as we pray and trust Him, and as we seek first His kingdom. We cannot be consumed with worry or greed when we fix our eyes on God's kingdom. We know that God will provide for His kingdom to advance, so we need not worry. We treasure our role in that advancement more than any affluence the world can offer. When the world sees our contentment, they should become jealous. When they see the kingdom advancing through our faith, they should be baffled.

When George Muller died, the Daily Telegraph reported that he had "robbed the cruel streets of thousands of victims, the jails of thousands of felons, and the poorhouses of thousands of helpless waifs." And how had he done this?

The Liverpool Mercury wrote, "How was this wonder accomplished? Mr. Muller has told the world that it was the result of 'Prayer.' The rationalism of the day will sneer at this declaration; but the facts remain."[47] Out of his personal poverty He had prospered the kingdom. The potential financial pitfalls became his platform.

God Expects Us to Be Examples

We have studied God's role in our finances. He owns it all and He will provide. But what is our role? What does God expect from

---

47 Ibid, 196.

us financially? We already saw that we must not love money or be motivated by any type of dishonest gain. But God will also hold us accountable for the way that we use the money that He has entrusted to us through honest means. Those in ministry are called to be good examples in how they manage their finances. Each couple must be an example of unity, integrity, good stewardship, and generosity.

The Devastation of Disunity

At the beginning of this chapter I told you how Mary Muller prospered because she was willing to put her husband and his ministry above her comfort and financial security. Now I want to tell you about another pastor's wife who did not pass the test.

Ann was tired of living on a tight budget. She had a constant desire for more than what her husband could provide for them on his pastor's salary, although it was coming in regularly and their needs were being met. She deserved better. Her husband wasn't managing their money well as far as she was concerned. She took a job to help provide for the family. Her respect and appreciation for her husband diminished. How could this happen? Bitterness crept in. This isn't how she wanted her life to turn out. She thought it was her husband's responsibility to provide for her. She began looking outside the marriage.

Another successful man started looking more appealing than her husband. He could give her what she thought would make her happy. He shows interest. She feels her heart being drawn to him. She begins to think that her marriage is a failure so she might as well admit it and start over. "The grass is greener" fallacy has taken over. She leaves her husband for this man and the devastation to the whole family is overwhelming—as well as to the kingdom of Christ!

There is nothing that can destroy us more than bitterness. It can eat us up inside. The consequences are devastating!

What are we to do if we see ourselves at any point in this picture? Take it to the Lord. Get alone with Him and tell Him just how you feel. He knows already. Let the tears flow. If there are no words, the Holy Spirit will pray for you with longings too deep for words. Turn your eyes back on the Lord. Confess the bitterness, the greed, and lack of contentment. Ask God for the will to accept whatever He wants for you. God can use your husband's seeming failures for good. (Perhaps there are no failures at all.) Yield it all to God. He knows what is best. Thank God for this test of your faith and trust Him to provide in His time. He knows what is best. Give up your own rights as to what you think you need to make you happy. Ask God to give you a life of obedience and faithfulness; keep up with your responsibilities and do the things that are required of you.

If we think that this couldn't happen, we are not aware of Satan's schemes. Paul writes, "Therefore let him who thinks he stands take heed that he does not fall" (1 Corinthians 10:12). We must guard our heart with all diligence for out of it flow the springs of life (Proverbs 4:23).

Satan would like nothing better than to work on our flesh and cause discord in our marriages over financial matters. We must not let him divide and conquer us. As couples, we come into our marriages from different backgrounds and differing ways of handling finances. These differences can cause severe tensions. We've all experienced them, but Christ can demonstrate His power to bring about unity among dissimilar people if we allow Him to.

Keep in mind that you are fellow heirs of the grace of life. (1 Peter 3:7) It's not "his" and "hers"; it is "ours." Whatever you do, you are in this together as one, united in heart and mind to live for God's glory in this important area of your finances, knowing it will take hard work.

If you are in a place to be able to help financially, and you both decide before God that it will bring glory to Him, you may decide to work to help get your family onto a sound financial footing. You shouldn't rule out that God might also want to provide without your working outside the home. He may want you to trust Him to provide. Even if we, as homemakers, don't get a paycheck, we work equally hard to provide for our families. The homemaker's work is a sacred task, equally important to her husband's calling. The important thing is to stay united.

Paul urges the believers,

> Each of us is to please his neighbor for his good, to his building
> up. For even Christ did not please Himself... Now may the God
> of perseverance and encouragement grant you to be of the same
> mind with one another according to Christ Jesus, so that with

one accord you may with one voice glorify the God and Father
of our Lord Jesus Christ (Romans 15:2-3a, 5-6).

If you can't come to a unity in regard to finances and this is causing
marital problems, you must seek counsel.

An Example of Integrity

The shepherd of the flock leads. Whatever he teaches, he must
model integrity. It is appropriate for the shepherd to let the flock
know about his giving, so they can have an example to follow. Bob
gives a sermon series on stewardship every year and often gives illus-
trations from how God has worked in our lives in this area. Bob has
always laid it all out there for the flock. He lets them know where he
is struggling and where he is following the Shepherd closely—and
how he wants them to follow. Paul used himself as an example. He
said, "The things you have learned and received and heard and seen
in me, practice these things, and the God of peace will be with you"
(Philippians 4:9).

How can he preach to others without being convicted and allowing
God to work in his own life? He challenges the flock to lay up treasure
in heaven where moth and rust do not destroy or where thieves do not
break in and steal (Matthew 6:19-21). They should see him doing the
same.

We learn from the bad example of Ananias and Sapphira (Acts 5:1-
15) that God requires integrity. Our outer life (our words and actions)
must match our inner life. We can put up a front of sacrifice and yet
be greedy and selfish and hoard everything for ourselves. God wanted
the church to be warned of hypocrisy right from its inception. He is
still serious about integrity today!

If your husband is sinning in the use of your funds, do not be like
Sapphira who covered up for her husband and shared in his fate. It is
up to you to bring it to the attention of the elders. It must be dealt with.
One pastor we know of left his church and community with unpaid
debts. That is a blot on the name of Christ. It is imperative that we
uphold a high standard of integrity in this area.

If we are expecting people to give us discounts and pay our way for things, or have the attitude that people owe us because we are in ministry, that can detract from our effectiveness as God's servants.

An Example of Good Stewardship

Are you an enterprising wife who knows how to make the money stretch? A good steward will actually multiply the finances through wise planning and good investments.

We learn from history that Martin Luther's biggest adjustment in marriage was with the family's purse strings.

He had never learned how to handle money. He once said, 'God divided the hand into fingers so that money would slip through.' He didn't want to accept anything not absolutely necessary, and he would give away anything not absolutely required. With Katie as his business manager, fiscal planning was introduced.[48]

As one biographer puts it,

> Frau Luther's thrift enabled the Luthers to "accumulate a considerable property, notwithstanding her husband's unbounded liberality and hospitality." At times she had to hide money to keep Martin from giving it away. Martin would invite students to come and live with them, but Katie insisted that they pay room and board. He came to appreciate her and once wrote, "The greatest blessing is to have a wife to whom you may entrust your affairs."[49]

I'm sure that we all want to be this kind of a blessing to our husbands and receive praise from the Lord for our good stewardship.

Over the years I found ways of stretching our income through canning and freezing fruits and vegetables given to us, sewing the drapes and curtains in our home, cooking from scratch, sometimes shopping at used clothing stores, using hand-me-downs for the children, having only one car for a period of time and not going into debt for things which we couldn't afford. My aunt Dorothy Coulombe, a pastor's wife for 50 years even sewed her children's clothes and raised her own fruits and vegetables to freeze and can. She was a great example to me in this area!

---

48 Petersen, *Martin Luther Had a Wife*, 26.
49 Ibid, 27.

Stewardship through Expert Counsel

We can seek wisdom from those who have become experts in this field. Our church makes the Crown Financial Ministries' courses available to the congregation on a regular basis. This is a course that is taught by those in the church who have already been through it with the books provided. It is important for the pastors or lay leaders to have taken this or a similar course in order to know basic biblical principles regarding money management. They can then share with their own children and others.

Stewardship through Budgeting

Instead of spending money without any plan of action, and then wondering why there isn't enough for the essentials, the wisest thing to do financially is to live by a budget—that is planned spending. Bob and I agree upon our budget after discussing the standard of living and financial goals that we want to live by. This will include the type of home we live in, the car we drive, how we will save for the future.

Have you sat down as a couple and worked out your financial goals that you want to achieve in all the areas mentioned above? Since we have to come to a consensus, we should pray for unity in knowing what God would have us do. "Can two walk together unless they be agreed" (Amos 3:3, NASB)?

Finances can be a very emotional issue and we often become tense or angry when there are disagreements. If we guide our decisions on biblical principles and yield to the Holy Spirit, He will help us work out our differences and come to some specific goals that will glorify Him.

Our financial situation is determined in part by our salary. The church that we serve, and many other churches, pay their pastors according to the pay scale of the public schools in their community. This is based on the mean income of the population, as these are public servants to the community with a comparable education to the pastors.

The philosophy behind this is that if the pastor lives like the mean income, it should result in more people being able to identify with him and vice versa. It is, however, up to the church leadership, guided by Scripture, how they use the funds entrusted to them.

Living within a budget requires self-discipline. Once a couple has set their budget categories, they must be faithful to live by them. Wives can significantly sabotage financial goals through mismanagement of the household funds. It is easy to follow our desires and societal norms and not follow our husband's leadership in financial matters. (The average woman in America has 35 pairs of shoes!)

In looking back, our son recounts that sometimes he felt like a "salvation army kid" because he didn't have the same quality of clothes, bike, haircut, shoes, or cars that his friends had. If our children don't have our perspective, they can feel cheated when they are called upon to have a different standard of living than their friends. We need to bring them to an understanding of why we handle our finances the way we do.

Stewardship through Avoiding Debt

Good stewards do not waste the Lord's money through accruing debt. Roget's College Thesaurus lists these synonyms for debt: liable, minus, owing, in hock, up against it, encumbered, insolvent, in the hole, broke.[50] When we are in debt we are working for the lender instead of getting ahead. This principle is stated in Proverbs: "The rich rules over the poor, and the borrower is the slave of the lender" (Proverbs 22:7).

Bob and I have set the goal to save for things needed and not go into debt for anything other than our home, which appreciates in value. This is in keeping with the Scripture, "There is desirable treasure and oil in the abode of the wise, but a foolish man swallows it up" (Proverbs 21:20).

It is not easy to wait for things that we would like that make our lives more pleasant—a new or newer car, a computer, furniture, a house, appliances, clothes, or any creature comfort or recreational activity. However, it is wise to save for what we want and not use credit cards, which accrue interest payments. You can pay twice as much for something bought on credit than if you bought with cash.

In order to be a disciple we must discipline ourselves for the purpose of godliness (1 Timothy 4:7). This is not a popular concept in

---

50 Roget, Peter Mark, Lloyd, Sue (ed.), "Debt." in *Roget's Thesaurus of English Words and Phrases*, (Harlow, Essex: Longman, 1982).

the church today. I know that it's easier to spend what we do not have in our society, as credit cards are so easy to use. Every time we go to the store we are tempted to yield to our desires, but God can give us self-control, which is a fruit of the Spirit. We can yield to the Spirit and be controlled in our spending.

When our children wanted to attend a Christian college, we decided that I would work two days a week for a Christian ministry in order to help with tuition. I have worked out of our home and it has helped us stay out of debt and keep to our goal. Our children graduated without debt. This freed up our son to take his first teaching position in a Christian school. It enabled our daughter to help her husband while he finished seminary and then head straight for the mission field a year after marriage.

Bob is the one who handles the finances in our marriage because he has made it a study and is better informed. Some wives are better at it. Bob uses computer software to record all of our expenditures and knows just where we are for tax purposes. He and I go over the budget together and he keeps me informed on where to cut and when we can spend a little extra. We chose to make funds available to make trips to South Africa even though it is expensive because we believe it is important to be able to have close ties with our children and grandchildren.

An Example of Generosity

Bob challenges our flock to give more than a tithe; therefore, we have made that our practice. The tithe is the bare minimum. We are to give as God has blessed us, and that is abundantly.

I am challenged by the account in the Gospels, which records Mary's sterling example of giving extravagantly! She broke her alabaster flask of very expensive perfume (worth almost a year's wages) and poured it on Jesus' head. Then she humbly used her hair to wipe Jesus' feet (Mark 14:3-9, John 12:2-8)! Jesus defended her against His frugal disciples saying that, "wherever the gospel is proclaimed in the whole world, what this woman did will also be spoken of in memory of her" (Mark 14:9). If only I could be more like her, giving extravagantly out of a heart of love—without hesitation.

Children sometimes lead the way with their heart to give. Our grandson Evan was so excited about the coins that his daddy gave him to put in the offering that he prayed at lunch, "Thank you Lord for this wonderful day to go to church and give money to You."

Since all we have materially we have together, our giving should be a joint effort. Do you share in the giving? Do your children participate in giving? There is a joy in bringing your gift and worshiping the Lord by placing it in the offering or mailing it off to a missionary. God loves a cheerful giver. We are part of God's "backwards kingdom" where it is more blessed to give than to receive.

It is so wonderful when we grasp that it all belongs to the Lord to be put to use for His kingdom. Then we freely and joyfully employ all that we possess for His glory! If we believe that God owns it all, then we will want to be good stewards of His money (with unity and integrity). If we believe that He will provide all that we need, then we will not be afraid to give generously—even with hazardous liberality, as one minister put it.

> Over and over Jesus is relentless in His radical call to a wartime lifestyle and a hazardous liberality. I say 'hazardous' because of that story about the widow. She gave her last penny to the temple ministry. Most of us would call her foolish or, more delicately, imprudent. But there is not a word of criticism from Jesus.... The point here is not that everyone should give everything away. The point is: Jesus loves faith-filled risk for the glory of God.[51]

Some friends of ours put this framed quote above their cabinet holding rare and beautiful objects as a reminder to themselves and to all who observe the beauty of their home and material possessions:

> I will place no value on anything I possess save in its relation to the kingdom of Christ. If anything will advance the kingdom of God, it shall be given away or kept only as by the giving of it or the keeping of it, I shall promote the Glory of Him to whom I owe all my hopes in time and eternity.
>
> —David Livingstone

---

51 Piper, *Don't Waste Your Life*, 110.

God Is All I Need

In 1894, George Muller found himself a widower for the second time, but he was able to say, "I am a happy old man! I walk about my room and say, 'Lord, I am not alone, for You are with me. I have buried my wives and my children, but You are left. I am never lonely or desolate with You and with Your smile, which is better than life!'"[52]

Muller had already parted with his worldly goods, now he was being called to take the next step and part with his family. Yet he was content, even happy. He was a man who had taken to heart this admonition, "Make sure that your way of life is free from the love of money, being content with what you have; for He Himself has said, 'I will never desert you, nor will I ever forsake you'" (Hebrews 13:5).

If Jesus is with us, that is enough! We can gladly sell all our possessions and follow Him. We can serve His people in humble means or in plenty. The God who owns it all will provide for all of our needs as He always has. He'll do this as we pray and trust Him seeking His Kingdom first and foremost in our lives. It is through His strength and enabling that we are examples to our flock in money matters.

He will satisfy us. Jesus said, "but whoever drinks of the water that I will give him will never thirst—ever; but the water that I will give him will become in him a well of water springing up to eternal life" (John 4:14).

We can show the world that we have drunk from the well of living water. We can invite them to the spring of eternal life. Our finances do not have to be a pitfall. Indeed, they can be a platform from which to proclaim Jesus Christ.

Remember, God is enough!

*Stretch

Let me tell you more about "Stretch." When our church plant was just getting started and there were about 50 people in attendance, the members started receiving encouraging notes and cards signed, "Stretch." They might say, "I sure appreciated your solo last Sunday. It ministered to my heart. Stretch" "I'm praying for you, that you will

---

52 Benge, *George Muller*, 193.

have God's peace in the midst of your trial. Stretch" "Your smile is such a blessing! Keep smiling! Stretch." The notes came from all over the U.S. and around the world. No one in the church was an airline pilot so it was quite a mystery. After the notes had been coming for a while, acts of kindness were added to it. People in our church were receiving visits from someone in a gorilla suit. He came to the door with a basket of encouragement for the whole family containing things for each member. Included was a note written on puzzle pieces, only readable after the pieces were put together, and as always signed "Stretch." One time a stretch limousine was used to make deliveries with Stretch dressed as a giant rabbit; clowns accompanied him.

Finally our whole church family got into the act. People received cash gifts hidden in various ways—in a box of donuts, in plastic eggs under a cloth chicken, in an envelope on the car seat, and so on. Bags of groceries were left on doorsteps as well as Christmas trees and big signs on the garage door, plants and flowers—all signed "Stretch."

One Sunday when we went out to our car after church, we were surprised to find two wrapped boxes—one for Bob with a pair of the best shoes you could buy, the other for me with a purse from Stretch. Bob's shoes were completely worn out and a new pair was on our "Bonus Prayer List," as we were on a tight budget at the time.

The timing was always part of the serendipity. A lady received a note of encouragement mailed from Thailand the day her husband was taken to jail for drug abuse. Money arrived the day a couple found out they were going to have a baby and didn't know how they could afford another child, and on the day the rent was due with no money to pay it. The unusual stories of Stretch visits are legendary in our church and they are not just a thing of the past. They continue to encourage our congregation to this day. Due to the anonymous nature of the gifts, all glory goes to the Lord. No one has ever found out who originated Stretch, but we are all grateful.

TAKING THE OPPORTUNITY TO DISCIPLE WOMEN

In our first pastorate I had grandiose ideas of what discipling women would be like. I envisioned women eager to learn all the things I had studied in seminary—apologetics, theology, church history, New Testament survey, and other wonderful subjects. I expected to be able to impart some of that wisdom to women who were thirsting for knowledge.

However, the first woman that I was called upon to disciple just needed help in dealing with her dismal life. Her husband was verbally abusive and very unkind to her, giving her no help at all with their three small children. They were poor. Their home was dark and the shades were always drawn. I could feel her depression each time I entered the door. I can still smell the old bacon grease in the air and see the dreary faces of her children.

This poor mother needed hope and help for a very unhappy

marriage and downtrodden life. What should she do? How could she have an abundant life in Christ? She needed a relationship with a woman who cared and would point her to the promises of God for her. Week by week as we met, her hope grew. She obtained strength from the Lord and His Word and help from the Body of Christ. She rose above her circumstances to serve her husband and children for the glory of Christ.

As the wife of a man in ministry you have countless opportunities to minister to women.

Women in your church will naturally look to you as a leader. Women in the community will look to you for help. Are you looking for them? Are you looking for every opportunity to make disciples? Whether you are seminary trained or a new believer, there is always someone who knows less than you. Find that person and pour into her life, and you will be blessed.

WHY MAKE DISCIPLES?

The simple answer to this question is that Jesus commanded it. He gave the mandate for disciples to make disciples with all the authority of heaven and earth backing Him (Matthew 28:18-20). As our Lord, He has absolute sovereign authority over our lives and His mandate to us cannot be over-emphasized. His disciples have been carrying out this command for centuries. If they hadn't, where would we be? Lost and in our sins! Now it is our privilege to carry and pass on the baton.

We must make disciples because the gospel has been entrusted to us as a precious treasure that we must not hoard. We must share it with the world. We can say with Paul, "...woe is me if I do not proclaim the gospel" (1 Corinthians 9:16). We have a stewardship.

We must make disciples because they will be our joy and crown (1 Thessalonians 2:19-20; Philippians 4:1). There is no way of knowing what the Lord has done with all of the seeds I have sown through teaching Sunday School classes or leading women's Bible studies. But I can know what God is doing—and rejoice—when I see one woman whom I have poured my life into serving the Lord with all her heart.

HOW DO WE MAKE DISCIPLES?

Rely on the Holy Spirit

We want to make disciples, not of ourselves, but of Jesus. The only way that we can know Jesus is through the testimony of His disciples whom the Holy Spirit used to write the Bible. Jesus promised them, "He [the Holy Spirit] will glorify Me, for He will take of Mine and will disclose it to you" (John 16:14, clarifying brackets mine). The only way that those we are discipling will see Jesus is if the Holy Spirit opens their eyes to see Him in the Bible.

The Holy Spirit gives us the power to become Christ's witnesses (Acts 1:8). Just think of what the Holy Spirit did to transform a band of hiding, cowering disciples into an army of evangelists. They were a very unlikely group.

> Christ here tells them ... that their power for this work should be sufficient. They had not strength of their own for it, nor wisdom nor courage enough ... Christ's witnesses shall receive power for that work to which he calls them; those whom he employs in his service he will qualify for it, and will bear them out in it.[53]

When the Holy Spirit turned Peter, the humble fisherman, into a preacher, 3000 souls were added to the church on the first day (Acts 2:41).

So is it only the super-Christians like Peter who can see the Holy Spirit work through them to be bold witnesses? No! All Christians have been baptized with the Holy Spirit at the time of their salvation (1 Corinthians 12:13; Romans 8:8-9). Our natural tendency is to trust in ourselves, but we must rely on the power of the Holy Spirit working in our lives and in the lives of those we disciple to do great and mighty things. Paul gives us his priceless example of faith in the all-sufficient One. "I have been crucified with Christ, and it is no longer I who live, but Christ lives in me. And the life which I now live in the flesh I live by faith in the Son of God, who loved me and gave Himself up for me"

---

53 Henry, Matthew. 1706. *Matthew Henry Commentary on the Whole Bible.* Vol. 6. https://www.blueletterbible.org/Comm/mhc/Act/Act_001.cfm. Accessed September 4, 2024.

(Galatians 2:20). It will not be us, but Christ in us through the power of the Holy Spirit who will accomplish His purposes in the lives of those we seek to disciple.

The Holy Spirit will lead us to those whom He wants us to disciple and He will do the work in and through us.

Pray

The apostle Paul thought that prayer was essential to making disciples. He prayed without ceasing for his disciples and he commands us to do the same for our brothers and sisters (Romans 1:9-10; Ephesians 6:18). This kind of alert, persevering, continuous prayer is a tall order. But it is how we will partner with God to see Him work. He exhorted the believers at Ephesus, "praying at all times with all prayer and petition in the Spirit, and to this end, being on the alert with all perseverance and petition for all the saints" (Ephesians 6:18). We must pray that God will show us someone to share the gospel with. We must pray that the Holy Spirit will then convict her of sin. Pray that God gives her faith in Christ's work on the cross for her and that He births her into His family. Pray for her growth in grace and in the knowledge of Christ.

In most of his letters Paul shares with the believers how he has been praying for them. He doesn't pray for mundane things but for deep spiritual growth. If we pray these prayers for the women we are discipling, we will be helping them immensely (Romans 1:9; 1 Corinthians 1:4-9; Ephesians 1:15-21; Ephesians 5:17; Philippians 1:3-6, 9-11; Colossians 1:9-14; 1 Thessalonians 1:2; 2:13, 5:23-24; 2 Thessalonians 2:16-17).

Start at Home

Here is a little poem about our first disciples as mothers:

She Follows Me

A little girl who follows me
A careful mom I want to be,
A little woman follows me;
I do not dare to go astray
For fear she'll go the self-same way.

I cannot once escape her eyes.
What e'er she sees me do she tries
Like me, she says she's going to be—
That little girl who follows me.
I must remember as I go
Through summer suns and winter snows,
I am building for the years to be—
That little girl that follows me.

—Author Unknown

Let's not in any way neglect our most natural and first disciples. If we do not do a good job with them, eventually no one else will want to follow us either.

Reach Out to the Lost

Jesus commanded us to make disciples of all nations. He set the example. He came to seek and to save the lost. He reached out to many needy women who had been cast aside. There was Mary Magdalene—the demon-possessed, the woman at the well—an adulteress, and Mary—a prostitute who anointed His feet. His love changed their lives. He also reached out to the upper-middle class—women like Martha and Mary, and the rich women who cared for the disciples as they traveled. He chose those who would follow Him and lovingly discipled them. He took them where they were and brought them to where He wanted them to be as His followers.

Women, if we are going to make disciples we must seek the lost. Rather than limiting our influence to within the church, we can build bridges of friendship to the lost in our neighborhoods and communities. We can get involved in reaching out to women wherever they may be. They may be in a group who quilt or who are on a PTA committee or sports team. They may be young women who attend the schools where our children attend—some with tattoos or given to drug use. They may be Goths or homosexuals. They may be in prison. We can't give up on such people. The need is too great.

There are all sorts of ways to develop relationships through serving. It may be through a mentoring program for the teen moms or an after-school tutoring program. It may happen through an English-as-second-language program, health clinic, job-skills training, rescue mission, or prison. In these situations it will probably mean going out of your comfort zone. It certainly did for me. But if the love of Christ constrains you, you will risk it.

We are to obediently go and make disciples as we go about life. What more exciting way could there be to live than to be constantly giving out the gospel of Christ? This good news can free people from their sin and its consequences—hell forever—and give them eternal life that glorifies God! The lost and needy are all around us in our community and in our churches. If we are reaching out and showing the love of Christ, they will be more likely to turn to us when they have needs. Then we may have the wonderful privilege of leading someone to faith in Christ. We can watch God give her new birth, give her forgiveness for guilt, holiness for sin, hope for despair, light for darkness, eternal life for eternal death. This is the first thrilling step in discipleship.

Invest in the Future Leaders

Jesus prayed all night before He chose His twelve disciples. Those few handpicked men would follow Him for three years, record the Scriptures, and die spreading the good news about Him so that millions would be saved. You want to choose those types of disciples. You may want to look for more mature believers in your church to disciple to the next level of leadership. As a disciple-maker you can be ushering in new "babies" and mentoring other "mothers."

If you are a senior pastor's wife, you can be investing in the other pastors' or elders' wives. If you are a young woman, you can mentor the leading girls in the youth group. Look for those women in your church with bright eyes full of questions. Look for the ones who are eager to serve. Look for the ones who are faithful in the little things. Make time for them and your time will not be wasted. Have we caught hold of Paul's principle set forth in his letter to Timothy? He said, "And the things which you have heard from me in the presence of many witnesses, entrust these to faithful men who will be able to teach others also" (2 Timothy 2:2). Paul modeled this over and over again. Timothy was just one of the faithful men he discipled.

Point Her to the Scriptures

If you are discipling someone you led to the Lord last week or an old believer, your job is not done until she knows how to obey all that Christ has commanded (Matthew 28:20). If you give her the Bible, you give her all she needs. "All Scripture is God-breathed and profitable for teaching, for reproof, for correction, for training in righteousness, so that the man of God may be equipped, having been thoroughly equipped for every good work" (2 Timothy 3:16-17).

But you might say, "This is a never-ending job. When will she ever know all of Scripture and obey all that Christ commands?" You're right. The Christian life is all about growth from the time of our new birth until we are finally glorified. That is why we always need to be making disciples and being discipled. God will show you when your disciple needs you less and is ready to continue her maturing more independently. Until then keep pointing her to Scripture.

The Bible equips us as disciplers to deal with situations that may seem way over our heads. We need not be intimidated. We have real answers, not out of our own wisdom or understanding. We have God's sufficient Word as our ultimate resource.

We don't have to depend upon our own experience. We don't have to have experienced a broken marriage or been a drunkard or drug user. We don't have to know a lot about postmodern theology. We have a divine guide for any situation we might encounter to equip our sisters and us for every good work. Isn't that incredible!

Peter reiterates what Paul says,

> seeing that His divine power has granted to us everything pertaining to life and godliness, through the full knowledge of Him who called us by His own glory and excellence. For by these He has granted to us His precious and magnificent promises, so that by them you may become partakers of the divine nature, having escaped the corruption that is in the world by lust.
> (2 Peter 1:3-4)

The promises of God are there for the taking! Promises such as "Come to Me, all who are weary and heavy-laden, and I will give you rest" (Matthew 11:28); or "If you ask Me anything in My name, I will do it" (John 14:14). These can apply to the affluent woman struggling with stress and million-dollar decisions, or the new convert trying to give up cocaine, or a young mom trying to cope with sick kids. We need to teach each woman how to tap into the resources that are hers in Christ and the wisdom that God will supply for every situation. All we have to do is open the treasure chest and show her where to find the jewels.

You don't have to have the gift of teaching to be able to disciple someone. There are many ways to point her to the Word. You can encourage her to come every time the Word is being preached. You can go over her notes with her and ask her if she has any questions. You can help her to apply what she is hearing. You can encourage her to get into a ladies' Bible study. The advantage of these kinds of groups is that they often provide formal teaching and the encouragement of interaction with other believers as they share their lives and pray for each other. Each one's spiritual growth is important to each member of the group.

Meeting regularly one-on-one with a person may be the most effective type of discipleship. It is life-on-life. In this context you can zero in on her particular needs and focus all your attention on helping her. You can just show her how you have your quiet time and encourage her to do the same. You can read through a book on spiritual growth together. You can choose a course of Bible study based upon the specific goal you have in mind—to learn how to grow as a new believer, to do a particular ministry, to master a spiritual discipline, to overcome a particular habitual sin or to handle a difficult situation.

You may want to work through a book of the Bible together. For new believers, a good book to use is Mark or John. One of the simplest forms of study is to read the portion of Scripture and answer the following simple questions about it: (1) What stands out to you? (2) What is the key verse or theme? (3) What did you learn about Jesus? God? (4) What does He want you to do (sin to avoid or command to obey)? (5) What don't you understand? You can help her find answers. Starting with this kind of inductive Bible study will give her confidence in God's Word alone. You can choose to keep it simple. We need not complicate the basics of the Christian life or make complex what God has made simple.

Once she has mastered a gospel you can move on to teaching her how to study other genres of Scripture. You can teach her how to interpret a parable by looking for one main point. You can teach her how to interpret Proverbs by taking them as general truths to gain wisdom from; not as absolute promises to claim.

You may choose to do a topical Bible study to zero in on her interest or need. For instance, you might take the topic "wife" and look up all the verses dealing with a godly wife. Other topics such as submission, discipline, forgiveness, fruit of the Spirit, and love make good studies. There are many good Bible guidebooks to help in these types of studies.

The apostle Paul encourages us to be persistent in our study of God's Word when he writes, "Be diligent to present yourself approved to God as a workman who does not need to be ashamed, accurately handling the word of truth" (2 Timothy 2:15). It takes hard work to understand the Word of God so as to faithfully teach it accurately and clearly. False teaching leads people astray and tears down the body of Christ. Good teaching makes them strong and discerning.

Make Use of Good Tools

These tools can aid us in our study of Scriptures:

- Concordance—which you can use to look up all the verses that have a certain word in them.

- Commentaries—which gives explanation and some application. It is very important to use reliable commentaries that are true to an evangelical interpretation of Scripture.

- Bible with study notes—which gives dates, the historical background and setting, and commentary explaining the text.

- Bible dictionary—which gives word definitions according to how they are used in the Bible.

- Computer software—which can have all of the above. Websites—sermon notes, ministry helps, etc.

- Different translations—good for comparing wording for better understanding.
- A Bible with cross references—good for comparing Scripture with Scripture.
- Biblically based books—usually topical.

We usually learn the most when we have to teach something to someone else. As we study the Scriptures to faithfully teach them to the women we are discipling, we will both be blessed.

Hold Each Other Accountable to Memorize and Apply Scripture

Every time we teach God's Word our goal is application. Jesus didn't say that we should make disciples "teaching them all that I have commanded," but "teaching them to keep all that I commanded you" (Matthew 28:20). You and I know for certain that Bible studies are not for knowledge alone. They are to bring us into conformity to the life of Christ. We need to be praying as we read and study God's Word: "Lord, what do you want me to learn from Your Word today about Yourself?" "Father, how does this apply to my life?" "What changes do You want to make in me?" "Lord change me according to Your Word!" We need to teach our disciples to hear God's Word this way. Otherwise we are just making them more deluded—thinking they are strong when they are weak. James exhorts us, "But become doers of the word, and not merely hearers who delude themselves" (James 1:22).

We need to meditate on passages to let the truth affect our inner convictions so that we will be able to act on it in our lives—to be doers of the Word. God directed His children through Joshua, "This book of the law shall not depart from your mouth, but you shall meditate on it day and night, so that you may be careful to do according to all that is written in it; for then you will make your way successful, and then you will be prosperous" (Joshua 1:8).

One way to do this is to memorize Scripture. It is a means of keeping us from sin (Psalm 119:11). The Holy Spirit uses Scripture to convict us and remind us to live in obedience. We can help the ladies we are discipling to make a Scripture memory plan and carry it out.

Let me encourage you to hold each other accountable. This is one of the best ways for bringing about change in our lives. We can share our specific goals. Then, we can lovingly ask our sisters how they are doing at achieving those goals. If we want to let God's Word transform us more and more into the image of Christ, then we will need to make ourselves vulnerable with one another, pray for one another, and ask one another hard questions.

Growth in obedience is the area where discipleship should shine. A preacher has little knowledge about how much of his sermon is being applied. But a discipler can get in there and say, "We're not moving on until we have applied this."

Address Sin Issues

As you grow closer to the woman you are discipling, you may see areas where she is straying from the path of obedience. It is your responsibility to come alongside to help carry her burden and get her back on track (Galatians 6:1-2). It's never easy to address issues of sin in another, but we must do it if we mean business about discipling.

This verse from Proverbs recently came true in my life: "He who reproves a man will afterward find more favor than he who flatters with the tongue" (Proverbs 28:23). A dear friend thanked me again for speaking the truth in love to her when she was away at college dating an unbeliever. I had written her a letter pleading with her from Scripture not to continue in the relationship. Although we had a strong friendship at the time, she told me that she tore up the letter and was angry that I would so boldly meddle in her affairs. However, the Lord used it to help her to do the right thing. That very week she broke up with her boyfriend and later married a godly young man. They have now been in ministry for many years.

What gives us the boldness to "meddle" in other people's lives? Our overriding love for them is based on Christ's lordship over our lives. We were on the path leading to destruction and He intervened to rescue us. We can share with our erring sister where we fail and how God forgives and puts us on the path again. We need God's grace and forgiveness every day of our lives, just as she does. "We love, because He first loved us" (1 John 4:19). We show that love sometimes by addressing sin. "Better is reproof that is revealed than love that is hidden. Faithful are the wounds of a friend, but deceitful are the kisses of an enemy" (Proverbs 27:5-6).

Pray the Scriptures

As we teach women how to listen to God through the Bible, we must also teach them how to talk to God through praying according to His will. "And this is the confidence which we have before Him, that, if we ask anything according to His will, He hears us. And if we know that He hears us in whatever we ask, we know that we have the requests which we have asked from Him" (1 John 5:14-15).

The surest way to know that we are asking according to His will is to pray the Scriptures. By claiming God's promises in prayer, we know that He will answer. It is good to go to prayer after reading some of the promises God gives us about hearing and answering our prayers (Matthew 6:5-7; Mark 11:24; John 15:7; James 5:16). We can pray the Scriptures that deal with our own sanctification. For instance if God is convicting you on your grumbling spirit, you can pray Philippians 2:14, Lord, help me to "Do all things without grumbling or disputing." You can also pray Philippians 4:4: Lord help me to "Rejoice in the Lord always." God loves to answer these types of prayers and make us more like His Son. Let's pray these kinds of faith-building prayers with the women we are discipling.

Do we need to pray with our disciples for specific requests for material needs and personal desires as well? Yes, because we talk to God as our Father. If we ask for bread He will not give us a stone (Matthew 7:9). It is exciting to keep a prayer journal or 3x5 cards of the individuals prayed for to record what God does. How refreshing it is to hear the prayers of a new believer laying things out in faith before God without all the jargon that we so often use in prayer!

Her faith will grow as she relies on God for everything and sees God answer specific prayers. Her trust and understanding of God can even grow as you help her to accept His negative answers. You can point out to her how Paul asked three times for his thorn in the flesh to be removed and God said, "No, my grace is sufficient for you" (2 Corinthians 12:9).

Encourage Her to Make Disciples

We know that we have truly made a disciple when we see her using her gifts and making disciples. We rejoice like grandmothers rejoice over their grandchildren.

We can train our sisters to be fruitful by letting them come alongside us in ministry. First we model ministry for them. Then we let them help us. Then we watch them as they do the ministry and we give feedback. Finally, we turn them loose to do it on their own and train others. Most of us have learned ministry just that way. My mother taught a Good News Club in our home as I was growing up. I watched her and then copied her. Our daughter watched me and copied me. By the time she was in high school she was leading many Good News Clubs on her own and teaching others. This is the biblical model of discipleship. This equipping process multiplies our efforts. Whatever ministry you are involved in, make sure that you have an apprentice alongside you.

POSSIBLE MINISTRIES FOR WHICH WOMEN CAN BE DISCIPLED

- Mentoring younger women
- Sunday School teacher
- VBS worker
- Children's choir leader
- Junior church leader
- Youth worker
- Women's ministry director
- Kids clubs coordinator
- Women's Bible study teacher
- Following up new believers—one-on-one Bible studies
- Counselor to women and children
- Christian education director
- Worship team member

- Hospitality to missionaries
- Secretary
- Financial secretary
- Ministry to unwed teen moms
- Ministering at a rescue mission
- Neighborhood Bible clubs
- Prison ministry
- Teaching English as a second language
- Prayer chain leader
- Meal ministry

Friend, I hope that I've encouraged you with all the opportunities to disciple women! But you may be feeling a bit overwhelmed, wondering how you are going to fit discipling women into your busy life. The good news is that discipleship is all about modeling. Everything you need to teach your disciple is just what you need to be doing for your own spiritual growth. You can't help but share the good news with the lost. You need to be studying the Scripture and applying it to your life. You need to be praying and confessing sin. You need to be using your gifts in the church. So start with just one woman. Love her with Christ's love. Then just let her walk beside you. Invite her to come over while you are cooking or cleaning the house or taking the kids to the park. Share with each other what you are learning at church and in your quiet times. Make her your apprentice as you teach Sunday School. Let her see the real you. Then you can say with Paul, "Be imitators of me, just as I also am of Christ" (1 Corinthians 11:1). And remember, He is not far away. He is right by our side as we are making His disciples. He promised, "and behold, I am with you always, even to the end of the age" (Matthew 28:20).

TAKING THE PRIVILEGE TO COUNSEL WOMEN

As the wife of a man in ministry, you may hear these kinds of cries for help, "Jan's mother just died and she is battling with depression, could you stop by and visit her?" "My husband moved out and I don't know what to do; can I come see you this week?" "I think our thirteen-year-old daughter might have an eating disorder; what should I do?"

Can you answer these cries for help? Should you answer them or would it be better to refer these ladies to the pastor, or better yet to a professional who knows how to deal with their deep mental and emotional needs? In this chapter, I want to show you that you do not have to refer them to someone else. You have the resources to give the best kind of help to these women who are desperate for counsel.

In the last chapter, we saw that it is our responsibility as ordinary Christians to be making disciples. Now I want to address a specific aspect of making disciples. That is teaching them how to obey God in the crises of life. Our society calls this kind of help, counseling.

There are many types of counseling available in the world. The various procedures flow out of a plethora of psychological theories. Many Christian counselors try to base their counsel on these psychological diagnoses and remedies. Unfortunately, this is like trying to build a house on shifting sand instead of on the rock of God's Word.

Psychology means "the study of the soul." This is not an area where all theories stand on level ground. The Bible is uniquely sufficient to address problems with the human soul. It is the counselor's manual. God says, "Counsel is mine and sound wisdom; I am understanding, might is mine" (Proverbs 8:14). The Bible can diagnose the heart better than any psychology textbook can. "For the word of God is living and active and sharper than any two-edged sword, and piercing as far as the division of soul and spirit, of both joints and marrow, and able to judge the thoughts and intentions of the heart" (Hebrews 4:12).

So we see that the Bible can show us the root of our problems. It can also lead us to the cure. "The law of Yahweh is perfect, restoring the soul; the testimony of Yahweh is sure, making wise the simple" (Psalm 19:7). If we want to give people God's answers for their problems, then we need to give them biblical counsel. This will not come in an easy prescription such as, "Take this Bible verse three times a day and all your depression will go away." But with careful study and application, God's Word is all we need.

Just what is biblical counseling? It is discipleship. It is an intentional relationship in which we walk alongside other believers in order to encourage, equip, and challenge them in love to grow to be more like Jesus through the study and application of His Word.

Who needs biblical counseling? We all do. We need it for comfort. We need it for guidance. We need it for reproof. Scripture warns us to "See to it brothers, that there not be in any one of you an evil, unbelieving heart that falls away from the living God. But encourage one another day after day, as long as it is still called "Today," so that none of you will be hardened by the deceitfulness of sin" (Hebrews 3:12-13). Sin is deceitful. Any of us can have blind spots, which will grow into dangerous habits of sin if left unaddressed. We each need other Christians to be exhorting us daily. That is biblical counseling. We need it and the women all around us need it.

We can get biblical counsel on our own from our personal study. We can get it from the pulpit and class settings. But there are times when people need personal attention. Sometimes the person needing counsel may ask for help. Sometimes you may need to initiate when you notice that someone is hurting or falling into sin (Galatians 6:1-2).

Many women are willing to share their deep problems with us because of our position as their pastor's wife. They trust that we will be sympathetic to them in their need. They hope that we will be able to give them some direction spiritually and practically. But many other women will need us to make the first move toward them. In their pain, they may not have the courage even to ask for help.

I had the privilege of counseling a woman who had recently lost her husband. She was in need of some tender loving care and some straightforward advice. We took a drive to a beautiful spot by a river and we talked about her future. She had been withdrawing from the church so I had taken the initiative of setting up the time together. She gave me permission to hold her accountable to stay faithful in the church body.

So how do you know if you are ready to offer biblical counseling to the person who asks for it or if you are equipped to boldly go after the lady who needs it and is afraid to ask?

Who is competent to counsel? The apostle Paul answers this question for us. "But I myself am also convinced about you, my brothers, that you yourselves are full of goodness, having been filled with all knowledge and being able also to admonish one another " (Romans 15:14). Who is able to admonish other believers? Is it only the pastors or the professionals? No, all believers are able to admonish one another. Some of us may be more gifted at edification than others. But we are all competent to counsel. The more full of goodness and knowledge of God's Word we are, the more competent we will be.

You may be a young pastor's wife, but chronological age is not the most important thing to consider; maturity in the Lord is. Those who are more spiritually mature are to teach and be examples for those who are less mature in the faith. Our daughter Michelle was asked to counsel a woman and her 22 year-old daughter who is in a psychiatric ward. Michelle writes, "Things like this sound so out of my league but I'm so glad that you have taught me how sufficient Scripture is so that I won't turn down an opportunity to see God do great things despite my inexperience."

Whatever your age, as a woman you even have an advantage over the pastor in your church when it comes to counseling women. It is better for you to counsel a woman than for him to counsel her just because of your gender. Women can easily become attracted to a male counselor who takes the time to listen to their problems and help them spiritually, especially if they don't have a husband who is leading them in this way. When counseling is woman-to-woman you eliminate all such distractions and temptations. By relieving your husband of any long-term counseling relationships with women you are not demonstrating a lack of trust in him but a wise love for him and for your sisters.

Since counseling is not just for an elite class of spiritual leaders or professionals, you should try not to counsel alone. You want to be part of an army of counselors in your church. Besides, you cannot do it alone. Sometimes we are bombarded by so many problems that women are dealing with around us that it can cause us to feel like we're on overload. It would be impossible to begin to minister to all of their needs. But if we are each faithfully pouring into a few lives and equipping them to counsel others, all of the needs can be met. The Holy Spirit will guide us as to who He wants us to help.

If you are new at biblical counseling, sit in with a pastor or elder or a more experienced counselor and learn from him or her. Once you have gained experience, you can bring another sister in to observe you in counseling situations. Counselees usually don't mind having another person sitting in if you get their permission. Then when you as counselors debrief about the session you can learn from each other's insights. This multiplies your efforts as you disciple other counselors.

What about the really tough cases? Some would say that the Bible is a great source of devotional food but it doesn't address issues that people deal with in the real world such as depression, addictions, and personality disorders. They say people need a psychologist who can delve into a person's past and can bring real healing of damaged emotions through psychotherapy and drug therapy.

If that is true, then Christians a few hundred years ago were consigned to live defeated lives. But Peter writes the opposite,

> seeing that His divine power has granted to us everything pertaining to life and godliness, through the full knowledge of Him who called us by His own glory and excellence. For by these

He has granted to us His precious and magnificent promises, so that by them you may become partakers of the divine nature, having escaped the corruption that is in the world by lust. (2 Peter 1:3-4)

We don't have to rely on man's diagnostic manual to help us deal with the difficult disorders. We have "His divine power." We don't have his divine power just to help us get saved and give us fire insurance from hell. We have his divine power for everything pertaining to life and godliness. God hasn't called us just to cope with life. He has called us to "become partakers of the divine nature." His magnificent promises can get us there.

Yes, we will encounter situations that make us tremble, wondering how in the world this problem should be handled. We may need to get help from someone more capable in handling the Word of God. But let's not turn the person over to someone who will leave God out of the picture and use secular thinking and methods. We must remember that we have the active and powerful Word of God that brings truth and conviction to bear. There is no other deeper source of truth!

Let me tell you about one pivotal counseling experience that demonstrated to me the power of God to change a life. All it took was simple biblical counsel and a big commitment of time. When I first started counseling Lucy the situation looked hopeless. The courts had decided that she was totally dysfunctional and had to be cared for in a group home. They had given custody of her daughter to the father. She was on a mile-long list of psychotropic drugs.

Lucy had known Christ and walked with Him before she had fallen into sin. We started dealing with the sin in her life, first through confession of the sin of fornication and the root sin of not loving and following Christ with her whole heart. The relationship with her Savior was restored. Then she confessed the sin to the young man and he in turn confessed his sin against her and this brought reconciliation into their relationship. Her burden of guilt was lifted and she began the process of growth in her walk of obedience. We met weekly for discipleship looking into the Scriptures and identifying sinful patterns of thinking and acting. We dealt with issues one strand at a time. Changes were taking place.

When I saw that Lucy was growing in Christ, my husband and I obtained a lawyer to get visitation rights for her. The judge granted them as long as I was there to observe her as she spent time with her daughter for two hours a week for the next two years. She and I also continued to meet during the week for discipleship. With the help of a Christian doctor, she was able to get off most of her medication. She was able to develop a good relationship with her daughter and the father, which continues to this day. She was able to build a new life. That was many years ago. What rejoicing takes place when the prodigal returns to the Father!

The secular counseling and drug therapy were superficial and powerless to help Lucy. It was through the enlightening of the Scriptures and the Holy Spirit's power that her life was totally transformed. With this heightened level of confidence that was produced in me, I began a ministry to single mothers that I have been directing for 14 years, training mentors to do what I did with Lucy. I have seen that the resources we have as women who know Christ and apply God's Word are sufficient to address and meet the needs of those who have bigger problems than we could imagine! God took that small measure of faithfulness on my part and multiplied it into an international outreach to teen moms through Young Life called Young Lives. What a joy to see hundreds of young women given hope and help in the Lord Jesus through this ministry, by God's grace!

Biblical Counseling Methods

Biblical counseling is a skill that must be developed as we grow in Christ and become better disciple-makers. There are many wonderful resources available in this field. But you have to be discerning because there are also many pseudo-Christian counseling resources. If I have whetted your appetite and you are hungry to see God transform lives through His Word, then please dig into some of the books that I have recommended in my reading list. For now, I offer the following brief overview of the methods of biblical counseling.

You Gather Information

"He who responds with a word before he hears, it is folly and shame to him" (Proverbs 18:13). We need to be careful listeners if we are going to be able to apply the scalpel of God's Word to the specific problems of people. All of the necessary information won't be obtained on your first time together. More will come out each time you meet. Take notes to help you remember what you have talked about, and what issues to tackle in future sessions. Seek to get to know her through probing questions, not ones that can be answered with a yes or a no.

Start by getting right to the point and asking, "What is the problem or particular trial that you are dealing with?" You have to know what is causing the trouble or grief in this woman's life. It is not necessary to delve into a person's past or subconscious. It is enough to deal with the facts of the situation and the counselee's conscious responses to it.

Then you may ask, "What have you done about the problem?" What has been done may actually complicate the problem. What has been done or what is being done may overshadow or conceal the actual heart issue that needs to be addressed.

Next you might ask, "How can I help you?" Get her expectations of you. Does she just expect you to be a sounding board for her to use to sort out her own thoughts? Does she want you to be a sympathetic listener who will justify her behavior because of the abuse that she has suffered? Does she want you to give her a quick fix for her marriage? You can only help her if she wants actual help and not just a listening ear.

You can only help her if she wants to know God's answers from His Word and is willing to go to work doing things His way. Before you start counseling, you have to be sure that you are both headed in the same direction. Your goal is to help her to become more like Christ. The other people who may have caused the problem are not there. She cannot change them but she can ask God to change her. Your goal is to direct her to what she can do about the situation. Through asking her about her expectations you will know where to start in explaining your goals and being sure that you are on the same page.

You Give Hope

We can offer people hope that the world does not have. You can counsel a woman who just found out that she has AIDS and send her away rejoicing saying, "Today I heard the worst news and the best news of my life. I found out that I am dying but I also found out that my sins can be forgiven and I can have eternal life." You can encourage women that God is in every situation and He is in it for good (Romans 8:28). You can motivate women to persevere knowing that God's ways work every time.

First make sure that your counselee has the hope of salvation and the Holy Spirit's power to help her to overcome. Then if she is a believer, share some of the promises of God with her including 1 Corinthians 10:13.

Her problem is common to other women.

It is not too much for her to bear. You can weep with her over her heartaches and show real comfort and concern. However, you have to stay out of the pit to offer the hand up. There is hope for the worst situation. God is sovereign. God can use this for good and His glory.

God will provide a way of escape that she may be able to bear it.

Share God's faithfulness in your own life and give the comfort, which you have received from the Lord to be able to comfort her (2 Corinthians 1:4). As you share how Christ's grace worked itself out in a similar situation, it shows her how she can also rely on it. You can begin with, "In my own life…" or "In Joni's life…" This is applied theology.

You Go to the Word

Find out what the Scripture says about the problem. Select one strand of the problem to deal with and go to work to find the biblical solution. When we look into the mirror of Scripture we usually see sin in the reflection. But this should actually give us hope because once we see the mess in the mirror; we can go to work fixing it. If our counseling just shows her how she is a victim of her past or her circumstances or her unmet needs, then there is no hope. But if our counseling shows her the sin that she needs to deal with and the biblical process of change, then there is hope. Christ died so that she could be freed from that sin.

Blame shifting needs to stop. She needs to examine her own life in light of God's Word and deal with her own sin even if it is only a small part of the problem.

We must think in biblical terms. Our society uses euphemisms for sin that make people slaves of sin instead of helping them to deal with it. If you are a kleptomaniac or an alcoholic or a co-dependent, then there is no hope for you to change. But God says that those are the sins of stealing, drunkenness, and man-pleasing. He calls us to put off those sins and put on working and giving, being filled with the Spirit, and fearing God. We are able to change in specifics, not generalities. Paul sets the example for dealing with specific sins such as lying, stealing, and bad language in Ephesians 4:25-32. He tells his "counselees" how to put off these actions and replace them with holy actions. We must encourage our counselees to lay aside the old self and the sinful pattern of thinking and living (Ephesians 4:17-22). Stop sinning. Change! God desires for us to be holy as He is holy. This is the process of sanctification—of being more and more conformed to Christ's image.

The Word of God goes to the heart of the problem. Depression may be the symptom of self-absorption and disappointment that things didn't turn out the way the counselee wanted them to—not faith and trust in God's sovereignty. Anger, fear, and worry may be the symptoms of a heart that desires control. Surface problems need to be traced to their root cause. Then we can tear down our idols and replace them with love for God that will enable us to have holy desires. If we desire His will over our own, we cannot stay depressed. If we trust His sovereignty, we cannot be angry at the way things turned out or worried about the future.

These changes of heart and habit do not happen easily. They come through the renewing of the mind (Ephesians 4:23). She renews her mind by putting on the new self—thinking and desiring and doing what God wants. This comes through daily practice, not a one-hour counseling session. She renews her mind by thinking God's thoughts after Him—meditating on His Word. As her mind is filled with Scripture, the Holy Spirit will continually convict her. She will see how her sin grieves her Savior and she will repent of it, confess her sin before God, and seek to obey Him. It is amazing how many counseling cases are ended when the counselee just learns to meditate daily on God's Word on her own.

You Rely on the Power of the Holy Spirit for Change

The Holy Spirit is the Source of all holiness. He produces the fruit in the life of each believer—love, joy, peace, patience, kindness, goodness, faithfulness, gentleness, and self-control (Galatians 5:22-23). Psychological therapies don't even try to produce these kinds of results. Their greatest goal is to make you functional. But biblical counseling, or discipleship, strives to make you like Christ through God's enablement.

You Hold Her Accountable

Biblical counsel is useless if it isn't put into practice throughout the week. That is why accountability is so important. Homework assignments help the counselees to apply what they have learned. Phone calls during the week may help to spur them on and show them that you really care about their progress.

- Write out her assignment so it is specific and concrete. (Keep a copy so you can hold her accountable.)
- Have her memorize one or more verses from Scripture that address the problem, and have her meditate on them during the week.
- Have her write a prayer personalizing it and praying it back to God.
- Give her a few practical examples on how to apply Scripture.

Example:

Suzie's husband, Harry, is not showing love and is instead, being very unloving.

- Biblical principles—get the log out of her own eye first (Matthew 7:1-5); win him without a word by her behavior (1 Peter 3:1-6).

Assignment:

- Have her read some from the Bible every day. Begin memorizing Matthew 7:1-5 and 1 Peter 2:21-3:2 to have her mind renewed.
- Have her write a prayer personalizing these passages and pray them back to God constantly through the day.

- Assign her to keep a "Logs List" of her own failures in the marriage based on Matthew 7:1-5. Be specific. We change in specifics. God forgives each one of our sins and failures. Remember to ask for His forgiveness. Next week have her work on a specific plan for laying aside the bad habits and for putting on godly habits in order to bring honor to Christ. We must focus on the motives behind this—"Am I doing this to honor Christ or only to please myself?"

- Ask her to do an extra-loving thing each day for Harry realizing that she can only love him as she loves God first. Pray for that love.

- Have her pray throughout her day for God to work in her own life. If she is just changing the outward things and not her inner attitudes and desires, then God is not honored.

- Assign her to read something pertinent to the problem such as chapter 1 in *Creative Counterpart* by Linda Dillow or *A Woman After God's Own Heart* by Elizabeth George, and be ready to discuss it next week.

Meet in one or two weeks to check up on her progress. If she has not done her homework, then you need to assess what response she needs. We are called to "admonish the unruly, encourage the faint-hearted, help the weak, be patient with everyone" (1 Thessalonians 5:14). If she continues to reject your counsel by failing to do her homework, then you have to discontinue meeting. If she has no desire for accountability, nothing will be accomplished. It is not fair to give her any indication that she can continue to live with the knowledge of what God wants her to do without obedience. You cannot support her in that.

If she is diligent in following through with the homework, you should meet with her until you see new heart attitudes and patterns of obedience established in her life. This may take six or eight weeks or it may take several months. For a few sessions, have her make her own assignments with homework and memory work. Then turn her loose to tackle the rest. As she has learned to continually practice the godly response in the problem areas you have helped her with, these new responses will extend to all the other areas of her life. You can have periodic check-ups after that to see how she is doing. What a joy to see her changed life!

You Celebrate Victories

Seeing a woman turn from self back to her Savior is the "pay" for all your work. This is a time for rejoicing when she has evidenced real heart changes and demonstrated new patterns of obedience through answered prayer! We are there to hold a party when lives are transformed.

You Leave the Results with God

Does everything always end up the way we hope it will? Sometimes we plant seeds and never see the fruit; in fact they turn away from the Lord and us. I have seen many teen mothers, and other women who I have counseled over the years; turn back to their sinful ways. It breaks our hearts, but we are not responsible for the outcome. We are only required to be faithful.

WHAT IF THE COUNSELEE HAS BEEN SINNED AGAINST BY ANOTHER CHURCH MEMBER?

According to Scripture, a person can choose to overlook a transgression. "A man's insight makes him slow to anger, and it is his honor to overlook a transgression" (Proverbs 19:11). However, if the person is not able to overlook it any longer and/or the sin is such that it needs to be confronted, the Lord has given us the method to address it.

Jesus knew that offenses would come within His church so he outlined a process to handle them. It is found in Matthew 18. Let's look at the passage and see what can be done.

The Process of Church Discipline
(Found in Matthew 18:15-20)

Step 1

The offended one goes in private to the other to draw him to repentance. If the offender listens, then reconciliation takes place. If there is no repentance, and therefore no reconciliation, the next step is carried out.

Step 2

The offended one takes one or two fellow Christians to the other to listen, establish the facts, and encourage repentance, and reconciliation.

Step 3

If this does not bring about repentance, then it must be told to the church. This would involve bringing it to the elders. The elders have the special task of watching over the welfare of the flock (Hebrews 13:17; 1 Thessalonians 5:12-14).

It is the responsibility of the elders to tell it to the whole body so that they will listen to them. This is so the members can seek him out and seek to reprove him. It is to be done in the spirit of meekness (Galatians 6:1-2) and in love (Ephesians 4:15), letting that person know that God will judge (Hebrews 12:4-11), and that he can be restored and that God can use this for good (Romans 8:28-39).

If he does not repent, that person is to be put out of the church and treated as a non-Christian. He is officially turned over to Satan for the destruction of the flesh (1 Corinthians 5:5). It is a time of humility and mourning over this person and their sin, and a time of recognizing that it could be me, but for the grace of God. It is a time to pray for that person.

If the person repents, then he is forgiven and restored to fellowship. Paul talks about church discipline that was exercised in Corinth. He says, "Sufficient for such a one is this punishment which was inflicted by the majority, so that on the contrary you should rather graciously forgive and comfort him, lest such a one be swallowed up by excessive sorrow" (2 Corinthians 2:6-7).

There is nothing that brings more hope than the process of church discipline. It takes care of unresolved issues in relationships between believers. God never intended for people to be in good standing in the church who are causing havoc and tearing down the name of Christ. It preserves the honor of God's Name. God disciplines His children and He expects the church to carry out discipline among its members as well. It is one of the most loving things that God does for us when it is carried out according to His plan. Reconciliation is more important than offering a gift to God (Matthew 5:21-26).

An Example:

Suzie has sought to get the "logs out of her own eye" through the above assignment. She has prayerfully sought to be what God wants her to be in the marriage. Her husband's treatment of her becomes even worse. He swears at her and the children and accuses her of things of which she is not guilty. In one day he calls her almost 50 times during the day to see where she is so he can direct her behavior. There is no pleasing him. He orders her out of the house and changes the locks.

Suzie tells Harry that she would like to go with him for counseling at their church. (He is a member in good standing in the church, and the worse he treats her the more he gives.) He refuses, insisting that it is her problem, not his. She tells him that she will be bringing elder Jim to talk with him about the situation.

Jim talks to Harry and tells him that things have to change. He tells him that as a believer, he has the responsibility to love his wife as Christ loved the church giving Himself up for her. He asks him to attend counseling with his wife. Harry refuses.

Jim tells him that he will be taking it to the elders in following the process of church discipline. He reads him the passage in Matthew 18 warning Harry not to cut himself off from Christ's church. If Harry responds negatively and Jim gives him a few days to think about it and there is no response, it goes to the elders.

The elders seek to contact Harry and if he responds and seeks help to be what God wants him to be in the marriage, then the marriage is saved. If he doesn't respond, then he is put out of the church. Once the church has taken action and he is placed outside the church, he is then to be treated as a nonbeliever. Suzie need not pursue a divorce, but she should remain single praying for Harry to return to the Lord. Should he continue to choose to live apart or seek a divorce, then she is not under bondage and is commanded to let him go and she is free to remarry (1 Corinthians 7:15).

It has been made clear to Harry that he cannot consider himself to be a follower of Jesus Christ and continue in sin. It has been made clear to the children that their father is not to be considered a Christian if he persists in this kind of a pattern. Christ is not to be disgraced by Harry claiming His name and not being willing to live a life of obedience. Church discipline is necessary for the purity of the body of Christ and for its testimony in the world.

Scripture gives guidance for any situation that can be encountered in life, and, if followed, will bring resolution and peace in its application.

One seasoned biblical counselor ends his book on counseling by saying,

> Two things always come to my mind as I finish teaching this material. First, I am hit with the utter simplicity of biblical personal ministry. It is not a secret technology for the intervention elite, but a simple call to every one of God's children to be part of what God is doing in the lives of others. It is living in humble, honest, redemptive community with others, loving as Christ has loved, and going beyond the casual to really know people. It is loving others enough to speak the truth to them, helping them to see themselves in the mirror of God's Word. And it is standing with others, helping them to do what God has called them to do. It is basically just a call to biblical friendship! It is embarrassingly simple: Love people. Know them. Speak truth into their lives. Help them do what God has called them to do.[54]

I hope that you see now that you can answer those cries for help that come to your ears. Sin complicates life. People are hurting. But you have the map, the salve, the remedy. God's answers are not easy, but they are plain. When you delve into Scripture as your counseling manual, you will find a well that never runs dry and refreshes you as you pour it out for others.

---

54 Paul David Tripp, *Instruments in the Redeemer's Hands* (Phillipsburg, New Jersey: P&R Publishing, 2002), 274-275.

LIVING IN THE PLACE OF HONOR, LOVE, AND REWARD

Not long ago, as I stood beside Bob and we blended our voices in a duet of praise from the front row, and then as he stepped up and preached the Word of God so gently, yet clearly and forcefully, my heart swelled with love for him and gratitude to God for making me his wife. I was thinking that I couldn't be happier, more fulfilled, or blessed!

Susannah wrote about her feelings following C.H. Spurgeon's proposal of marriage to her 40 years later, referring to her journal written on August 2, 1854:

> To me it was a time as solemn as it was sweet; and with a great awe in my heart, I left my beloved and hastening to the house and to an upper room, I knelt before God and praised and thanked Him with happy tears for His great mercy in giving me the love of so good a man. If I had known then how good he was and how great he would become, I should have been overwhelmed, not so much with the happiness of being his, as with the responsibility which such a position would entail.[55]

Honor of the Calling

We have looked at our responsibilities of being one with a shepherd

---

[55] Charles Ray, *Mrs. C.H. Spurgeon* (Edinburgh, Scotland: CrossReach Publications, 1905 Reprint 2020), 37.

and now I want us to consider the honors. What an honor it is for us to be married to a man called out by God and placed in a role of equipping the saints for the work of ministry! We are fellow-laborers with them, one in life and purpose, gratefully (hopefully, not arrogantly) sharing in the honor of their calling.

Just how did our husbands get to be in ministry, in this place of such honor?

We can thank and praise our Lord that it was by His marvelous grace that He called them to this great task of serving His body. Jesus Christ, as the Head of the church, assigned gifted men. First, the 12 apostles—all who had seen Him risen from the dead—and Paul, uniquely set apart as an apostle to the Gentiles. Building upon the foundation of their ministry Christ called evangelists to proclaim the good news of salvation to unbelievers, and pastors and teachers (understood to be one office) to be shepherds who instruct the flock. He gifted pastor-teachers to build up His church so that they might be mature and properly equipped for their service (Ephesians 4:11-13). These men are also called elders, bishops, overseers, or shepherds (Titus 1:5-9; 1 Timothy 3:1-7, 1 Peter 5:1-2). Do you see where your husband fits in? It's an important calling and gifting he has from Jesus Christ!

In the book of Acts we see the historical account of when the church first ordained elders, or pastor-teachers, who began to have a leading role in the church (Acts 11:30; 14:23; 16:4). The church was instructed by the apostles to ordain elders, or pastor-teachers, by the laying on of hands—a symbolic way to affirm their call to ministry (1 Timothy 4:14). It was not something to be done hastily, but after a thorough time of testing to know if this person had the character qualities and preparation needed for this significant role in the church (1 Timothy 5:22).

The Bible makes the character qualities necessary for this position very clear. He must be blameless, faithful as the husband of one wife, temperate, sober-minded, not violent nor greedy for money; he must be gentle, not quarrelsome nor covetous. Out of his inner life that pleases God flows good behavior, hospitality, and the ability to preach and teach God's Word and to manage his own house well. He must not be a novice or prideful and he must have a good testimony with those outside the church (1 Timothy 3:1-7). It is absolutely necessary that our husbands as Christ's under-shepherds live this kind of a blameless life. Along with the inner desire for this office, their outer lives must measure up. That is why it is such an honor to be as one flesh with a man of such integrity.

Paul wrote about his own calling to ministry, "of which I was made a minister, according to the gift of God's grace which was given to me according to the working of His power. To me, the very least of all saints, this grace was given, to proclaim to the Gentiles the good news of the unfathomable riches of Christ" (Ephesians 3:7-8). Paul was not inflated with pride because of his position. Instead he praised God for His ability to use such a frail vessel. He also said, "For woe is me if I do not proclaim the gospel" (1 Corinthians 9:16b). He knew that God's chastening would be his if he were unfaithful to his call.

What a truly humble servant Paul was, realizing his own unworthiness apart from the grace of God, and that his ministry was all of God's doing. There was no false humility. It is important to keep in our minds that "No man can make himself a minister of God because the calling, message, work, and empowering of genuine ministry to and for God are His prerogative alone to give."[56] It is God who placed our husbands in ministry. The honor first and foremost goes to Him!

Is it right then for our husbands to receive honor? It is if it is directed back to its source. Paul wrote Timothy that the elders who rule well were to be considered worthy of double honor, especially those who work hard at preaching and teaching (1 Timothy 5:17).

We are reminded every four years of the great honor Olympians receive when they win the gold. The great apostle Paul would have known about those events and so did the Greeks to whom he was writing. He wrote,

> Do you not know that those who run in a race all run, but only one receives the prize? Run in such a way that you may win. Now everyone who competes in the games exercises self-control in all things. They then do it to receive a corruptible crown, but we an incorruptible.
> (1 Corinthians 9:24-25)

---

56 John MacArthur, *The MacArthur Study Bible*, (Nashville, Tennessee: Word Bibles, 1997), 1806.

It's certainly not wrong to go for the gold!

What will we do with those crowns in heaven? We'll cast them before the throne of God saying, "Worthy are You, our Lord and our God, to receive glory and honor and power, for You created all things, and because of Your will they existed, and were created" (Revelation 4:11). He alone is worthy of praise and honor!

One way to test ourselves to see if we are giving the honor back to God or craving it for ourselves is to see how we respond when we don't get it. We can become used to being honored and find ourselves looking for it and expecting it. We will be disappointed when it is not there.

One such occasion stands out in my mind. After ten years serving in our first church we were given a farewell that would rival the finest funeral service. In fact, Bob and I both thought it must have been like attending one's own funeral. There were the eulogies, the tears, and the goodbyes. Afterwards, there was a sumptuous feast of the most delectable cream cakes, fruit breads, and open-face sandwiches that the predominantly Norwegian ladies were so adept at making—all served in the finest style. We were honored to the utmost!

Then we came to the installation service for the church that we were going to plant. What a contrast. No fanfare, no frills. It was held in a small chapel with only a few people in attendance. The very plain sandwiches, some of which I had brought, were eaten in the courtyard on paper plates. I hate to admit my feelings of disappointment when it didn't quite measure up to the style to which I had become accustomed. We can look for the praise of men to our own detriment.

Jesus said, "Beware of doing your righteousness before men to be noticed by them; otherwise you have no reward with your Father who is in heaven" (Matthew 6:1). Paul understood Jesus' teaching and wrote, "But he who boasts is to boast in the Lord. For it is not the one who commends himself that is approved, but the one whom the Lord commends" (2 Corinthians 10:17-18). If we too realize that God's holiness is our standard and He is our judge, then we have nothing to boast in but His grace.

Pastor John Piper warns us severely not to prize the praise of men,

> Oh, yes, I've known what it is like to call the praise of men an
> act of love and justify this craving with the readiness to give the

same. How satisfying it does seem—this love among ourselves of mutual admiration! But now (thanks to your mighty grace!) I see it is an imitation. It has its roots in Eden long ago.[57]

He points out that pride can raise its ugly head in our hearts and we can desire praise and glory when all the glory needs to go to our blessed Lord. How could anything that we do hold a candle to what He is and has done for us?

This wise pastor continues,

> How could I put my eye to some great telescope, designed to make me glad with visions of the galaxies, and notice in the glass a dim reflection of my face and say, Now I am happy, I am loved? How could I stand before the setting sun, between the mountain range and the vastness of the sea, and think that everlasting joy should come from making much of me?[58]

To Him goes all the praise and glory now and throughout all eternity! Let's direct any praise that we receive to Him.

Love and Thanks

Most pastors are loved and thanked by their congregations. Hopefully, the people are showing their appreciation to us as an expression of thanks to the Lord Himself, and we should consider it so because we are merely His servants. The apostle Paul reports that the believers "honored us in many ways," on the island of Malta (Acts 28:10).

Paul received their honor and provisions gladly. Paul did not reject this honor like he did in Lystra when they wanted to honor him as a god (Acts 14:12-18). He thanked the Philippians also for their care for him saying, "Not that I seek the gift itself, but I seek the fruit which increases to your account" (Philippians 4:17). We must not rob people of the joy of giving to the Lord through blessing His workers.

There are many ways that a congregation demonstrates its love for its pastor. We have been privileged to serve very loving congregations who constantly are expressing their appreciation. The notes

---

57 Piper, *Don't Waste Your Life*, 184.
58 Ibid, 186.

telling us how God has used His Word in their lives and thanks for the ways we minister to them are truly valued. I keep a basket of these uplifting cards and notes in my kitchen as a reminder of the love of our people.

Here is one such note of appreciation we received after organizing a group of ten couples to visit one of our elders who had just found out that he had cancer and would need to undergo chemotherapy. Each couple brought something to put in the basket of encouragement we gave him at the end of the evening. His wife wrote this note:

> I just want to let you know how much Lee and I appreciated the surprise encouragement-gathering in our home earlier in the summer! The basket of goodies was very much appreciated, as was the framed picture of our marred savior—Jesus holding His special lamb. Sometimes a picture will speak louder than words (this is a great example). So far it remains in our kitchen where we can be reminded often of His special care for us! Thanks for making Lee feel so loved and supported during this incredibly difficult time in his life! I don't know what we would do without the body of Christ.

This is another expression of gratitude from a dear friend whose son is in prison:

> Thank you so much for going to all the trouble of inviting the ladies and putting together such a lovely lunch. I was so very blessed and encouraged to know there are sisters in Christ who really do care and pray for my family and me.
>
> Thank you for the book (*Trusting God Even When Life Hurts* by Jerry Bridges), I am enjoying it. There is a wonderful peace that is beyond understanding when we choose to trust God rather than focus on what seems to be reality. Knowing that God's reality transcends what we can see, touch and feel. The confidence that He will 'Make all things work together for good' gives me the will to face each new day and all that it might bring.
>
> Thanks for caring for the flock in such tangible ways.

There are other ways churches show appreciation. For instance, our church staff was recently honored by a lovely meal prepared by two couples in the church to express their love for us. At our once-a-year church in the park, our pastoral staff was given a basket of cards of appreciation along with gift certificates for dinner. When Bob's mom was not expected to live, they flew him to see her. Even the verbal thanks after the service for the message makes us feel loved and appreciated.

Sometimes it is difficult to know how to take a compliment. We must graciously receive the thanks, knowing that by God's grace He does use us. If we dismiss the expressions of thanks, or minimize what we have done for the person who has expressed appreciation, that actually can detract from God's glory. We don't want to depreciate the work that God has done in a person's heart.

When people compliment my husband on his sermon, he just smiles and says, "Praise the Lord!" That is a good way to accept the compliment and also direct the praise in the right direction.

Lasting Fruit

There is nothing to compare to the absolute joy and reward of seeing people growing in the Lord. Paul calls them his "joy and crown" (Philippians 4:1). Making an eternal difference in people's lives is cause for rejoicing!

What a joy to reflect on the many couples that God brought together and Bob united in marriage, and to see them honoring those vows and living for God's glory. There are the ones who grew up in the church and who have gone out to serve Christ like Sarah and Jon ministering in Thailand. There are people like Ellen and John, and so many like them, who jumped right in with both feet the minute they came to the church—looking for needs to follow up on with no prompting, hosting a home Bible study, and shepherding God's people.

There are people like Ann and Jim, neighbors in our first church who came to faith in Christ, who have continued to hold a neighborhood Bible study in their home for over 20 years. There are individuals like Kathy, who is a ministry wife raising her children for God's glory. There are people like Jim and Pat, who came to Christ 30 years ago when they came for counseling and have formed a national crisis-pregnancy-biblical training ministry.

Then there are regular, ordinary church members who go about their lives in a normal every-day way doing thousands of unseen deeds of love and kindness that no one ever notices. They love and care for their families. They are ordinary people demonstrating a Spirit-driven, extraordinary love for God and people. It is seeing their faithfulness that is a rich reward. We must remember to give all the glory to God, because He is the One who has accomplished the work in the hearts of people.

When you are discouraged, stop and make a list of the people who God has allowed you to impact and who are flourishing in the Lord. Praise God for them and ask Him for more. Those are prayers He loves to answer.

Community Respect

Another way that our husbands are honored and respected is as a member of the clergy in the community—although this seems to be diminishing as our country drifts from its Christian moorings. However, in most cases our husbands hold a place of trust as moral leaders and spokesmen for what is right and just. My husband is able to write a column for the local newspaper several times a year, and is looked to as someone with ideas worth honoring.

Our husbands have access to the community through many different doors. They can serve as chaplains in the police force, in hospitals, or for sports teams. The community often calls upon its ministers when there is a tragedy or a celebration. They must take advantage of these opportunities while they can and we must be eager to let our husbands serve the community as doors open up.

We must also value the trust and respect of the community and be careful not to lose it. They are always watching us. Let's be holier and happier than they ever expected and we will continue to receive their honor.

Respect from Our Children

When our husbands are thanked and honored, we appreciate it, particularly when it comes from our children—our first disciples.

Here is a sweet note written to Bob, which he keeps in his Bible:

> Dad, I am proud to call you my dad. You have shown me what
> it is to live your life with the fruit of the Spirit. I can always call

you for advice and know that a listening ear is on the other end. Thank you for instilling in me fear and love for God. Your life has been one of a faithful servant to the Most High and I pray that my life will reflect the glory of God as much as your life has. I don't know that I have told you this lately or since I have moved away from home, but I miss you and your 'Rise and Shine' song in the morning.

Love you, Dad!

Reward and Honor from Jesus Christ

More than the temporary acknowledgement that we receive from people, we have the eternal reward of our Lord and Savior to look forward to. Even if your church is thankless, your community doesn't pay its clergy any respect, or your children are ungrateful for you or the position you hold, you can look forward to the reward and honor you will receive from the highest person in and beyond our realm—Jesus Christ.

There will be a time when "The kingdom of the world has become the kingdom of our Lord and of His Christ, and He will reign forever and ever" (Revelation 11:15). At that time He will reward His saints—those who fear His name, small and great (Revelation 11:15, 18). Jesus said, "Behold, I am coming quickly, and My reward is with Me, to render to every man according to his work" (Revelation 22:12).

Eternal Life

Jesus assured us, "And everyone who has left houses or brothers or sisters or father or mother or children or farms for My name's sake, will receive one hundred times as much, and will inherit eternal life" (Matthew 19:29; cf. Mark 10:28-31).

Those are realistic words; they face the facts squarely. There will be separation from loved ones and from property. And Mark adds "along with persecutions." Yet, in the midst of the loss and trials, Jesus in His own time and way promises to provide not only the rewards of the age to come, but now also with new brothers and sisters and family in Christ, and farms and houses as well.

Harriet Newell epitomized this aspect of leaving her family behind for the sake of the gospel. She was a young missionary bride who left her home in Haverhill, Massachusetts to reach the lost in

India in 1812. She died along with her infant child from sickness contracted on the stormy seas. The letters and journal of this modest, unambitious young woman were used to ignite a missionary zeal in America when missions were first being launched. They reveal her deep desire to turn her eyes from vanity to searching the Scriptures and listening to the instructions of those who taught her the way of life. I received and eagerly read a ninth edition, printed in 1830. What an inspiration to see Harriet's love for Christ and her desire to give herself to reaching the lost on every page of her journal! Here's just one example:

> June 30, 1812 My whole soul was melted into compassion for impenitent sinners. [She tells how the pastor of a church she attended in India had spoken on Jesus weeping over the city of Jerusalem.] Can I ever again feel regardless and unconcerned for their immortal souls?
>
> > *Did Christ for sinners weep,*
> > *And shall our cheeks be dry?*
> > *Let floods of penitential grief*
> > *Burst forth from every eye.*
>
> Did Jesus say to sinners, 'Oh that thou hadst known, in this thy day, the things that belong to thy peace,' and shall I smile upon them while in the road to ruin?[59]

The pastor who preached her funeral message (contained in this little volume) used Matthew 19:29 to reassure those who leave all for the sake of the kingdom of Jesus Christ. In his message he told how that during her sickness she talked in the most familiar manner, and with great delight, of death and the glory that was to come. She was looking to her reward of being with Christ. This reward has motivated the saints of all the ages to do great exploits for their King.

Rewards in Heaven

God has prepared a special reward for our husbands, described as a crown of glory, for shepherding the flock of God—not for monetary

---

59 Newell, *Memoirs of Her Life*, 105.

gain or for power, but as examples. This reward is described as an unfading crown of glory, which will be presented by the Chief Shepherd Himself (1 Peter 5:1-4).

Jesus promised a reward for us wives as well by saying,

> He who receives you receives Me, and he who receives Me receives Him who sent Me. He who receives a prophet in the name of a prophet shall receive a prophet's reward; and he who receives a righteous man in the name of a righteous man shall receive a righteous man's reward.
> (Matthew 10:40-41)

To welcome Christ's ambassadors is the same as welcoming Jesus and God the Father. That act of love will be richly rewarded when it is done in His name and for His glory. My husband ("a righteous man") is spoken of here and so when I care for him I will receive the same reward as will be given to him.

I know so many ministry wives who are unsung heroes, faithfully serving alongside their husbands, many times totally behind the scenes. Each one makes it possible for her husband to have an effective ministry. She is doing the bulk of the child rearing and running of the home. She loves and supports and prays for her man so he has the backing at home to minister to others. She has an indispensable role! Her reward is coming!

What a God we serve! "For God is not unrighteous so as to forget your work and the love which you have shown toward His name, in having ministered and continuing to minister to the saints" (Hebrews 6:10). No tear we ever shed in His service is ever wasted. He keeps all our tears in a bottle (Psalm 56:8). If we go forth with tears, planting seeds, we shall doubtless come again with rejoicing, bringing our sheaves with us (Psalm 126:5-6).

Let's look at all the other ways that we can receive honor from God (John 5:44).

Jesus promises rewards for:

- Being persecuted for His sake (Matthew 5:12; Hebrews 10:32-36)
- Loving those who don't love us (Matthew 5:44)

- Charitable deeds done in secret (Matthew 6:4)
- Private prayer (Matthew 6:6)
- Fasting and not letting it be known (Matthew 6:18)
- Giving even a cup of cold water in Jesus' name (Matthew 10:42)
- Works (Matthew 16:27); works done with Jesus as the foundation (1 Corinthians 3:14)
- Planting and watering the seeds of the gospel—rewarded equally (1 Corinthians 3:8)
- Loving our enemies (Luke 6:35)
- Lending without expecting anything in return (Luke 6:35)
- Doing what we do heartily as to the Lord and not to men (Colossians 3:23)
- Not casting away our confidence in Him (Hebrews 10:35)
- Endurance in doing God's will (Hebrews 10:36)
- Holding to the truths of the gospel (cf. 2 John 8)
- Not getting off track doctrinally (Colossians 2:18)
- Disciplining our bodies (1 Corinthians 9:25)
- Loving His appearing (2 Timothy 4:7-8)
- Enduring temptation successfully (James 1:12)
- Dying to self; serving Christ; following Him (John 12:25-26)

What are we to learn from all these references to rewards? God is going to reward us without a doubt. We don't know what these rewards are that He has promised, but we do know that the rewards that Jesus gives will be commensurate with His deity, love, and power, and they include "glory, honor, and immortality" (Romans 2:7).

It is important to have faith in God who rewards. We cannot please God unless we prize Him and His rewards above everything else. In that great chapter on the heroes of faith it says, "And without faith it is impossible to please Him, for he who draws near to God must believe that He is and that He is a rewarder of those who seek Him" (Hebrews 11:6).

Just consider what motivated Moses to give up his high worldly position in the courts of Egypt and the passing pleasures of sin to obey God's call. Scripture tells us it was the reward he would receive from God (Hebrews 11:24).

The apostle Peter tells us that we can greatly rejoice, be exuberant even, if we are going through trials because the genuineness of our faith is being tested and we will be rewarded if it passes the test. The reward is praise, honor, and glory at the revelation of Jesus Christ (1 Peter 1:6-7).

God's glory will be revealed to us in heaven. Paul said, "For I consider that the sufferings of this present time are not worthy to be compared with the glory that is to be revealed to us" (Romans 8:18). If we suffer with Him, we will indeed be glorified with Him (Romans 8:17). What greater reward could there be than to see Him and be made like Him (1 John 3:2)?

In the great allegory *The Pilgrim's Progress* that John Bunyan wrote from prison, we catch a glimpse of how focusing on our reward can help us to overcome Satan. One of the most terrifying parts of the journey comes when Christian must face Apollyon. Let's break into their conversation:

> Christian: To tell you the truth, Mr. Apollyon, I like His (the King of all princes, Jesus Christ) service, His wages, His servants, His government, His company, and His country much better than yours and all you can promise—and you have never been one to keep your promise. I am His servant, and I will follow Him.
>
> Apollyon: That is pure sentiment. Consider again in cold blood, what you are likely to encounter in the way you have chosen. You know that, for the most part, His followers suffer reproaches, perils, weariness, stripes, stonings, imprisonment, pain and death, all because they oppose me and my kingdom. Think how many of them have been put to horrible death! And your Master never came from His mysterious, invisible, exalted dwelling place to deliver them. How can you count His service better than mine? Not many of my servants have ever been martyred. All the world knows very well that I deliver, either by power or by fraud, those who have followed me, from your Master and His power. And be sure I will deliver you.
>
> Christian: When He, for a time, does not deliver His servants from trouble, it is for their good; it strengthens their faith and

their love for the right, and affords an opportunity for them to show the sincerity of their love and add to their rewards. And as for the death you speak of, it is only temporary. He delivers His servants out of death, and gives them a perfect life beyond. His servants do not expect immediate deliverance from the petty dangers and discomforts of this present perishing world, but are willing to wait on the Lord, knowing full well that they shall be more than well rewarded for all their sufferings, when He comes in His glory with all His holy angels.[60]

Just think of it! The One to whom all honor is due, is going to honor us—not because we are special in ourselves but because of His grace. Jesus makes this amazing statement, "If anyone serves Me, the Father will honor him" (John 12:26b).

Imagine the joy that will be ours when we will have the honor of being in the presence of the One who is the light of heaven. We will share in His holiness and have no more struggles with sin. We will be free from pain and sadness that cause tears to flow—free from wrongs and disappointments.

We will be honored by the preparation He made of such a beautiful place for us described as streets of gold, foundations of gems, and gates of pearl. We will drink from the crystal stream. We will be Home in our Father's house that Jesus has gone to prepare. What an honor! Scripture tells us, "Things which eye has not seen and ear has not heard, and which have not entered the heart of man, all that God has prepared for those who love Him" (1 Corinthians 2:9).

Even as the 24 elders cast their crowns before the throne saying, "Worthy are You, our Lord and our God, to receive glory and honor and power, for You created all things, and because of Your will they existed, and were created," we will join that great chorus alongside all those to whom we have ministered (Revelation 4:11). Our praises will be to our King of kings and Lord of lords—the Lamb upon the throne. Our joy shall be at its peak forever!

> but thanks be to God, who gives us the victory through our Lord Jesus Christ! Therefore, my beloved brothers, be steadfast,

---

60 John Bunyan, *The Pilgrim's Progress*, (Chicago, Illinois: Moody Press, 1964), 58.

immovable, always abounding in the work of the Lord, knowing that your labor is not in vain in the Lord.
(1 Corinthians 15:57-58)

If we have been steadfast, immovable in the Lord's work, we will be able to say with Paul at the end of our journey,

I have fought the good fight, I have finished the course, I have kept the faith. In the future there is laid up for me the crown of righteousness, which the Lord, the righteous Judge, will award to me on that day, and not only to me, but also to all who have loved His appearing.
(2 Timothy 4:7-8)

What a joy it is to run the race side by side with our husbands! You and I as wives of men in ministry have been blessed beyond our imagining to be united to men who are called by God to do His work on earth. That great preacher, Charles Spurgeon, described the marriage that God had given him by writing:

Happy woman, happy man, if heaven be found on earth, they have it... At last, two are so blended, so engrafted in one stem, that their old age presents a lovely attachment, a common sympathy, by which its infirmities are greatly eliminated and its burdens are transformed into fresh bonds of love. So happy a union of will, sentiment, thought, and heart exists between husband and wife that the two streams of their life here wash away the divided bank and run on as one broad current of united existence till their common joy falls into the ocean of eternal felicity.[61]

To be one with a shepherd can actually be a foretaste of heaven on earth. May God give us His wisdom to understand our role and give us His grace to spend and be spent because of the love we have for our indescribably wonderful Lord Jesus. No sacrifice is worth mentioning in light of His magnificent rewards. I pray that this book has helped you to dig into God's Word, look at examples of the past and see how you, as a wife of a man in ministry, can live the life that is most rewarded now and for all eternity, for God's eternal glory!

---

61 Charles H. Spurgeon, *C.H. Spurgeon's Autobiography Volume 1 The Early Years 1834-1859* (Banner of Truth Publications Reprint), 185.

APPENDICES

ACCOUNTABILITY QUESTIONS

- Are you regularly spending time in the Word of God and prayer?

- Are you working on a particular area of growth in your walk with Christ and how are you progressing in it?

- Do you and your husband regularly read the Word of God and pray together? Do you keep a weekly date night or at least some time alone together seeking to make your relationship stronger in the Lord?

- Are you actively seeking to disciple your children?

- Have you purposely spent time with an unbeliever, prayed for an opportunity to share Christ, and actually had a chance to give a witness if the Lord opened the door?

- How are you seeking to multiply your efforts by making another disciple?

APPENDIX B

CHARACTER QUALITIES TO WORK ON WITH YOUR CHILDREN

- **Attentiveness:** James 1:19; Proverbs 1:5, 4:1, 12:15

- **Responsibility:** Luke 16:10; Proverbs 14:23, 20:11, 28:20

- **Diligence:** Galatians 6:9; Proverbs 13:4, 14:23, 22:29

- **Gratitude:** Ephesians 5:20; 1 Thessalonians 5:18; 1 Timothy 4:4; Psalm 107:1

- **Patience:** 1 Corinthians 13:4; Galatians 6:9; Proverbs 14:29, 19:11

- **Wisdom:** James 1:5; Proverbs 1:7, 12:15

- **Loyalty:** Proverbs 3:3, 17:17

- **Selflessness:** Matthew 7:12; Philippians 2:3-4; Proverbs 19:17

- **Generosity:** Acts 20:35; 2 Corinthians 9:7; Proverbs 11:25

- **Forgiveness:** Matthew 18:21-22; Ephesians 4:32; Colossians 3:12-13; Nehemiah 9:17

APPENDIX C

A PLAN FOR DISCIPLINING A YOUNG CHILD

- Establish a prior standard. Give one warning spelled out very clearly. Delayed obedience is disobedience. Counting is out!
- Get on the child's eye level and use eye contact.
- Let the child know the consequences.
- Always follow through.
- Always discipline in private.
- Send the child to his or her room while you ask God for wisdom and calmness.
- Establish the child's responsibility: "What did you do?"
- Appeal to the child's conscience: "Was that kind? Loving? Generous? Honest?"
- Establish God as the final authority: "Did that please God?" "What would Jesus want you to do?"
- Reflect grief.
- Teach that God holds you responsible to discipline and that He disciplines you.
- Associate correction with love.
- Associate lack of discipline with hatred.
- When using a rod, use something that will not injure the child, such as a switch.
- The parent who disciplines should comfort the child.
- Pray with the child.
- Encourage him to ask for God's forgiveness.
- Ask him if he would like to ask your forgiveness or the forgiveness of the person he offended.
- See if there is restitution that needs to be carried out and help the child carry it out.
- Evaluate.

APPENDIX D

EPILOGUE

The Expectant Pastor and His Wife

When I say "expectant" I am not referring to a child, but a ministry. Graduating from seminary is the beginning of a period of expectancy. Let me relate our experience, which is probably typical of most couples entering the ministry.

During our senior year many inquiries were made regarding openings in the pastorate. We heard of many churches that needed pastors. We met with district superintendents and sent a tape of a message to one but no calls came to candidate. June came and we were thrilled to receive our degrees but full of wonder as to where we would be able to use them.

Then a call came to candidate in a small church in the country. I went through a struggle with my own desires when my husband wrote the letter accepting the invitation to candidate. I felt candidating was almost the same as accepting the call. Surely they would want us if we would agree to go there. (Every wife must feel that her husband's preaching is the best and anyone would want him as their pastor.)

Shortly after we accepted the invitation to candidate there we received another invitation to preach in a larger church in a metropolitan area. Naturally I got excited. This was more suited to the type of area I had envisioned us serving in. A university and a Christian college are in the city as well as a large population to be reached.

We went first to the country church. My husband preached his heart out. The people were warm and friendly—anxious to go on with the Lord. Some, where we stayed, talked about how things would be if we came. The woman of the house even asked me if I would teach the women's Bible class. We saw the parsonage nestled on a hill with the 19 other houses in the village. It was very old but we had visions of fixing it up should the Lord lead us here.

The next week Bob spoke in the city church. It is a beautiful church in a lovely city. The people were a bit reserved but showed us good Christian hospitality and friendliness. We left with the feeling however, that we would never hear from them again. The pulpit committee, which had interviewed us until 10:30 at night, seemed very cautious and even a little anxious at the thought of having such a young, inexperienced pastor. Could it be that the Lord wanted us to begin our ministry at the church in the country?

The word came—the country church did not vote to give us a call. They had 4 candidates to vote on and none received the necessary two-thirds vote. As we drove the 1,000 miles back to our base of operations at the seminary where our things were stored the thought started to creep in "If they didn't want us, who would?" But we encouraged each other with the knowledge that God had another place for us.

We drove another 2,000 miles to my state across the country and while we were there the door opened almost miraculously to speak in a church in an area I had always had my heart set on. It wasn't long before my husband had the same interest in the place. It is an absolutely beautiful area in which to live with a big university and a new subdivision around the church just waiting to be reached.

The people were enthusiastic about Bob's preaching and our spirits soared. We waited to hear if the pulpit committee would decide to have us back to candidate. The phone finally rang. It was negative. I could hardly keep the tears back. I fled to God's Word for reassurance, and He gave it to me. What a comfort to know that if the Lord opens a door, no one in all the world could keep it shut—not even the pulpit committee!

A couple of other possibilities for candidating came to us and then a phone call from the city church asking us to return to candidate for three weeks. What a surprise! Since we had decided to follow-through on the openings in the order in which they came to us, we decided to go back. So we crossed the county again wondering if this were the place where the Lord would place us, or if we would have to continue to try other doors.

We have spent 2 of the 3 weeks now. Bob has preached and taught, led prayer meetings and done the visitation. The people have had us in their homes almost every evening to get better acquainted. They are lovely Christians—hospitable people. They want to know us before they vote because choosing a pastor and his wife is a big decision. The pastor will minister to their spiritual needs, marry their sons and daughters, comfort their sick and sorrowing, and challenge and channel their energies for the Lord. The pastor's wife either enhances his ministry or detracts from it. We are being carefully scrutinized. It causes us to do some soul searching. Are we the people we should or could be in word and in deed?

Just as a young couple expecting their first child, who will thrust them into a whole new way of life as parents, even so are we. To enter the ministry is a whole new way of life. Expectant parents never know what lies ahead. There are joys innumerable and yet many trials in raising a family. So it will be in the ministry. We have already had a taste of some of these the two weeks we have been here. But we are excited. It is a new venture—one we have been preparing for and looking forward to our whole lives.

Older pastor's wives this summer have given me valuable advice. "Always go visiting with your husband during the day." "Be honest, don't play the role of a minister's wife. Be yourself." "Back your husband with prayer." "Enter into the work of the church whole-heartedly." None of these wives regret having lived in the parsonage. They have had useful lives alongside of their husbands. How great it must be to look back and see how God led and blessed all the way. (Even into that first church!)

Now we look forward expectantly. The future is in His control. Will we begin our ministry here in this established church or might He still call us to the country or someplace else? We rest in this promise: "Commit your way to Yahweh, trust in Him, and He will do it" (Psalm 37:5).

"Surely wait in silence for God, O my soul, for my hope is from Him" (Psalm 62:5).

Written while candidating at Trinity Evangelical Free Church, Teaneck, New Jersey on September 2, 1970. We accepted a call to this church and served it for almost 10 years.

The Relinquished Pastor and His Wife

Almost 10 years have come and gone and a more rewarding and fruitful ministry than we had ever imagined rewarded our expectancy. The years have flown by so fast that it almost seems like yesterday that we came so full of wonderment.

It was scary at first, meeting all the responsibilities of pastor and wife of this long-established church (which is celebrating its 90th anniversary this year). There were so many differing responsibilities besides just preaching—counseling, helping those in physical need, organizing, teaching, meetings *ad infinitum*, sharing and caring. There had to be time for the respect and confidence in us to grow. There were many personal lessons to learn. You had to be patient with us.

The Word of God went forth. First it touched our lives. It worked in us to show us where we needed to be more conformed to the image of His Son. Others were touched. Some were saved and many experienced growth. We came very close to some at our points of need. Many times we felt "poured out." We were hurting when you hurt. Our hearts were knit together.

There were so many joyous times. How were we so fortunate as to participate so closely in each marriage and feel the intense joy you shared? Each baby born and dedicated to God meant a happy sharing in one of life's greatest joys and a link with the next generation.

The times of personal crisis in our own lives were met with such loving support that we were able to come through strongly. In sickness and in health the body stood by to minister to us. We thought we were the ministers but you ministered to us.

When we experienced the death of those in our fellowship there was a great loss because we had grown to love each one. We shared your sorrows. Our lives have been greatly enriched by those precious ones He took to Himself while we were here. We also felt the great loss of those in our fellowship who moved away from us—and many there were.

The church's missionary families have become such a part of our lives. We could never sever our prayerful interest in each missionary we have supported over these past nine plus years.

Our young people, now seniors in high school, were only in 3rd grade when we came. How they have changed! But the thrill of seeing them go on with the Lord is our reward. Seeing some go into vocational service for Christ has been such a thrill!

The best years of our lives have been here. We have been at the height of our strength; our children were both born here; Bob's call to the ministry was confirmed here by his ordination and successful ministry, his doctorate was obtained, his book published for further outreach and ministry and we have grown.

Now it is time to leave—to go to another challenge, which the Lord has set before us. It breaks our hearts to leave this church. It is where we began, where we had no precedents, where we poured out our hearts and lives. The ties that bind are strong. They are the cords of Christ's love. These will never be broken. Miles will only separate us. Our prayers and thoughts and memories will always be for this church. And now we must relinquish you and be relinquished. May the Lord give us His grace!

Written the day before and read at our Farewell.

Recollections on our Farewell

A funeral service and a farewell service have so much in common that one of our parishioners said when referring to our coming farewell, "First will be the funeral where friends come from all over, then the time of refreshments and then the private viewing for the family to follow." And that was exactly what it was like. The beautiful, heart-rending music was there, the eulogy, the finality, and the tears. We had decided to go to another place of service and now we were dead to these dear people who had been the major part of our lives for the past 9 years. We would no longer be there to answer their calls, or to be their friend. It was as if we had died. We would be moving far away with the possibility of never seeing any of them again on this earth.

How could we have made such a decision to leave them when what they were saying was so intensely appreciative of all we had been trying to do? They loved us more than we knew.

My husband and I looked into each other's tear-stained faces and grasped each other's hand tightly for reassurance. The dye was cast. There was no turning back. This was it—our farewell. Our hearts were torn more than we ever imagined they could be. Some of those we had led to Christ (our spiritual children) were weeping along with many others. Some hugged us and tore themselves away. Others wrote notes, not trusting their feelings to speak. Old and young came up to say good-by and to thank us.

When all the testimonies had been given as to the effect of the ministry on their lives, poems were read and songs sung, one man said, "It's too bad a man either has to die or have a farewell for people to say such good things about him!"

We experienced the sadness of having attended our own funeral in parting with those dear people. Our emotions were drained. We will never forget it. It will be part of us until we leave this life. We decided then that we hope our next pastorate will be a long one.

Written a few days after our farewell service.

Beginning Again

After relinquishing and being relinquished by our former congregation, we are to begin again in our new church. It must be like starting out on a new marriage after a dear partner has died. All the love and devotion, which were poured into the other relationships, are over and now there is the promise to begin again. It is hard. Many years went into the strong love that was experienced before. Many experiences were shared together, which bound us together. Now everything is new. The trust has to be built. The love has to grow. It will take time. There is mourning over what has been lost, a natural feeling of having left our first love for another. There is sadness and a wondering if we did the right thing in leaving that congregation which was our life's blood.

We have the knowledge that God directed here. We have much to do to get established here in the work. There needs to be patience. People aren't going to be flocking to hear my husband's wonderful sermons or for counseling. It is a new town for us, a new area, and new people. We have been uprooted. There is a sense of shock.

We have to constantly discipline our minds not to look back to all the good times, the good friends, and family we left behind. We have to throw ourselves whole-heartedly into our new calling. God has gone before and is with us and behind us. He will give the increase, as we are faithful here.

I hope no one ever thinks it is easy for a pastor and his wife to change churches. It has been the hardest experience of our lives up to the present. We need God's healing power to heal the hurts of losing our old church family and His power to begin to love again.

Written at the start of our church-planting ministry February 1980.

Here We Are!

We now look back on 25 years of ministry with this congregation that began with eight couples meeting in a home. I'm now in the place of the older pastor's wife who gave me advice when we were just starting out. If you are just beginning or going through hard times, take heart, God will see you through!

This book has chronicled many of the lessons learned over the past 35 years of ministry. It is all by God's grace and mercy that we can look back and see fruit. He has done it all! We have many more beloved people with whom we have gone through the thick of life, who have supported and encouraged us on our way. What a joy it has been! We don't know what the future holds but He does, and that's all that matters.

Written at the (initial) release of this book, January 2005

Here We Go Again!

We didn't know what the future would hold but God did. He led Bob to continue his ministry by teaching Biblical Counseling at a Christian university on the graduate level, believing he could multiply his efforts for God in this crucial area. I was also able to teach there and disciple young women who were there to grow in Christ and in their effectiveness for Him. It is an absolute joy to see our students, all around the world who caught the love for Christ and His Word, sharing it with others. We never stopped seeing the importance of the local church and sought to keep involved in its ministries. Now we are moving to South Africa for our fourth and final season where we hope to serve in any way we can at Antioch Bible Church where our son-in-law serves as senior pastor. Although our bodies are wearing out and growing tired, we never retire from God's service. He is worthy of all the love and devotion that we can pour out now and one day when we behold Him in all of His glory. May we be found faithful until then!

Written for the new edition of this book 2024.

APPENDIX E

RECOMMENDED RESOURCES

Visit the Free Resources tab at 316Publishing.com
to download the list of recommended resources on Spiritual
Growth, Marriage, Discipling/Counseling, and more!

STUDY QUESTIONS

(By Mary Beeke)

———————

Since 1989, Mary Beeke has been a homemaker
and a pastor's wife to Dr. Joel Beeke, Pastor and Chancellor
of Puritan Reformed Theological Seminary.

Chapter 1: Understanding Our Role

1. Do you see your role as a pastor's wife as a "calling"? What is your attitude toward this position? What is your attitude toward your husband possibly changing careers? (Examples: joy, fear, excitement, anxiety, etc.)

2. Each of us has to find a proper balance between personal, family life, and church life. What are some factors that we should consider to find that balance? Read Romans 14:12, Colossians 3:23-24, Titus 2:3-5. If you know other helpful texts, please share them.

3. Have you discussed being a "worker at home" with your husband as far as working outside the home? What conclusions have you come to and how?

4. Based on Proverbs 31:10-31, name some blessings and encouragements that we receive from fulfilling our duties and calling at home.

5. Do you know a pastor's wife whose example you appreciate?

Chapter 2: Dealing with the Physical Demands of Ministry

1. What are some of the blessings of being a ministry wife? What are some of the challenges?

2. It is biblical to work with all our might (Ecclesiastes 9:10), but how important is it to rest from our labors (Psalm 127:2)? From the list, what are two ways that spoke to your heart, by which you can make sure you don't overextend yourself?

3. How can you, as a wife, help your husband to bear his burdens? Share a text from Scripture that is instructive or encouraging to you.

4. Name one positive effect that a balanced life in the ministry can have on our children. Name one negative effect an imbalanced life in the ministry can have on our children.

5. Read 1 Corinthians 12:12-26. What is one area of ministry that you are (or hope to be) involved in?

6. Pick one of the "Twelve Ways to Lessen the Physical Demands of Ministry" that you would like to implement right away. What concrete steps will you take to do this? Let someone hold you accountable to carry it out.

Chapter 3: Handling the Spiritual and Emotional Burdens of Ministry

1. What are some real-life examples of the spiritual and emotional burdens that you are called to handle as a pastor's wife, either in the past, present, or future?

2. This chapter focuses on living in Christ. From the first three sections how can we get strength and conquer our doubts from our personal relationship with Him? What is it about abiding in Jesus Christ that gives us encouragement for life and ministry?

3. God gives us means to learn from Him and to approach Him. Read the next 2 sections and share why living in God's Word and prayer is so important.

4. Gleaning from the last three sections, what hope can we find from the sufferings of Christ and His resurrection?

5. Can you suggest other ways of coping with the spiritual and emotional burdens of ministry (possibly some practical ways)? What scriptural texts have helped you?

Chapter 4: Not Falling Prey to the Success Syndrome

1. If we fall prey to the "success syndrome," what are some complaints that we might be having? What might the attitude of our hearts be? How will this affect our spiritual life?

2. The author lists four passions to put off to beat this detrimental syndrome and four passions to put on. Summarize them below:

   a. Put off:
      Put on:

   b. Put off:
      Put on:

   c. Put off:
      Put on:

   d. Put off:
      Put on:

3. If you are convicted about one of them, write out a prayer that would implore God to change your sinful passions in one of these areas to be one that glorifies Him.

4. Should we expect it to be easy? Why or why not? What are some practical ways we can obtain a long-term cure?

Chapter 5: Overcoming the Hurts that People Inflict

1. Why is it so difficult for us to have hurt inflicted upon us by other people? (What thoughts and feelings do we go through?)

2. What might God's goal be in sending us difficulties?

3. What are some ways to deal with the pain of church members changing churches that the author gives? Can you relate?

4. What are some of the ways to deal with the hurt of criticism, complaints, and gossip that the author describes for finding relief from this pain? Which is the hardest for you? Why are these things so important?

5. Talk about the ways of handling the pain of outright rejection.

6. Name one or two scriptural texts that can help when people hurt us.

7. Have you experienced difficulties similar to what has been discussed? How did you feel? How did you react? How did you find solutions?

Chapter 6: Coping with Loneliness

1. As a pastor's wife you probably have times of loneliness. What makes you the most lonely?

2. From this chapter, name and explain two ways of overcoming loneliness that you would especially like to implement.

3. What are some other ways that you have found helpful in coping with loneliness? What advice would you give to a young mother who is lonely? What Bible texts do you find especially helpful?

4. Have you thought about what your "consuming purpose" is? (See pages 80-81.) Please share about it.

5. How have you been able to deepen your friendship with your husband while in ministry to help dispel the loneliness?

6. Jesus Christ is the purpose for your husband being in ministry or studying for it. How can we direct our hearts, our emotions, and our thoughts so that we draw closer to Christ and bring glory to Him?

Chapter 7: Living by the Models for the Ministry Marriage

1. This chapter focuses on husband and wife being one, and then serving God together. What are two things that can threaten this oneness in a ministry marriage?

2. The author describes four different models for understanding God's design for our marriages. The first one is "The Mystery of Oneness".
   a. What is the source or foundation for this oneness?
   b. How is this oneness seen in our lives?

3. "The Love of Christ for the Church" is the second model.
   a. Explain the basis for this model, and then meditate on it.
   b. If you compare Christ's love for the Church to your own love for your husband, how are you inspired and motivated to improve?

3. The third model is "Christ's Dependency and Submission".
   a. Describe Jesus' dependency upon His Father.
   b. What can happen when we don't do this?
   c. How should we follow His example in our marriages, in relationship to God and to our husbands?

4. "Christ's Respect" is the fourth model.

    a. How is Jesus our example in this way?
    b. What are some specific ways that we are prone to violate this?
    c. How can we fulfill this mandate in our marriages?

Chapter 8: Maintaining the Ministry Marriage

A ministry marriage has certain challenges that other marriages might not have. Below is a list of the nine areas found in chapter 8 that help us to maintain unity in marriage. For each subheading do the following:

    a. Write either a short summary <u>or</u> tell why it's important.
    b. Write an experience you may have had related to this.
    c. Write advice or ideas related to this.

Try to fill in all the letter a's. Then fill in as many as you can think of for letter b and letter c. **You *don't* have to fill in *all* the blanks.** See #1 for an example.

1. Committing to close communication

    a. Prayer a priority!! Don't be too busy to talk with God and family.
    b. When I decrease my devotions, God usually reminds me by sending difficulties. He draws me back. Likewise, I need communication with my husband to keep close.
    c. Luther said, "I have so much to do today, I have to pray an extra hour."

2. Sharing ourselves

    a.

    b.

    c.

3. Listening

    a.

    b.

    c.

4. Building him up

    a.

    b.

    c.

5. Keeping confidences

    a.

    b.

    c.

6. Building a flourishing friendship

    a.

    b.

    c.

7. Fanning the flames of romance

    a.

    b.

    c.

8. Committing to faithfulness

    a.

    b.

    c.

9. Resolving conflict lovingly

    a.

    b.

    c.

Chapter 9a: Being the Ministry Mom, Pages 113-126

1. Why is expressing love, affection, and affirmation so important? What are some ways you express these in your family and in your culture?

2. What is one way that you find to be effective in training your children in the Word of God? Give one text that relates to this.

3. What can we do to train our children in prayer? What are some precious prayers your children have prayed?

4. Why is it so important to "walk our talk" or to "practice what we preach"? What happens if we don't?

5. Name a text from Scripture that supports disciplining our children. Name two ways that we can discipline. How do individual differences in children affect our discipline?

Chapter 9b: Being the Ministry Mom, Pages 126-136

1. How are you seeking to be active in the education of your children? What are some ideas for handling children who do not like school, or who have a difficult time learning? (See pages 126-127)

2. Why is physical activity important for a family? What are some ideas for family exercise? (See pages 127-128)

3. What are some family traditions that you have? What impact have they had on your family togetherness? What other traditions would you like to start? (See pages 128-129)

4. How can we honor God in the family in the area of the arts? What are some components of the Christian worldview? (See pages 129-132)

5. How can we do everything in our power to instill into our children zeal for serving others and for evangelism? (See pages 132-133)

6. How can we train our children for missions? What are various ways we can express a mission heart? (See pages 134-136)

7. If you have children old enough to move away from home, what helps you to release them? (See page 136)

Chapter 10: Attacking the Problem of Rebellious Children

1. What are some things the author and her husband learned through their son's rebellion?

2. Why is a child's rebellion not the parents' fault? How can a parent keep from self-recrimination?

3. As we evaluate ourselves, what are three different factors that might cause our children to rebel? Why are self-evaluation, honesty, and openness so important for our relationship with our children?

4. In what areas do you give your children some choice and freedom to make their own decisions? How does age and maturity play into these?

5. What is Satan's aim for our families? (See page 145.) How can we fight him?

6. Why and when should a pastor step back from his ministry, related to misbehavior of his children?

7. Name some scriptural texts to pray and cry out to God for your (rebellious or not) children.

8. What good can possibly come out of having to deal with a rebellious child or children so that you can even thank Him for this trial?

Chapter 11a: Being One in Purpose, Pages 151-160

Note: Each question is related to one subsection. Key words are in bold.

1. What does it mean to you to be one in purpose with your husband in the context of your marriage? What about in the context of the ministry?

2. Why is it necessary for a **shepherd** to **sacrifice**? In what ways is a shepherd called to sacrifice? What is the character of our sheep?

3. Compare a ministry marriage covered in **prayer** with one that is not. Do you want to covenant that you will pray for your husband faithfully for each of the areas of ministry entrusted to him as noted in the rest of the chapter? It would be good to journal your prayers and note specific answers.

4. What are some principles to keep in mind to motivate you and your husband to **lead by example**? What are some specific ways you can lead by example?

5. Name two aspects of the ministry in which **organization** is important. How can you as a wife, be a helper/helpmeet in this area?

6. What does it mean to **feed the flock**? How can you help your husband in this way?

7. As our husbands **equip others for service** in the church, how can we come alongside them?

Chapter 11b: Being One in Purpose, Pages 160-168

Note: Each question is related to one subsection. Key words are in bold.

1. There are certain individuals in our flocks that need more shepherding or **counsel**ing than others. What kinds of situations can we expect in this way?

2. In what ways must our husbands **guard the flock,** and how can we help them?

3. We are all sinners, so some members might need **discipline** at times. What support can we give to our husbands in these situations?

4. How might you be involved in **going after the lost sheep** with your shepherd-husband?

5. As a pastor's wife, what role can you fill in **caring for the hurting**?

6. What are some ideas for methods and manners of communicating with the flock? (See pages 165-167)

7. How **important** is it to be a shepherd of Christ? We wives are not the shepherds, but we have a supportive role. What is the most important thing you have learned from this chapter about being "one with your shepherd?"

Chapter 12: Exercising Hospitality

1. What is your favorite text in Scripture related to hospitality?

2. Why is showing hospitality so important for Christians? Is it even more important for the minister and his wife? Why or why not?

3. Who is a mentor for you in showing hospitality either from Scripture or someone you know?

4. What are some obstacles to showing hospitality that you experience?

5. What do you enjoy the most about showing hospitality?

6. What are some factors that limit our hospitality?

7. Name one sacrifice and one reward that come with being hospitable.

8. Share one hospitality tip that you found helpful from the chapter and from your own experience.

Chapter 13a: Managing the Money, Pages 185-194

1. What are some important biblical principles the author gives that can guide you when you handle money? How does this affect the attitude of your heart?

2. In what ways must ministry couples be examples in the area of finances? Why is it so important?

3. In God's providence, pastors are not usually wealthy. What do you think is the reason for this? How can we learn contentment?

4.   How is prayer related to managing money? (See pages 189-191)

5.   Money matters can cause stress in our lives. What is the cause of this stress? What is the cure for this stress?

6.   What is the balance between wisely and carefully managing your money and not being overly anxious about God's provision?

7.   Please share one resource you find helpful, **or** one practical tip that helps you manage money.

8.   Can you share a story of God providing in a time of need, **or** a story about a mentor of yours in the area of money management?

Chapter 13b: Managing the Money, Pages 194-204

1. Is it more important for ministry families than for other families in the church to follow biblical mandates for handling money? Why or why not?

2. What will our attitude be if we are in unity with our minister husbands in the area of finances? What if we are in disunity?

3. What can we do to safeguard this unity in our marriages?

4. Describe one action that demonstrates integrity with our finances. Name one biblical example or text that speaks to financial integrity.

5. What does Scripture say of good stewardship? What is your favorite way to exercise good stewardship?

6. What is an advantage of budgeting? Of avoiding debt? Of getting financial counseling?

7. It is hard to be generous when we have little money, but what does God say about this subject? How important is tithing?

8. What thoughts and feelings arise in you when you read of the example of George Muller?

Chapter 14: Taking the Opportunity to Disciple Women

1. Discipling women can take on many forms. From your experience or from observation, what are some ways that women disciple other women? How important is it?

2. What do we need to understand about the role of the Holy Spirit in discipling? How does this affect our discipling?

3. What do we need to understand about the role of Scripture in discipling? How does this affect our discipling?

4. What place does prayer have in discipling? How does this affect our discipling?

5. What are some general goals in discipling?

6. What discipling are you doing now that you desire to continue? As a pastor's wife (present or future), what opportunities would you like to take for discipling?

7. How do you wish to grow? Do you need someone to mentor you? Are you studying and growing to be a better discipler? If so, share your plan.

Chapter 15: Taking the Privilege to Counsel Women

1. Find a verse that shows we can rely on Scripture to counsel others. Find another text that helps us to understand human nature.

Note: Mrs. Somerville lists steps for biblical counseling methods. The following questions address each step. Key words are in bold.

2. Why is it important to **gather information**? What types of information should you gather?

3. How would you **give hope** to someone you are counseling?

4. Please share an example of how you have used the **Word** of God to address a problem while counseling someone, either in your home or in an actual counseling situation.

5. What are the results when we **rely on the power of the Holy Spirit for change?**

6. Why is **accountability** so important in counseling? What are some ways to hold your counselee accountable?

7. Give an example of how to **celebrate a victory** with a counselee.

8. Why is it important to **leave the results with God,** whether they are good or bad?

9. Briefly, what are the steps to take when a **church member sins against another church member?**

Chapter 16: Living in the Place of Honor, Love, and Reward

1. Compare and contrast the honor of being a pastor's wife with the honor of being a non-Christian wife of a worldly CEO.

2. How is honor and love shown to us? How should we react? What are some of the pitfalls of this honor that we should be wary of?

3. From the perspective of a church member, what guidance does Scripture give for showing honor and love to the pastor, his wife, and family?

4. There will be times in ministry where we receive dishonor, no love, and no reward. What type of situation might we expect? How should we deal with it?

5. What is God's perspective on honor, love, and reward to ministers? What is God's perspective on His honor?

6. Why is it so important to keep the eternal perspective? What do heavenly rewards mean to you?

7. Hopefully we have been inspired and excited to fulfill the role of ministry wife, looking forward to the honor of casting our crowns before our King. What Scripture is your source of inspiration and how would you like to finish the race with your shepherd husband?

"

IT IS **THE BEST**
ENGLISH TRANSLATION
I HAVE EVER READ

—

John MacArthur

"

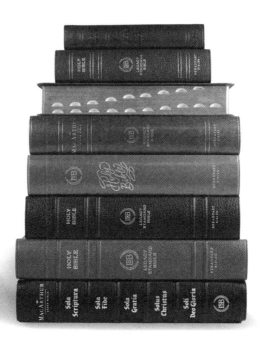